Praise for *The Adaptation Adva*

Heather McGowan and Chris Shipley are prophets of the Fourth Industrial Revolution. Their extraordinary insights and tools challenge and empower organizations, leaders, and people across society to thrive in a future marked by exceptional technological and societal change."

—Major General James Johnson,
U.S. Air Force (ret), former Director of Air Force Integrated Resilience

The Adaptation Advantage brings sense to the sometimes confusing and scary world of change. McGowan and Shipley give us permission to be entrepreneurial by exploring the nature of opportunity and a natural pathway to engagement. Ambiguity is our friend in a world that understands change as a chance to improve lives. The authors beautifully weave macroeconomic phenomenon with a prod for introspection. Their book is a "self-help meets personal empowerment" treatise. Reading this book is a therapy session with motivational power. You'll want to reread it again and again.

—Stephen Spinelli Jr., PhD.,
President, Babson College, co-founder of Jiffy Lube

The Adaptation Advantage is fueled by the power of an elegant idea: our ability to learn and adapt is inseparable from our sense of identity. And as automation driven by machine intelligence remakes our world, the need to continually transform our identities becomes the very foundation of human growth—and how we thrive. McGowan and Shipley have wrapped a vivid and immensely readable narrative around this idea. My advice: read it!"

—Randy Swearer, PhD.,
Vice President of Learning Futures, Autodesk

In *The Adaptation Advantage*, McGowan and Shipley deliver a powerful message for corporate leaders about success in the future of work. Learning and identity are not only intertwined but fundamental to any organization's ability to adapt and create value. How exciting to read a book built on the core premise that learning unleashes our human potential while also driving competitive advantage.

—Sean Gallagher, PhD.,
Executive Director, Centre for the New Workforce, Swinburne University

The Adaptive Advantage needs to be on every educator's bookshelf, preferably dog-eared with highlighted pages, guiding their efforts to reorient the education system into continuous and future-focused learning. McGowan and Shipley's advice is both simple and profound—our students' competitive advantage is their exponential and expansive capacity as humans to adapt, advance, and add value, rather than to compete with artificial intelligence that mimics their genius.

—Tonya Allen,
CEO, Skillman Foundation

The Adaptive Advantage lays out a clear, compelling case to stop defining ourselves by our jobs, to extend formal education into lifelong learning, and to let curiosity lead us through the arc of our working lives. That way we remain resilient no matter how forceful the waves of change become. Most books about the future of work put automation at the center of the story. McGowan and Shipley put humans at the center—as well they should. Many essential capabilities can't be replaced…creativity, collaboration, judgment, sensemaking, empathy, and other forms of social and emotional intelligence are uniquely human. And while technology will continue to evolve the way we work, we have immense agency to determine and design what we do and why we do it.

—Sandy Speicher,
CEO, IDEO

The Adaptation Advantage tackles head-on the most critical challenge facing all of us in the near future: Where do we find purpose and prosperity in a world that increasingly feels beyond anyone's control? The extent to which we adapt to a radically shifted concept of "work" will inevitably be determined by our ability to rethink learning – away from a fixed-term preparation for employment, to a continuous way of living. Accordingly, this vital book offers a road map to the oldest question of all: How, then, should we live? Among a growing cadre of dystopians, it's refreshing to hear a much-needed optimistic analysis from McGowen and Shipley.

—David Price, OBE,
Best-selling author of *Open: How We Will Work, Learn, and Live in the Future*

An insightful comprehension of the velocity and force of the multi-tiered and numerous elements of change offer leaders the insight and capability to creatively lead transformations. Resilient and adaptive learners will be the change-makers of the future. How thrilling to read the book that potentially allows us to embrace change as a propellant versus a weight.

—Lynne Greene,
Former Group President, Estee Lauder Companies

McGowan and Shipley's *The Adaptation Advantage* nails it. Adaptive identity requires letting go – letting go of a job or skill set identity in order to thrive in a world of rapidly changing societal norms and technologies. This is required reading for all students of service science, such as myself.

—Jim Spohrer, PhD.,
IBM Director, Cognitive Open Technologies

In a world of exponential change, we all need strategies to help us continually adapt. With *The Adaptation Advantage*, Shipley and McGowan have given us the user manual.

—Gary A. Bolles,
Chair for the Future of Work, Singularity University

Heather McGowan and Chris Shipley have crystalized what the future of work looks like and it is good news for us humans, providing we embrace change, get comfortable with the unknown, and keep adapting and learning. That last bit bodes well for the business events industry, which is the ideal vehicle for professionals to develop and maintain an agile learning mindset, to retool and retrain, and to hone the uniquely human skills—like creativity, empathy, and communication—that will ensure our future success, individually in our careers and collectively as a species.

—**Sherrif Karamat,**
President and CEO, Professional Convention Management Association (PCMA)

Twenty years of research have shown me the importance of bringing humans to the forefront of the future of work. By recognizing the centrality of human potential, *The Adaptation Advantage* illuminates the value of resilience, adaptability, and the qualities that make us uniquely human in the future of culture, work, and self.

—**Vivienne Ming, PhD.,**
Theoretical neuroscientist, founder, Socos Labs

The Adaptation Advantage is the clearest, most compelling, and most original examination of the present and future workplace. Packed with powerful data-driven insights and provocative examples, this book is a masterclass in how individuals and organizations can and must develop the capacity to change fast and learn faster. McGowan and Shipley offer sage advice and wise counsel on every page, and it's imperative that you take their lessons to heart. But the big surprise in this book is that it's not about learning to live with more robots, but rather learning to become more human. Whether you were born digital or born analog, *The Adaptation Advantage* is your indispensable resource for thriving in a world that is transforming as you read this.

—**Jim Kouzes,**
Coauthor of *The Leadership Challenge* and Executive Fellow at the Center for Innovation and Entrepreneurship, Leavey School of Business, Santa Clara University

This book is an essential guide for anyone who seeks to understand what it means to be human in the age of intelligent machines. The sources of advantage in the future of work have shifted to our uniquely human capabilities. Heather and Chris urge us to go on an inward journey to uncover who we are and consider how we manifest our passion, character and collaborative spirit as our most enduring and sustainable means of making positive progress as people, leaders, and institutions.

—**Dov Seidman,**
Author of *HOW* and founder and chairman of LRN and The HOW Institute for Society

This book will change the way you see yourself within the future of work, give you very practical ideas for leading in that new but unknown world, and leave you genuinely inspired about what the future holds.

—**Peter Sheahan,**
CEO, Karrikans Group

The paradigm of pursuing higher education is shifting. For example, American workers are now getting a job to go to college versus going to college to get a job. In this must-read, Heather and Chris effectively describe these and other trends that are playing out across corporate America today. In a world where rapid learning and adaptation are essential to prepare for the future of work, we need leaders across industries, disciplines, and functions to work together to become champions of human potential.

—**Rachel Carlson,**
CEO and co-founder of Guild Education

In a world where we are drowning in information, and misinformation, clarity is power. Many jump on the fear bandwagon around the future of work, but Chris and Heather have done their homework, the thinking, and crafted a vision for how humans can adapt and thrive, with supreme clarity. They tackle this subject with original thinking and substance.

—**Annalie Killian,**
Vice President Strategic Partnerships, sparks & honey

Speed is the only constant in today's world. That much is clear to all of us. We read tomes upon tomes deploring it or analyzing it, but most of it is opinion and editorial whereas Heather and Chris break it down into clear, actionable concepts and better yet, anchor them with science and examples so plentiful that this book will become your absolute go-to when you mean to school others in the potential perils and opportunities of VUCA.

—**Duena Blomstrom**
Author, co-founder, and CEO, PeopleNotTech Ltd.

The digital revolution is overturning careers as well as companies. This book will be an essential guide to the future of work for both individuals and organizations.

—**Mark Bonchek,**
Chief Epiphany Officer, Shift Thinking

The Adaptation Advantage paints a vivid and compelling picture of a future of work in which the most successful and fulfilled participants will be those who continually learn and relearn in order to adapt to accelerating social, economic, and technological change. As a result of these changes, our current system of higher education is being presented with exciting challenges and opportunities to evolve to support that increasingly dynamic societal and work force future.

—**Russell L. Moore, PhD.,**
Provost and Executive Vice Chancellor for Academic Affairs,
University of Colorado, Boulder

Microchips cannot and will not replace relationships. Your next job starts where the robots stop. Learn to embrace that handoff. The best way to do that, Heather and Chris argue, for both individuals and organizations, is through rapid learning, unlearning, and adaptation. Heather and Chris's book is an indispensable guide to how to navigate this new era in the workplace.

—**Thomas L. Friedman,**
Foreign Affairs Columnist, *New York Times*

LET GO, LEARN FAST, AND THRIVE IN THE
FUTURE OF WORK

the
adaptation
advantage

**HEATHER E. McGOWAN AND
CHRIS SHIPLEY**

WILEY

For general information on our other products and services or for technical support, please contact our Customer Care Department within the United States at (800) 762-2974, outside the United States at (317) 572-3993 or fax (317) 572-4002.

Wiley publishes in a variety of print and electronic formats and by print-on-demand. Some material included with standard print versions of this book may not be included in e-books or in print-on-demand. If this book refers to media such as a CD or DVD that is not included in the version you purchased, you may download this material at http://booksupport.wiley.com. For more information about Wiley products, visit www.wiley.com.

Library of Congress Cataloging-in-Publication Data:

Names: McGowan, Heather (Consultant), author. | Shipley, Chris, author.
Title: The adaptation advantage : let go, learn fast, and thrive in the
   future of work / Heather McGowan and Chris Shipley.
Description: Hoboken, New Jersey : John Wiley & Sons, [2020] | Includes
   bibliographical references and index.
Identifiers: LCCN 2020001497 (print) | LCCN 2020001498 (ebook) | ISBN
   9781119653097 (paperback) | ISBN 9781119653059 (adobe pdf) | ISBN
   9781119653172 (epub)
Subjects: LCSH: Labor supply—Effect of technological innovations on. |
   Work—Forecasting. | Manpower planning. | Organizational change.
Classification: LCC HD6331 .M34 2020 (print) | LCC HD6331 (ebook) | DDC
   650.1—dc23
LC record available at https://lccn.loc.gov/2020001497
LC ebook record available at https://lccn.loc.gov/2020001498

Printed in the United States of America

SKY10032985_020222

For my wife, Pat, from whom I learn every day; for my family, who supports my learning adventures; and especially for my brother Jonathan, who models persistent adaptation every day. —Heather

Nancy Latta has always understood that identity and joy come from work well done and so very much more. Shirley Shipley embarked on life-changing learning when most mothers of five would have opted for a well-deserved nap. My work on this book is for them. —Chris

CONTENTS

FOREWORD:
FROM FLAT TO FAST TO SMART
TO DEEP

There are a lot of snappy, shorthand ways I could summarize Heather and Chris's book, but my favorite is this phrase that they use to encapsulate the essence of what they are saying: the abiding cliché and dominant news headline in the workplace these days is that the robots are going to take your job. What you learn from this book, though, is that, yes, indeed, robots can take your job. But if we're smart, they can also guide you to and define your next job. Because whether it's robots or automation or digitization, two things are true and always will be: there will always be another technological advance that will devour existing jobs—and, yes, those advances will be coming faster and faster. But we will always need humans to translate and augment the latest technology and we will always need humans to make meaning, joy, and connections that entertain us, inspire us, and connect us the moment we put our technology down. Microchips cannot and will not replace relationships. Your next job starts where the robots stop. Learn to embrace that handoff.

The best way to do that, Heather and Chris argue, for both individuals and organizations, is through rapid learning, unlearning, and adaptation. These skills are the new normal. Rapid learning, by the way, is not just about how to augment machines as they spin off new jobs, but how to augment humans as they stay the same, always craving meaning, joy, and new forms of entertainment and connections in every new epoch.

Rapid unlearning and adaptation are both about how we embrace and absorb new skills and how we let go of old ones. To be able to do both effectively and constantly, they argue, requires a mind shift and an identity shift—a letting go of "who we think we are" and a regular reinventing of yourself. I find this the most original aspect of their book—the important role that identity plays in how and how much we can learn and adapt at the steady pace demanded by this age of acceleration.

Heather and Chris argue that those who do it best will be those who allow themselves to be vulnerable, forcing themselves to be more open to the new and to the other. And that is not always easy under any conditions, but it is especially challenging when social norms are rapidly changing, or new immigrants are arriving with greater speed and numbers, and your identity—your sense of home, work, and norms—feels like it is under assault. That people today all over the world are reaching for walls to slow down the pace of change and protect their identities is not an accident.

I will let them tell you the rest …

If there is anything I can contribute from my own research and writing, it's the conviction that the technological forces that are requiring such rapid learning, unlearning, and adaptation—this new normal—are not going away. Indeed, they just keep getting faster and touching deeper into more areas of daily life, commerce, governance, and science. Why?

The short answer is that technology moves up in steps, and each step tends to be biased toward a certain set of capabilities. Around the year 2000, for instance, a group of technologies came together that were biased toward "connectivity." Because of the dramatic fall in the price of fiber-optic cable, thanks to the dot-com boom, bubble, and bust, we were suddenly able to wire much of the world and, as a result, *connectivity became fast, virtually free, easy for you, and ubiquitous.* Suddenly I could touch people I could never touch before and I could be touched by people who could never touch me before. I gave that moment a name. I said it felt like "the world is flat."

Around 2007, another set of technologies came together that had the effect of making the world "fast." This was also driven by a price collapse—a collapse in the price of computers, storage, software broadband, and smartphones. This enabled us to do a huge number of complex tasks on the cloud with just one touch on a mobile device. We took friction and complexity out of so many things. Suddenly, with just one touch, on an Uber or Didi app, I could page a taxi, direct a taxi, pay a taxi, rate a taxi, and be rated by a taxi. With just one touch! *Complexity became fast, virtually free, easy for you, and invisible.*

Indeed, the year 2007 was a remarkable year. In 2007, Steve Jobs introduced the iPhone. Facebook opened its platform to anyone with a registered email address and went global in 2007. Twitter split off onto its own platform and went global in 2007. Airbnb was born in 2007. In 2007, VMware—the technology that enabled any operating system to work on any computer, which enabled cloud computing—went public, which is why the cloud really only took off in 2007. Hadoop software—which enabled a million computers to work together as if they were one, giving us "Big Data"—was launched in 2007. Amazon launched the Kindle e-book reader in 2007. IBM launched Watson, the world's first cognitive computer, in 2007. The essay launching Bitcoin was written in 2006. Netflix streamed its first video in 2007. IBM introduced nonsilicon materials into its microchips to extend Moore's Law in 2007. The Internet crossed one billion users in late 2006, which seems to have been a tipping point. The price of sequencing a human genome collapsed in 2007. Solar energy took off in 2007, as did a process for extracting natural gas from tight shale, called fracking. Github, the world's largest repository of open source software, was launched in 2007. Lyft, the first ride-sharing site, delivered its first passenger in 2007. Michael Dell, the founder of Dell, retired in 2005. In 2007, he decided he'd better come back to work—because in 2007, the world started to get really fast. It was a real turning point.

Today, we have taken another step up to another platform: now the world is getting "smart." And it is being driven by still another price collapse—the collapse in the price and size of sensors. Now we can put sensors—"intelligence"—into anything and everything. We can put intelligence into your refrigerator, your car, your lightbulb, your toaster, your front door, your golf club, or your shirt. And with that intelligence, we can make your car drive itself, your refrigerator stock itself, and your shirt talk to your doctor and then tell your grocer which healthy foods to deliver to your home. And we can do all of that now with "no touch." It all just happens by sensors talking to machines and vice versa. The other day I got a text message on my cellphone that said I had an appointment in my office in 30 minutes, but I was still 35 minutes away by car. It made me smart—or at least aware—with not even a touch, because it was sensing from my smartphone and GPS where I was, how far I was from my next meeting, and who that meeting was with when.

So what's the next platform? I believe that when the world gets this flat, fast, and smart, what happens next is that it starts to get deep. How so? Well, when your shirt has sensors in it that can measure your body functions and then tell your e-commerce grocery store what foods are right for your particular body type and DNA and then order them for you at Walmart and have them delivered by an autonomous vehicle or drone to your refrigerator and restock them when the refrigerator announces that you are running low—that's "deep." And that's where we're going. Deep is the ability to hit that precise target you are looking for—no matter how small or hidden—in the precise context you are looking for it and then impact that target—heal it, fix it, track it, extract it, illuminate it, fake it, or destroy it—with an accuracy that a decade ago would have been dismissed as science fiction.

And that is why, in my opinion, *deep* is the word of the year. Have you noticed how many things we are now describing with the word deep?—deep mind, deep medicine, deep war, deep fake, deep surveillance, deep insights, deep climate, deep adaptation.

We discovered that we needed a new word, a new adjective, to describe the fact that "deep technologies" have two qualities that we could tell were a difference in degree that was a difference in kind. One is physical. Deep technologies literally get imbedded deep inside your neighborhood, your home, or your bedroom. Having Siri or Amazon Alexa in your bedroom is deep. Having 5G wired into the streets of your neighborhood is deep. Having a shirt that monitors all your key bodily functions is deep.

The other quality is existential. Deep technologies can reach into places so deep and produce outcomes, insights, and impacts so profound and accurate that we also needed a new adjective to describe them. Deep technologies are almost God-like in their powers to hit precise targets in medicine or war; to find the right needles in the right haystacks of data; to manipulate the right atoms and cells in science; to create machines that can defeat any human in chess, Jeopardy, or Go; or to fake any face, voice, or image—always with an accuracy or at a depth that was considered science fiction just 15 years ago. And that is why deep technologies also need to be governed in new ways, because they can be used for so much more good or evil in so many new ways.

As the world has gone from flat to fast to smart to deep, it is overturning and melting traditions, foundations, and bonds in every realm of our lives—how we work, how we communicate, how we learn, how we educate, how we conduct business, how we conduct trade, how families communicate with each other, and how governments control their people—to name but a few. In my opinion, this inflection point may in time be understood as the single biggest and broadest inflection point since Guttenberg invented the printing press. And you just happened to be here. And it's not over—in fact, it's just getting started.

Heather and Chris's book is an indispensable guide to how navigate this new era in the workplace.

—Thomas L. Friedman
Foreign affairs columnist, the *New York Times*

INTRODUCTION

Breaking with Identity to Seize the Adaptation Advantage

"Human beings are works in progress that mistakenly think they're finished," psychologist Dan Gilbert famously observed in a 2014 TED Talk viewed by more than 4.5 million people.

It's in that space, between work in progress and finished, that workers find themselves today. We are incredibly well prepared for the past, and woefully unready for a future of work that has yet to be defined. This in-between space can be—and is—unnerving when the future is so difficult to see. "Most of us can remember who we were 10 years ago," Gilbert says, "but we find it hard to imagine who we're going to be, and then we mistakenly think that because it's hard to imagine, it's not likely to happen. When people say, 'I can't imagine that,' they're usually talking about their own lack of imagination, and not about the unlikelihood of the event that they're describing."[1]

But change *is* happening, and happening at a rate that is only getting faster. The good news is that we can change, too. And while that might seem like a scary proposition, it's important to realize that we are already very, very good at changing. Again, from Gilbert's TED Talk: "The person you are right now is as transient, as fleeting, and as temporary, as all the people you've ever been."

Read that again: *As all the people you've ever been.* There is hidden wisdom in Gilbert's assurance, a wisdom that finds itself at the heart of this book. Each of those "people you've ever been" is a version of a personal identity that has evolved over your life—a child, a student, a partner, an athlete, a traveler. Yet, when it comes to work, we cling to a professional identity to direct our understanding of work and career. We are executive or entrepreneur, teacher or technician, politician or plumber. We are boss or crew, leader or team member, foreman or lineman. That identity plays a critical role as a social signal and is, in many cases, the basis for self-esteem.

It's also an anchor that makes the necessary reimagining of work much, much harder than it needs to be. It is the barrier to making the crossing from the past of work to the future of work. But cross we must because the future is coming at us faster than we can understand it. If we're going to keep up, we'll have to adapt. Indeed, the ability to adapt is our key advantage.

The first step to seizing that advantage is letting go of professional identity, and in that letting go, tapping into our imaginations to reimagine ourselves and our work.

So What's Changing?

In a word: everything. In his eloquent foreword, Tom Friedman made the case that we are moving from flat to fast to smart to deep because of the exponentially expanding capabilities of technology. To his list, we add two more, seemingly at odds, elements of change: *invisibility* and *visibility*. On one hand, we can see things now that were hidden before. The data that flows like water brings insight into just about everything. On the other hand, we no longer see the working of everyday things that have been made invisible through automation. Our thermostats jumps to our preferred temperature when we walk into our homes. Already our phones and computers download and update software without our intervention. Driverless cars, one day soon, will automatically arrive to whisk us to our scheduled appointments, and groceries will be delivered to our doors from orders placed by a smart refrigerator that senses we are out of milk or need eggs.

With all this visible and invisible technology coming at a rate that is fast and only getting faster, what is a person to do? Who are we in the context of a rapidly transforming digital revolution?

In truth, we are all works in progress and we need to imagine, or rather reimagine, work. In order to do that, though, we're going to have to confront who we think we are, at least professionally, so that we can reimagine, and reimagine again, and again, who we are in the context of a changing future of work.

That's a tall order. And that's why we wrote this book: to help you better understand what is happening to work and why it matters to you. In doing so, we hope you'll gain the adaptation advantage.

How Did We Get Here?

The old model that parsed life into sequential steps of education, career, and retirement (Figure I.1) is blurring. Once, we were "educated" early in our lives enough to get us on a 40-year career ladder that we climbed until we retired and then, by design, soon after died. Today, considerable leaps in human longevity have stretched that career phase out a decade or longer.

A single dose of "education"—a process that infers an end state of being "educated"—isn't sufficient for a career arc that looks more like a spiral. Instead, we need to swap education for learning, a continuous state of discovery and reinvention. Work, then, leverages that learning and the work itself becomes another form of learning. And retirement? Societally, we neither planned for nor funded the 20 or 30 years of retirement that is the reality of our longer lives. Simply, we need to imagine

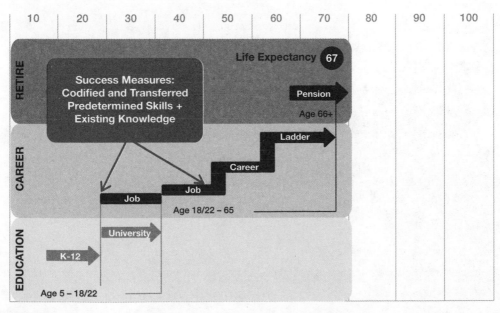

Figure I.1: The Old Economy

a different model that blends these three bands of life, mixing learning, work, and retirement in an iterative cycle that spans 50 or 60 years or more (Figure I.2).

We've talked about this old economy/new reality dichotomy in hundreds of talks, workshops, and conversations, and something finally struck us. Many listeners accepted the old economy as their reality and assumed the new reality existed only for their children or grandchildren. Not so fast, friends. The truth is that many of us will have to leap from the old economy into the new reality, and with that leap we'll have to navigate from a professional identity bestowed by degree and experience into a new identity we create for ourselves (Figure I.3). In short, we will all need the adaptation advantage. This is something we'll talk about in detail throughout the book, but especially in Part II.

How Big Is the Challenge?

In a 2019 report, IBM projected that 120 million people in the 12 largest economies alone would need to retrain in the next three years in order to keep pace with rapidly changing technological capabilities impacting work.[2] The Organisation for Economic Co-operation and Development (OECD) 2019 Employment Outlook predicted that

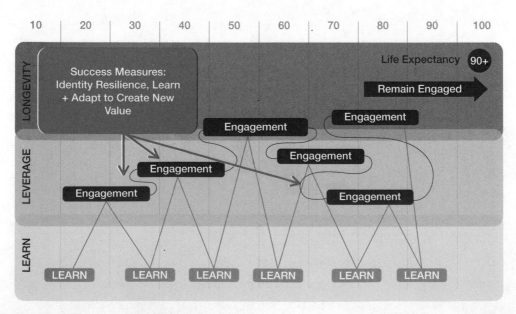

Figure I.2: The New Reality

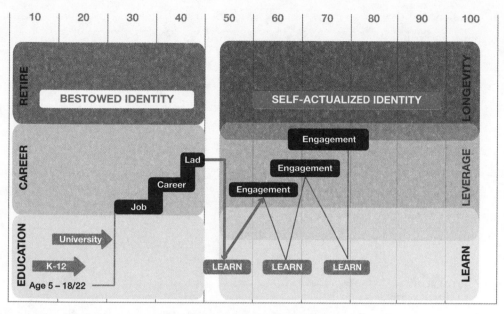

Figure I.3: The Leap from Old Economy to New Reality

14% of jobs could be lost and 32% transformed through automation and that 60% of all workers lacked the necessary information and communications technology (ITC) or computer skills for that new work.

And this isn't just a future state. The labor market, the OECD determined, has already transformed, resulting in a profound loss of middle-skill jobs. Specifically, the 20 years between 1995 and 2015 saw a 20% decline in manufacturing jobs and a 27% increase in service jobs that do not require little training or education.[3] The greatest shift thus far has been in technology's ability to consume routine work, giving rise to nonroutine work (Figure I.4). This shift has restructured the physical labor market and very soon it will upend the knowledge labor market as well. In short, the OECD describes a world of work rapidly transforming while most of us are flat-footed, unprepared to respond, let alone proactively adapt.

In 2013, the famed but flawed Frey-Osborne model predicted that 47% of work tasks in the United States could be automated. Some argue that the numbers in the Frey-Osborne model are not entirely reliable because the formula did not account for the cost of labor or capital, the impact of political resistance, or whether replacement technology could actually free workers to focus on other tasks,[4] which are all criticisms that the framework's authors acknowledged. Even so, the report

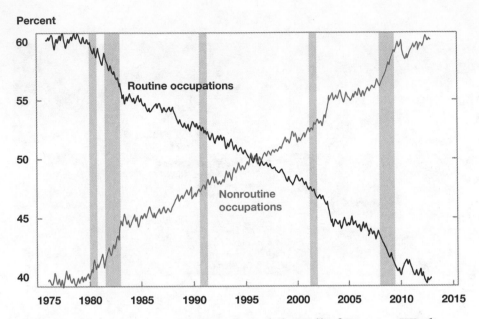

Figure I.4: The Rise of Nonroutine Work and the Fall of Routine Work

Note: The bands indicate recessions as defined by the National Bureau of Economic Research.

Source: U.S. Census Bureau, Current Population Survey.

caused a bit of panic, as people saw a future that evaporated their jobs. Automation *does* replace some jobs, but mostly automation *alters* jobs. IBM CEO Ginni Rometty puts a fine point on this distinction: "I expect AI to change 100% of jobs within the next five to 10 years."

Rometty isn't alone in this prediction. The World Economic Forum places the value of digital transformation to the Fourth Industrial Revolution at $100 trillion over the next decade.[5] A 2018 survey of 10,000 workers in the United Kingdom conducted by Barclays LifeSkills identified a significant employability skills gap. In the report "How Employable is the UK? Meeting the Future Skills Challenge," Barclays found that nearly 60% of adults lack all the core employability skills needed for the future world of work, notably among them proactivity, adaptability, and leadership.[6]

It should be no surprise, then, that our old measure of potential success—IQ (intelligence quotient)—has given way to EQ (emotional intelligence quotient) and is shifting yet again to AQ (adaptability quotient). In the 1980s, skills learned in a university or on the job held their relevance for nearly three decades, about as long as

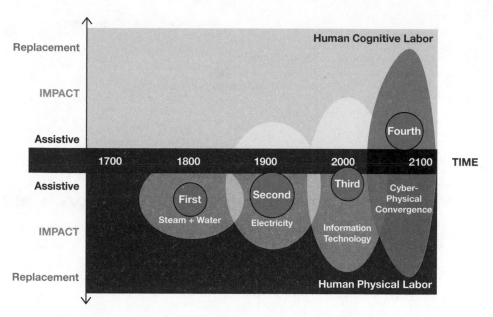

Figure I.5: The Fourth Industrial Revolution Reshapes Work

a typical career arc. Today, skills have a shelf life of less than five years, according to researchers at the World Economic Forum.[7]

The First Industrial Revolution was marked by the steam engine and the Second Industrial Revolution brought electrification and the division of labor; together, these first two revolutions created tools that supplemented muscle. The Third Industrial Revolution delivered tools, in the forms of computer technology, that assisted our mental labor. Now, we are entering the Fourth Industrial Revolution, steeped in advanced software and real-time data and offering tools that augment, and in some cases even replace, human cognitive labor (Figure I.5). Unlike the capital-intensive machines and robots that replace manual labor, the tools of this economic transformation are relatively cheap. They will scale very quickly and be incredibly cost effective. Are we ready? The answer is decidedly no.

The Adaptability Gap

Even as advanced tools and data become increasingly available, we are failing to harness the potential of that technology. Technology is growing exponentially, yet business productivity grows linearly (Figure I.6). The management consulting firm

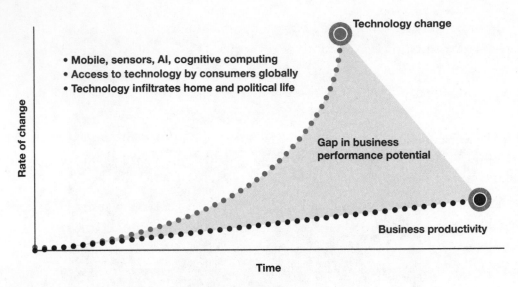

Figure I.6: Bersin/Deloitte's Productivity Gap

Source: © Deloitte University Press | Dupress.Deloitte.com | Josh Bersin.

Deloitte first noted this divide in its *Deloitte Human Capital Trends* report. "Data from the US Bureau of Labor Statistics and other sources," the report noted, "show that productivity growth remains low despite the introduction of new technology into the business environment. In fact, since the 2008 recession, growth in business productivity (gross domestic product per hour worked) stands at its lowest rate since the early 1970s (1.3%)."[8]

Why the gap? The Deloitte report attributes it to "human capital strategies—how businesses organize, manage, develop, and align people at work."

That gap does not appear to be narrowing. At IBM, for example, the company reported that the average of 4 days of training needed to close the skills gap in 2014 had jumped to 36 days by 2018. That works out to between 14% to 16% of all working hours now required for skills training just to stay current.

Amid Rapid Change, Keep Calm and Adapt On

The future of work need not be a dystopian nightmare. Rather, with careful planning and some essential policy interventions, this future could unleash the potential of humanity to create more and more meaningful work for everyone. The key is preparation for rapid cycles of adaptation and learning.

In order to better understand how to optimize adaptation, we began looking deeply at the questions surfaced by an unknowable future of work nearly five years ago. Finding the answers has taken us around the world (literally) to talk with hundreds of people who work by every definition of the term "job." Whether "experts" in economics, psychology, design, or human factors or just "experts" in doing amazing work every day, these individuals have shed a bright light on the challenges we all face when the world moves faster than we're accustomed to.

Dr. Jeffery LePine, professor and PetSmart Chair in Leadership at the W.P. Carey School of Business at Arizona State University, studies organizational behavior, specifically of teams and adaptability. Professor LePine helped us see the difference between two concepts often conflated: flexibility and adaptability. LePine told us, "Flexibility is the ability to pivot from one tool in your toolbox to another or from one approach to another. Adaptability requires you add something. Adaptability may require you to drop that tool and forge a new one or drop that method, unlearn it and develop an entirely new one."

That insight became our guide for this book, and we hope this book will be your guide to becoming more adaptable and to thriving in the future of your work. The book is designed for easy reading. Each chapter begins with several key points, and we've included dozens of figures that we hope make concepts easier to understand. Skim them from chapter to chapter and you'll be off to a good start.

If you take away nothing else, please absorb these three key points for the book itself:

1. The future of work, for both individuals and organizations, relies on rapid learning, unlearning, and adaptation.

2. To successfully learn and adapt, we have to be willing to let go of "the way we have always done it" and equally, if not more difficultly, "who we think we are."

3. Navigating a world of rapid learning, unlearning, and adaptation requires that we become comfortable with ambiguity and vulnerability, allowing us to become champions of human potential in learning tours filled with unknowns.

Or as Peter Senge first wrote in *The Fifth Discipline*, "The ability to learn faster than your competitors may be the only sustainable competitive advantage."[9]

So What's in This Book?

We've organized this book into three parts to help you in learning how to adapt, thrive, and lead people into the future.

Part I: Adapting at the Speed of Change

In Part I, we walk you through the existential impacts of accelerated change driven by both exponentially growing technology and rapidly shifting cultural and societal norms. We posit that in order to learn, unlearn, and adapt, you will need to develop a comfort with ambiguity and open yourself to vulnerability.

Rapidly shifting norms—our racial and religious compositions and majorities, definitions and fluidity of gender, shifting demographics of all types, and diversity in our family units, among other social changes—have landed some folks smack in the center of an identity crisis while leaving others with a feeling of long-awaited inclusion. In Chapter 3, we explore all the ways you have already begun to adapt to illustrate that the process is underway. As change continues to accelerate, however, you will need to become more aware and more intentional in your own transformations.

The slowest rate of change for the rest of your life is right now. We are moving, in the words of Deloitte's John Hagel, from a world of "scalable efficiency" to a world of "scalable learning," in which we need to become more adept at working in emerging flows of knowledge rather than recycling stocks of knowledge we stored long ago. We highlight some companies with the adaptation advantage, those that are making early strides in modeling what it looks like to be a learning-centric company.

Part II: Letting Go and Learning Fast to Thrive

Since our central thesis is that to thrive in the future of work we will need to continually let go of old ways of doing things, including fixed occupational identities, in Part II we do a deep dive into identity formation and the traps we need to avoid. We'll look at the damage done by our social-normative question "What do you do for a living?" and explore ways we can move beyond this occupational identity trap.

Because we want to practice what we preach, we shared in Chapter 6 our experience with occupational traps, failures, and setbacks and how we've both emerged, adapted, and—we'd like to think—thrived as a result.

In Chapter 7, we propose a new foundation for adaptability, which includes a resilient identity, an agile learning mindset, and a strategy for nurturing our uniquely human capabilities. Some call these "soft skills"; we think they are what make us uniquely human. It's our hope that this foundation will best prepare you to acquire new capabilities and discard irrelevant skills when needed, and to continue doing so for the rest of your life, just like you add, update, and delete apps on your phone as your needs change. We round out Part II by taking a deep dive into the uniquely human, hard to automate skills we believe are the hallmark of the future of work for humans.

Part III: Leading People and Organizations in the Evolution of Work

While this book is for anyone, anywhere, who has a job or wants to have one, we want to prepare those who lead teams and companies for a future of work that organizes differently from structures of the past. In Part III, we plunge into leadership issues most germane for this future of rapid adaptation. Through stories of research that include cookies and chicken (trust us, it will make sense when you read it), we show how some of our prevailing notions of strong leadership are actually weaknesses as we move into the Fourth Industrial Revolution. In Chapter 10, we explain why organizations will thrive in the future if they adopt an almost maniacal focus on culture and capacity to achieve the adaptation advantage. And finally, in Chapter 11, we offer advice on how to recruit and organize talent for this rapidly emerging new world of work. By the time you reach this chapter, you won't be surprised to learn that conventional ideas about credentials, screening for past skills and experience, job descriptions, and even team homogeny may be a liability.

Who Is This Book For?

We designed this book with organizations in mind and specifically created sections for teams and leadership. We hope this book will provide guidance to the worker, the supervisor, the middle-level manager, the C-suite executive, the student, and the parent. We have sprinkled exercises throughout the chapters to help you plan and take actionable steps toward adaptation and the future of your work.

In short, this book is for anyone who intends to work in the future of work.

We welcome feedback and ask that you please share your stories with us. And please visit us at www.adaptationadvantage.com.

Notes

1. https://www.ted.com/talks/dan_gilbert_you_are_always_changing/transcript

2. https://newsroom.ibm.com/2019-09-06-IBM-Study-The-Skills-Gap-is-Not-a-Myth-But-Can-Be-Addressed-with-Real-Solutions

3. https://www.oecd.org/employment/future-of-work/

4. https://www.ft.com/content/c8901cc7-d879-3fb7-89ea-16aab9bec3e7

5. https://www.weforum.org/press/2016/01/100-trillion-by-2025-the-digital-dividend-for-society-and-business/

6. https://home.barclays/news/2018/10/barclays-lifeskills-to-help-tackle-uk-employability-skills-gap-/

7. http://reports.weforum.org/future-of-jobs-2016/skills-stability/?doing_wp_cron=1570891431.4452030658721923828125

8. https://www2.deloitte.com/content/dam/Deloitte/global/Documents/About-Deloitte/central-europe/ce-global-human-capital-trends.pdf, citing https://www.bls.gov/lpc/prodybar.htm

9. Peter Senge, *The Fifth Discipline* (New York: Doubleday/Currency, 1990).

Part I

Adapting at the Speed of Change

Key Ideas

1. In the midst of the greatest-ever velocity of change in technology, climate, and markets, we must become adept at adapting.

2. Dramatic shifts in cultural and social norms are challenging our sense of personal and professional identity, and our ability to navigate the identity crisis is dependent on our ability to define, own, and embrace the fundamental aspects and values of our complex selves.

3. The impact of technology on work can be alarming, but we have already begun to adapt. Our ability to continue to adapt with agility and without fear is fundamental to our future prosperity.

1 The World Is Fast: Technology Is Changing Everything and Planting Opportunity Everywhere

Key Ideas

1. We are in the midst of the greatest velocity of change in human history at the same time we are experiencing the greatest leaps in human longevity.

2. Three "climate changes" are happening all at once, *New York Times* columnist Thomas Friedman tells us. These changes are happening to technology, the climate, and the market, and they are reshaping politics, geopolitics, community, ethics, and work and learning. This book focuses on work and learning.

3. When everything starts shifting so quickly, we have to become adept at adapting.

Wait a Second

Change is coming at us with the greatest velocity in human history.

In the single second it took you to read that sentence, an algorithm executed 1,000 stock trades. Computers at the credit card network Visa processed more than 1,700 transactions, no doubt a few of them providing payment for the 17 packages that robots helped pack and ship from Amazon warehouses. Right now, 76,000 Google searches are returning tens of billions of results links. Nearly 9,000 tweets and 930 Instagram photos have been added to an already overwhelming cloud of content. And at this very moment, more than 2.8 million emails are being sent, not all of them by actual humans.

Technology is accelerating the pace of business at unthinkable speeds, so much so that the job you have today, the workforce you currently manage, or perhaps the job you are training or studying for now is changing as quickly as you read this page. In the next 18 to 24 months, the job you have today—if, indeed, it still exists at all—will be very different from what it is today. While technology experts from many different disciplines offer widely different views of the jobs gained or lost in a newly automated economy, IBM CEO Ginni Rometty captures the impact succinctly: "I expect AI to change 100 percent of jobs within the next five to 10 years."[1]

Despite this reality, our contemporary views of education, career, workplace advancement, and even retirement continue to plod along at a horse-drawn-carriage pace. If we can barely imagine a one-second's-worth digital deluge, how will we get our heads around the implications for so much change, let alone adapt to it?

While it's true that we are in the midst of the greatest velocity of change in human history, speed is only part of the problem. Change is coming at us from all sides. It's not just technology that's changing work; dramatic shifts in society and global economics are shaking up our worlds. And we've got to deal with them all at once; we've got to become adaptive.

We are entering the Fourth Industrial Revolution. The First Industrial Revolution was marked by the steam engine, the Second by electrification and the division of labor for manufacturing, the Third by computerization and the beginning of automation of physical labor, and now the Fourth by the merging of biological and cyber systems into a fully digitized economy. In this push to a digital world, any physical or mental task with a predictable, repeatable outcome will be handled by an algorithm. Objects will contain sensors connected to networks where data drives decisions in real time. Many aspects of the biological world will be augmented by robotic and cognitive technologies. In this world, our relationship to work is no longer a monolithic career based on a single dose of early learning and compiled experiences. Instead, our careers will be defined by a state of constant learning and adaptation as new technologies, applications, and data alter the current state (Figure 1.1).

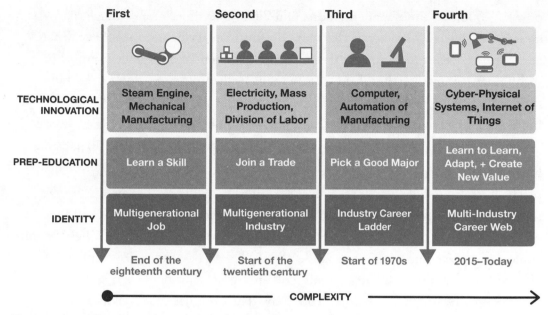

Figure 1.1: The Fourth Industrial Revolution

Celebrated *New York Times* columnist Thomas Friedman perfectly captures this moment in history in his most recent book, *Thank You for Being Late*. In it, Friedman argues that we are being buffeted by three simultaneous and interlocking "climate changes": technology, the environment, and the global economy. These changes, he suggests, are rapidly reshaping our world.

Technological Climate Change

In 1965, semiconductor pioneer Gordon Moore posited that the capacity of a silicon processing chip would double each year, writing in the journal *Electronics* that "there is no reason to believe [the rate of change] will not remain nearly constant for at least 10 years."[2] A decade later, Moore revised his forecast, predicting that processors would double in capacity every *two* years throughout the next decade.

Moore, it turns out, was not nearly far-sighted enough. More than 50 years later, Moore's Law continues to hold, even as the price of these now high-capacity processors continues to drop relative to their capabilities.

It's difficult to imagine the impact of Moore's Law, but consider this: the smartphone you no doubt carry everywhere has 100,000 times more computing power, 1,000,000 times more memory, and 7,000,000 times more storage than was aboard the *Apollo 11* spacecraft that carried astronauts to the moon. Yet even that comparison doesn't fully capture the impact of exponential change in computing technology, so imagine this: if the Volkswagen Beetle progressed along the same trajectory as semiconductors, that car today would be able to travel 300,000 miles per hour, get 2 million miles per gallon, and cost just four cents.

There is yet another way to understand the impact of technological change, however: the change that we are absorbing at work. In the late '80s and early '90s, professionals entered a workforce where the Internet had little commercial impact, software came on floppy disks, a mobile phone was the size of a brick, social media was an evening book club, and artificial intelligence was science fiction. These people could expect to climb a corporate ladder, be paid a 401(k), and retire comfortably after 2030. If that sounds like you, and you are reading this book as it was published a full decade before that milestone, you know that work has changed, and that you will need to change with it. You will need the adaptation advantage.

A Note about Artificial Intelligence

From sci-fi depictions of autonomous robots with a "mind" of their own to Apple's Siri answering our most basic questions, artificial intelligence (AI)—in pop culture and reality—has endured more than 30 years of hype, yet still comes up short of the bold promise of a broadly "intelligent" computing system.

Artificial intelligence is not one but dozens, if not hundreds, of component technologies. Throughout this book, we use the term "artificial intelligence" to discuss computing systems that are able to execute well-defined cognitive tasks. When a problem is specific and bounded, artificial intelligence techniques can solve it rather well.

In truth, a general AI—one able to fully mimic the complex thinking and manage the rapid context shifting of the human brain—is far from realized with today's technology. Rather than AI, we tend to think of this capability as silicon or artificial cognition, and we use that reference from time to time in this book.

But when it comes to computer systems taking on the cognitive tasks once exclusively the domain of humans, tasks that are very tightly defined and with outcomes predictably certain, we use the commonplace, if imperfect, artificial intelligence or AI.

Today's new workers were "born digital," grew up programming, carried their mobile phones to elementary school, and are beginning to think Twitter and Facebook are passé.

Where technology-driven productivity shifts were once absorbed across a lifetime, allowing workers to adjust at pace, they are now on an exponential growth curve where change drives workers from job to job, employer to employer, and career to career.

How we adapt to this much change may well be determined by our age. Science is just beginning to understand how our brains change with age, but most agree that fluid intelligence—our ability to rapidly and easily adapt to constant change—peaks at about the age of 20. Why does that matter? Well, if you were 10 years old when Internet technology became mainstream, you adopted smartphone technology at about the age of 20. Your parents, and especially your grandparents, met the challenge of this change much later in their lives. Adapting to ubiquitous wireless communications at 50 or 70 is a very, very different cognitive lift (Figure 1.2).

There is no reason to believe that the pace of technological change will slow, and we're going to need new skills to stick to the pace. Human adaptation has long been linear, each step equal to the last. Technology expands exponentially, each step twice

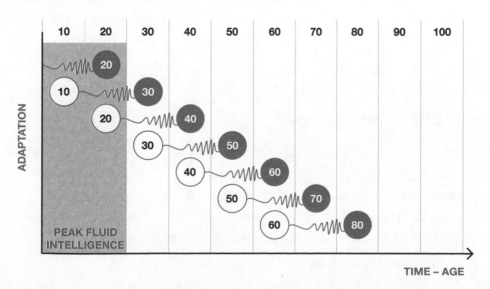

Figure 1.2: Age and Adaptation

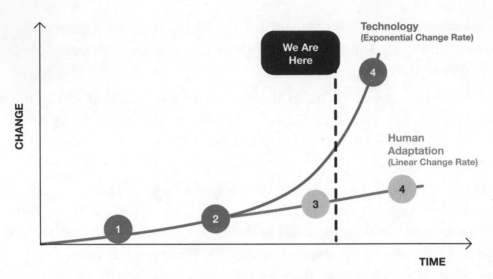

Figure 1.3: Human Adaptation Is Linear, Technological Change Is Exponential

the size of the one before (Figure 1.3). In fact, by all estimations, the slowest rate of change you will experience for the rest of your life is … right now.

What Does This Mean for Your Work?

Your work life will be one of constant adaptation. Every time you hand off a skill to technology, you must reach up to add capacity to your arsenal. We'll come back to this again and again throughout the book, but for now just let that idea set in. Understanding the need for continuous adaptation is the first step in achieving the adaptation advantage.

Environmental Climate Change

While politicians may debate the cause of and response to environmental climate change, scientists aligned to academies, governments, and non-governmental organizations (NGOs) around the world are clear on one point: our natural environment is changing at a rate faster than at any time in the past 7,000 years. Eighteen of the 19 warmest years on record have occurred since 2001.

For millennia, CO_2 levels had remained below 300 parts per million, until the 1950s, when atmospheric carbon dioxide surged to its current level of 412 million parts per million, their highest level in 650,000 years, according to NASA scientists.

The effects of environmental climate change increasingly are becoming evident. Sea ice is melting, contributing to sea level rise. In 2014, the global sea level topped 2.6 inches above the sea level of just 20 years earlier. Scientists at the US National Oceanic and Atmospheric Association (NOAA) predict that seas will continue to rise at a rate of about one-eighth of an inch per year, contributing to coastal erosion, devastating storm surges, and deeper in-land flooding.

In some regions, growing seasons will be longer. Others will face devastating drought. Hurricanes will be stronger. Heat waves longer. And the Arctic Ocean is expected to be ice-free by mid-century.

This environmental climate change, the *New York Times'* Friedman contends, is fundamentally reshaping our geopolitical and economic foundations. And while you might not directly link environmental climate change to work, the effect of shifting climate will have a profound impact on human habitation. The World Bank predicts that as many as 143 million people will become "climate migrants," leaving parts of the globe devastated by draught, floods, and failing crops.

Within the typical span of a 30-year mortgage, nearly $120 billion of US housing stock will be at risk from chronic flooding, according to an economic report published by the Union of Concerned Scientists. In other words, your house may be underwater, even if your mortgage is not. Worse, that number skyrockets to more than $1 trillion by the end of the century. Many of America's largest cities, including New York, Boston, Miami, San Francisco, and Los Angeles, are in grave jeopardy from sea-level rise, suggesting a profound disruption of the country's economy and, by extension, its workforce.

Scientists at the United Nations predict that we have just 11 years to make the significant changes necessary to avoid catastrophe.

What Does This Mean for Your Work?

There is no more kicking the can down the road. We can't just decide to deal with it later. As Friedman says, "Later is over." In its annual survey of CEOs in both 2018 and 2019, PricewaterhouseCoopers found that executives view climate change as the leading threat to business. Similarly, the World Economic Forum found that environmental risks account for three of the top five risks believed by executives to be likely to occur and among the top four risks believed to have the greatest impact on business.

Every company will soon be forced to adapt to avoid catastrophe or adapt to catastrophe itself. There is no denying that this will reshape how and where work is done.

Climate Change of the Market

In the analog economy, global commerce moved only as fast as a ship could transport a container across the sea, and that container could easily be regulated, inspected, and taxed as it moved from port to port.

Not so in the emerging digital economy. Bits flow across international boundaries at the speed of light. There are no ports of entry, customs inspections, or tariffs on digital goods. The adage "information wants to be free" may not always hold, but on the Internet, it certainly flows freely.

Consider the speed at which Airbnb took off in Cuba after the US Embassy opened there in 2015. Within three months, the homeshare service listed some 2,000 accommodations. It would have taken years for even the most ambitious hoteliers to build that many rooms for tourists eager to visit the formerly off-limits island nation.

The scale of global trading partners affects the pace of business growth, too. Uber grew quickly in the United States. When Uber took its ride-hailing service to Miami, the city reached 1 million riders in just two years. An important milestone, no doubt. When Uber entered the market in Shanghai, however, they hit the million-rider milestone in less than two weeks.

Of course, countries with large populations offer more scale than smaller ones, but consider this. While China and India support the largest *physical* populations, they rank only fourth and sixth, respectively, when you consider the rise of digital communities. Facebook, YouTube, and Whatsapp all host larger populations on their social media platforms. And they amassed those populations in under four years, not over centuries of human population growth (Figure 1.4).

Facing a residential population decline, Estonia digitized its economy and became determined to grow virtually. For 100 euros, anyone can become a digital resident of Estonia and, by extension, the European Union. While an Estonian digital passport doesn't convey the social and tax benefits of the country or the EU, if you want to establish a presence in Europe, open a European bank account, and

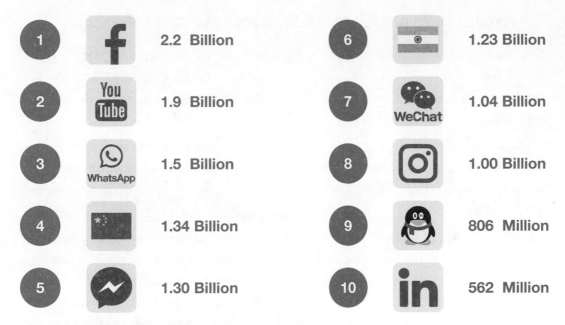

Figure 1.4: Top 10 Populations in the World

be paid in euros, you can become a digital citizen for about USD110. Best of all, the entire transaction is done digitally; you don't even have to travel to Estonia to become a part of the country's now growing virtual population. In fact, in just over five years, the virtual population of Estonia is growing significantly faster than its physical population.

As worldwide economies cross the bridge from analog to digital, every part of global business—currency, credentials, contracts, collaborations—will be backed by and amplified by digital technologies. If the speed of digital commerce seems breakneck now, when less than 20% of the US economy has transformed to digital, just imagine the pace of a fully digitized, global economy.

What Does This Mean for Your Work?

Nothing can slow digital flows. We now live in a world in which any company can tap into the human talent cloud to identify the highest-quality, lowest-cost actor (human or technological) for any given task. In this reality, you must focus on how you uniquely add value, leveraging but not competing with rising technology and your own access to the talent cloud.

The Force of Three Amplifying and Interlocking Climate Changes

The effects of these three climate changes have far-ranging implications that demand we rethink our relationship to work, careers, and how we prepare for them. They demand that we recast our identities, not in a rigid mold but with a flexible framework.

Again, the *New York Times'* Friedman is instructive here. The three climate changes reshape our world across five dimensions: politics, geopolitics, community, ethics, and work (Figure 1.5).

As entrenched as the US two-party political system seems today, Friedman predicts the concept of "left" and "right" politics will give way to an entirely new political system in order to provide effective and adaptive government in the face of complex changes. Our current, mostly binary choices—capital versus labor, big government versus small government—that define the left and right simply won't be relevant. Instead, these real and unstoppable climate changes will require a more nuanced and adaptive government if we are to adapt and thrive ourselves. Friedman predicts that the United States will need to craft a new political party that is circular and based on natural systems—in short, a political party that is adaptive to changing social and environmental forces.

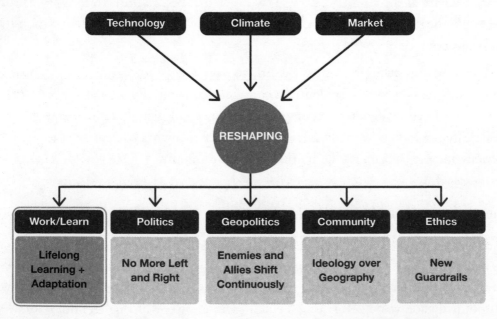

Figure 1.5: Friedman's Three Climate Changes Reshape Our World

Moreover, our economy is interdependent with those of nations around the world, tying the United States to economic partners who are not always our closest allies. Where community once meant the people who lived and worked nearby, community has slipped physical ties to include the people we've connected and formed bonds with online, people we may never even meet in person.

As data and automation take on bigger roles in our lives, we must become intentional about defining the ethical guardrails between society and autonomous technology. Humans face fuzzy decisions every day; most of us navigate complex social ethics and cultural mores to make those decisions as fairly and effectively as possible. How will we program autonomous technology to make humane choices? What code will give a driverless car, for example, the judgment to crash into a lamppost, potentially endangering its passenger, rather than hitting a pedestrian in a crosswalk? Will developers be incented to optimize their algorithms to favor business over workers? What data will we use to train machine learning systems without bias? These are the type of critical questions that humanists and technologists must work on together.

And finally, there is work, arguably the dimension across which this shape-shifting has the greatest impact. More than political ideology, geopolitical economics, ethical technology, or even community affiliation, work is deeply personal. Work is deeply engrained in our psyche. It drives our sense of value, purpose, and identity. If work shifts, we shift.

And shift it will.

We have entered what is often referred to as the Fourth Industrial Revolution barely able to keep pace with the velocity of change. Prior economic transformations—agrarian to mechanized production, for example—were absorbed over many decades, even hundreds of years. An apprentice could enter a trade, master his craft across a lifetime, and pass those skills on to his sons and daughters. Family businesses thrived across generations, so much so that surnames, most notably for those of European descent, often described the family's work: Carpenter, Baker, Smith, Parson, and so on. In the past century, one might reliably begin and end a career with a single company, perhaps even performing the same job. If you were born at the time of the steam engine, you had two or more generations to absorb the impact of that change, but if you are born today you will have to adapt to three, four, or five paradigm shifts within a single generation—that is where the velocity of

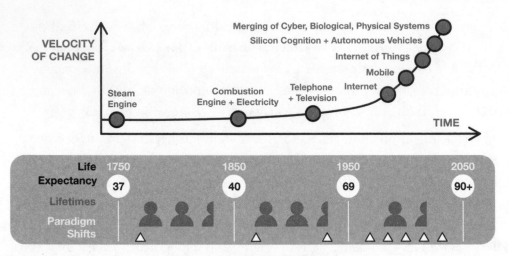

Figure 1.6: The Velocity of Change Requires Adaptation

change meets our expansive human longevity, and this is why we need the adaptation advantage (Figure 1.6).

That's no longer the case. Indeed, the market is now retiring the last generation to view longevity at a single company or even in an industry as a virtue. We are now well into an era where specialization gives way to neogeneralism and lifelong learning. We are entering the fifth era in human history, an era that overlaps and maps to pre- and post-industrialization. It gets a bit confusing, so let's sort it out. In the eras of hunter/gatherers and agrarians, humans needed a wide array of skills to subsist, let alone thrive. As the industrial era unfolded, humans could specialize, share, and trade their work. The information era shifted physical labor to knowledge work and drove even more specialization, storing up knowledge from classrooms and work experience. As we enter the augmented era in which we partner with sophisticated technology, knowing must give way to learning (Figure 1.7). The path through education, work, and on to retirement is no longer a straight line, if it's even a line at all. Human beings must adapt, and quickly, yet our institutions, workplaces, and work policy are firmly stuck in the past. If we continue to ignore the clear signs that the future of work is fundamentally different from the past, we'll find ourselves wallowing in unemployment, underemployment, and dispirited workers and workplaces.

To avoid that fate, we must find a new path, one that loops through the traditional notions of work, learning, and retirement in a continuous and adaptive

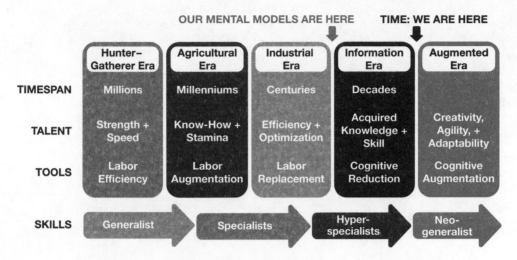

Figure 1.7: The Fifth Era in Human History

Source: Concept of Augmented Era © Jeff Kowalski, CTO Autodesk.

cycle. Where we once learned to work and then used that learning to build a career over decades, now we must work in order to continuously learn to recognize and embrace the challenges and opportunities that these climate changes present. Working to learn is the cornerstone of the adaptation advantage.

That will be the biggest, most essential shift of all.

Notes

1. https://www.cnbc.com/2019/04/02/ibm-ceo-ginni-romettys-solution-to-closing-the-skills-gap-in-america.html
2. Gordon E. Moore, "Cramming More Components onto Integrated Circuits," *Electronics,* April 19, 1965.

2 The Only Things Moving Faster Than Technology Are Cultural and Social Norms

Key Ideas

1. While technology is moving at a breakneck pace, shifting social and cultural norms are actually moving faster and impacting us more deeply than the widespread adoption of quickly emerging technologies.

2. For many, individual personal and professional identity have been disrupted by some of these demographic, social, and cultural changes. For those experiencing an identity crisis, it is almost impossible to learn and adapt to change.

3. Psychological security will be dependent on our abilities to define, own, and embrace the fundamental aspects and values of our complex selves undeterred by external changing norms.

Shifting Ground Beneath Our Feet

The exponential growth in technological capability explains much about the changes we experience at work, but it hardly accounts for the profound changes we're seeing today in so many aspects of everyday life, changes that inevitably also affect the workplace. Despite, or perhaps because of, the networks that bind us together, societies seem more divided. A smoldering discontent is easily fanned into outrage and anger. Even as empirical evidence shows trendlines that indicate a healthier, wealthier, even happier world population, many people believe the opposite to be true.

But why?

The simple answer is identity. Our identity is formed and reinforced at an early age. We identify with family, place, culture, ethnicity, and, perhaps above all, work. Consider the questions we commonly ask in conversations. We ask children, "What do you want to be when you grow up?" College applicants are asked, "What is your major?" before even setting foot on campus. And who hasn't broken social ice by asking someone, "What do you do?"

That may well make for easy social conversation, but the danger of tying our personal and professional identities together is significant. How can a child imagine a future self in a world changing so fast that many jobs of the future don't yet exist? As the lifespan of many skills grows increasingly short, how wise is it to pursue a tightly defined curriculum when neither life experience nor future visibility provides any real signpost for moving forward?

How can we reasonably ask young people to focus on a future self when, according to research by the Foundation for Young Australians, they will likely have 17 jobs across five different industries in their now much longer career arc?[1]

And when we ask an adult, "What do you do?" we are asking that person to further embrace a professional identity. What, then, happens when that identity is threatened?

These questions, it turns out, are traps. They stand in the way of learning and adapting as work environments and opportunities shift and change (Figure 2.1). Instead, we should focus on learning and agility, heeding the guidance of IBM CEO Ginni Rometty, who suggests, "an average skill, particularly in technology, has got a half-life of three to five years. So, what do you do? You actually won't hire for skills anymore, you will hire for propensity to learn."[2] In other words, you will hire for the adaptation advantage.

Anchoring identity in occupation will become increasingly dangerous to be sure. Still, we need to put the future of work and work identity in a large context. The truth is that many other aspects of our identity are becoming unmoored as well.

What's happening?

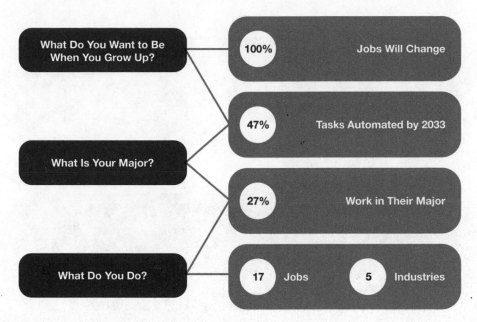

Figure 2.1: Outdated Questions Set Traps

Data sources: Frey-Osborne Model, Federal Reserve Bank of New York, and the Foundation for Young Australians.

The answer is that the only thing moving faster than technology is culture. Rapid shifts in social norms are tearing at our individual and social identities, leaving many of us struggling to answer the three basic and oft-asked questions that establish our identity and orient us in the world:

1. Who are you?

2. What do you do for work?

3. Where are you from?

From Linear and Local to Exponential and Global

Answering those questions isn't quite as simple as it once was when we lived in a world in which change was nominal and influence and impact were local. Adapting to shifting norms was relatively easy when change was linear, a series of sequential steps—1, 2, 3, 4, 5. Now, driven by accelerated growth and adoption of technology,

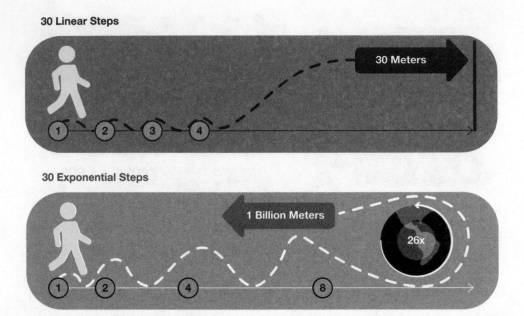

Figure 2.2: The Difference Between Linear and Exponential Progress

Data source: Singularity Hub.

change has taken an exponential pace, each step increasing the magnitude of the prior one—1, 2, 4, 8, 16, and so on. At an exponential pace, the first few steps feel comfortably manageable, but the further along the scale, the divergence explodes. You may be adjusting now but buckle up; the slowest rate of change you will feel for the rest of your life is right now!

Not all that long ago in human history, we only really knew what we could see and experience in a day's walk. New ideas about everything from fashion to religion to politics once took years, if not decades, to migrate from one region to another. Now, ideas move at the speed of light in our hyperconnected and interdependent world. What happens on the other side of the world impacts our economy, our stories, and even our jobs.

Let's dive a little deeper into some of these differences (Figure 2.3).

Race

Within our lifetimes, the United States and many other developed countries will see their white majority evaporate. In fact, recent census data project that by 2045, white/Caucasian may no longer be the majority race in the United States.[3] It wasn't

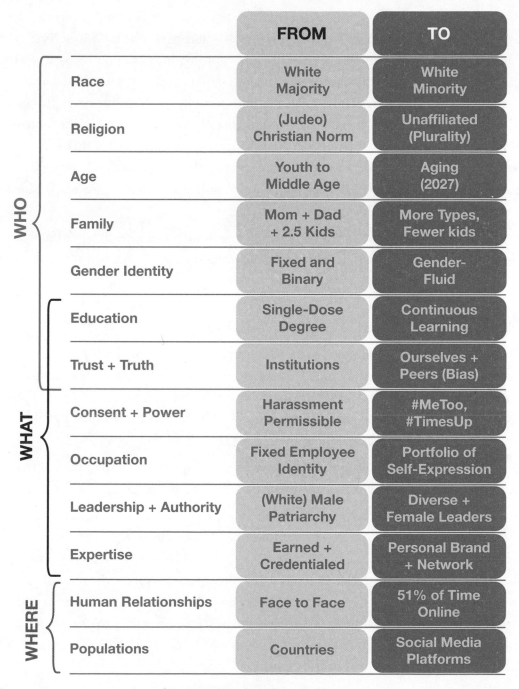

	FROM	TO
Race	White Majority	White Minority
Religion	(Judeo) Christian Norm	Unaffiliated (Plurality)
Age	Youth to Middle Age	Aging (2027)
Family	Mom + Dad + 2.5 Kids	More Types, Fewer kids
Gender Identity	Fixed and Binary	Gender-Fluid
Education	Single-Dose Degree	Continuous Learning
Trust + Truth	Institutions	Ourselves + Peers (Bias)
Consent + Power	Harassment Permissible	#MeToo, #TimesUp
Occupation	Fixed Employee Identity	Portfolio of Self-Expression
Leadership + Authority	(White) Male Patriarchy	Diverse + Female Leaders
Expertise	Earned + Credentialed	Personal Brand + Network
Human Relationships	Face to Face	51% of Time Online
Populations	Countries	Social Media Platforms

WHO — Race, Religion, Age, Family, Gender Identity
WHAT — Education, Trust + Truth, Consent + Power, Occupation, Leadership + Authority, Expertise
WHERE — Human Relationships, Populations

Figure 2.3: Dimensions of Societal and Cultural Change

that long ago that a large family was beneficial, especially for families who made their living in farming and other labor-intensive small enterprises. The advent of birth control and planning, coupled with agricultural automation, urban migration, and the skyrocketing expense of raising children brought a marked decline in the average household size. Today, a decline in fertility rates, coupled with immigration from non-European countries, is radically changing the racial composition in the United States and other developed countries. And there's no reason to believe that these shifts won't become even more dramatic as people migrate by choice to escape unstable governments, seek better economic opportunity, or flee areas whose changing climate has made them less suitable for human sustenance.

Those whose identity is strongly tethered to a homogeneous racial or ethnic community are seeing that identity becoming unmoored.

Religion

The United States was founded on the idea of religious freedom, yet we have long been a country dominated by Judeo-Christian norms. So-called "blue laws" dictated business practices on Sundays. Religion was injected into our national language ("One Nation Under God" and "In God We Trust") and our community practices (prayer before civic meetings and at the start of the school day, for example).

That foundation is shifting. The United States is rapidly becoming marked by both a plurality of religions and an absence of religious affiliation at all.

In the United States between 2009 and 2019, according to Pew Research, the share of adults who identify as Christian declined from 77% to 65%, while the share who claimed no religion at all rose from 17% to 26%.[4] In 2019, Harvard graduated the first class with more declared atheists than declared Christians, the most since its founding in 1636.[5] According to research by Pew, Christianity will cease to be the world's largest religion in the next 50 years or so. Islam is expected to grow twice as quickly as the world's population from 2015 to 2060, and Muslims will outnumber Christians in the second half of this century.[6]

For many whose identity is centered on a particular faith, that pillar may be shaken as that faith is less and less a shared experience among all the peers they interact with.

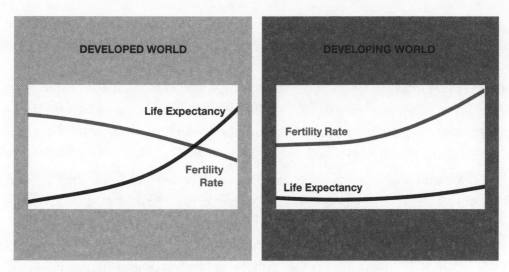

Figure 2.4: Shifting Population and Aging Trends Worldwide

Data sources: UN Department of Economic and Social Affairs, World Population Prospects 2012, Bureau of Labor Statistics, World Bank.

Age

Our once youthful society is aging. In only a few generations, we've seen life expectancy grow from about 40 years in 1850 to 69 years in 1950 and likely 100 years or for those born in 2050. And even as the United States experienced a recent dip in longevity, due in large measure to obesity, addiction, suicide, and homicide, the overall trend toward increased longevity is expected to continue. This extension of life, coupled with declining birth rates, reshuffles age demographics and dramatically disrupts our social and economic constructs. In the United States and elsewhere, for example, our social safety net was built for a lifespan of less than 70 years, assuming a worker would retire at 62 and die by the age of 68 (Figure 2.4.). Now, according to the United States Department of Labor, 4.4% of those over 85 years old were engaged in the workforce in 2018, up from 2.6% in 2006, while workers 30 years old and younger are staying out of the labor force at rates we have not seen since the 1960s, before women joined the labor force in masse. This shift in retirement age is evident no more clearly than in the American Association for Retired Persons, or AARP. One of the world's largest nonprofit membership organizations with 38 million members, AARP kept its acronym and changed its name to the American

Association for Real Possibilities to signal the shift from retirement to later-in-life encore careers. In 2019, AARP joined forces with the World Economic Forum and OECD in a global initiative called Living, Earning, and Learning Longer to encourage employers to rethink their relationships with older workers, a topic already on the agenda of the 2021 World Economic Forum in Davos. These leading organizations are signaling a profound shift in how we think about people in our society whom we have long considered "retirement age."

In the United States, we build and market products and services for the coveted 18- to 44-year-old age group, even as demographers predict that by 2027, just a few years from now, more people will be over the age of 65 than under the age of 14. According to the US Census Bureau, the number of adults over 65 is on track to double between 2000 and 2030; those over 85 are the fastest-growing segment of the US population.

In Asia, and particularly Japan, where more than 12% of the population is over 75, these shifting demographics are having a profound impact. Will there be an adequate labor force to sustain the economy and enough caregivers to tend to the elderly?

In parts of the developing world, advances in and access to medical care have reduced the infant mortality rate but have not as dramatically increased overall life expectancy. The lack of readily accessible birth control, the desirability of large families for providing agricultural labor, and the relative lower cost of raising children is driving overall fertility rates considerably higher than in developed countries. So while the developed world is adapting to aging societies, youth booms in the developing world demand a different adaptation. In the Middle East and Northern Africa, 66% of the population is under 25. In Egypt, 50% of the workforce is under 30.

We can expect these trends to continue, and while developed and developing worlds may have to adapt differently, it is now imperative to rethink work, retirement, and how we structure all aspects of our societies from city planning to social safety nets, and even products and services designed to accommodate dynamic age redistribution. And we need to start rethinking now. The baby born today with a life expectancy of 100 years or more will grow into new and adapting social structures. More urgently in need of a reimagined future is the 55-year-old woman who launched her career some 30 years ago, planned to retire at age 65, and expected to live into her 70s. It's quite reasonable to assume that she will outlive that expectation by a decade or more.

For her, and likely most anyone born in the United States after 1965, we need to pool our collective strength and imagination to jettison our increasingly old-fashioned idea of work and retirement and begin to plot a new future that weaves the strands of learning, work, and "retirement" through a long and productive life.

Family

For much of the twentieth century, the word "family" evoked images of Mom, Dad, 2.5 kids, and maybe a dog. Today, that view is not so easily conjured. Declining fertility rates in the developed world[7] have all but made extinct the middle child. In 2016, 40% of children in the United States were born outside the institution of marriage, up from 28% in 1990.[8] The once "nuclear" family is giving way to extended families, as grandparents, aunts, and uncles engage in primary caregiving for children and aging adults. Children living with only one parent account for 27% of families. Some 6 million Americans are children of LGBTQ-identified parents, and the rise of marriage equality globally is spawning families of choice rather than biology.

These reconfigurations of family challenge the boundaries of traditional values when those values are exercised in unfamiliar ways.

Gender Identity

Gender identity was long fixed and binary. Check a box: Are you male or female? Not so anymore. Gender identity is changing perhaps faster than any other social construct. In a word, gender is now fluid. In various business, academic, government, and other forms, you may be asked to declare your personal pronoun preference. After your name in your email signature line, you may simply offer: She/Her/Hers or He/His or They/Theirs. By the end of 2019, 14 states in the United States offered "X" in addition to "M" and "F" as options in answer to gender questions, up from only three states the previous year. People of Latin American dissent once referred to themselves as Latino (male) or Latina (female), and now more frequently use Latinx to signify liberty from a gender marker. Take the London Underground public transit today, and you will be greeted with "Good Day, Everyone" where "Ladies and Gentlemen" were welcomed until mid-2017. "We have reviewed the language that we use in announcements and elsewhere and will make sure that it is fully inclusive, reflecting the great diversity of London," said London mayor Sadiq Khan at the time.

In Fall 2019, both Merriam-Webster and the Oxford Dictionary added "they" as a third-person singular pronoun for nongender binary individuals. A few months later, Merriam-Webster selected "they" as the word of the year for 2019. The shift from fixed to fluid gender identity is being fueled by younger generations, Pew Research discovered. By the end of 2019, 35% of Generation Zers and 25% of Millennials reported knowing someone who uses gender-neutral pronouns. Compare that to 16% of Generation X, 12% of Boomers, and 7% of the Silent Generation who report the same.[9]

Gender identity is core to both personal identity and our ability to relate to and connect with others. What was once largely "obvious" is now cautiously questioned, changing one more touchstone in the identity framework.

Truth and Trust

From the advent of radio and then television, a handful of networks and media delivered the daily news, mostly objectively, thanks in large part to the Fairness Doctrine that required broadcasters to give equal time to opposing views in order to secure their broadcast license. When CBS newsman Walter Cronkite signed off his broadcasts with the signature line "And that's the way it is," his viewers believed him. In fact, in a 1972 poll, Cronkite was named the most trusted man in America.

Fifteen years later, the much-debated Fairness Doctrine was no more, repealed by the FCC. New networks with obvious political opinions on both sides of the aisle made the scene, and before long, "fact" and "analysis" swam in the same pool. You could find a "truth" that best fit your personal ideology simply by changing channels. An unregulated Internet—no broadcast license required—proved fertile ground for ideologies out of the mainstream, giving voice to fringe ideas and further blurring the line between fact and fiction. With social media's ability to amplify and target information, true or otherwise, it's no wonder that trust in media has withered.

Over the past decade, according to a survey conducted by Gallup for the John S. and James L. Knight Foundation's Trust, Media and Democracy initiative, 69%

of Americans say they have lost trust in the media. Not surprisingly, respondents trusted media in varying degrees according to their personal political leanings, further entrenching themselves in political tribalism.

The proliferation of news sources and the inclination to cherry-pick facts and reject uncomfortable "truths" has eroded a once-common American experience: the day's news delivered by a trusted news anchor. It's just one more way our common identity has frayed.

At the same time we're witnessing a decline in trust in both government and media, we're seeing a rapid decline in church membership. Losing faith in our fundamental social structures signals a crisis in belonging, one that underpins a loneliness epidemic (Figure 2.5). In 2019, the health insurer Cigna surveyed 20,000 Americans and found that nearly 47% reported feeling alone or left out. This phenomenon is not unique to the United States. More than 40% of Britons reported that their primary sense of company is a pet, leading the UK to create a government-level position to combat loneliness. A government study in Japan found that more than a half a million people had gone at least six months at home without human contact.[10]

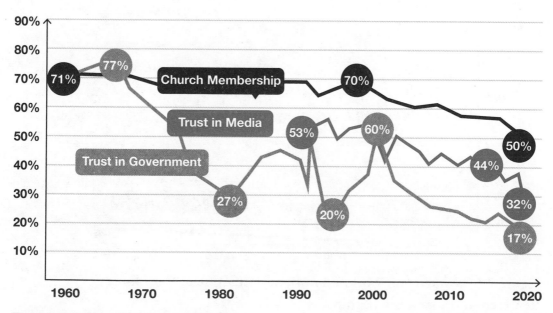

Figure 2.5: Membership and Trust

Data sources: Gallup (church membership and trust in media), Pew Research (trust in government).

Consent and Power Shifts

Women entered the workforce en masse in the 1970s and now, almost 50 years later, we are seeing the dramatic (if slowly attained) shift in how women and men are treated at work. Women are earning increasing respect, power, and authority in the workplace, academia, and all walks of life (Figure 2.6.).

Far from the power dynamic of the *Mad Men* era, women score higher than men on a vast majority of leadership competencies, according to research published by *Harvard Business Review*.[11] (The same study noted that we have much more work to do to bridge the advanced degree and leadership gap for underrepresented minorities.)

Women now far outnumber men among recent college graduates in most industrialized countries.[12] Indeed, women have outnumbered men in degree attainment in the United States for the past 20 years. In 2015/2016, women earned 61% of associate's degrees, 57% of bachelor's degrees, 59% of master's degrees, and 53% of doctorates.[13] In 2019, university-educated women, for the first time,

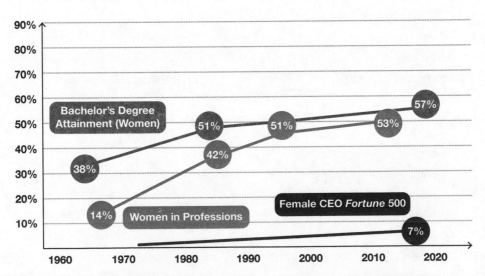

Figure 2.6: Women and Work: Educational Attainment, Workforce Representation, and Leadership

Data sources: Equal Employment Opportunity Commission (women in professions), National Center for Education Statistics (degree attainment by women), Catalyst (*Fortune* 500 CEOs).

outnumbered university-educated men in the workforce in the United States.[14] Despite this pipeline of talent, and with a workforce that is 47% women as of 2019, only 5.4% of the CEOs of S&P 500 companies[15] and 7% of *Fortune* 500 CEOs[16] are women. If you consider venture-backed startups a pipeline to leadership of quickly scaling businesses, the numbers are not yet there for women, either. In 2017, just 2% of venture capital funding went to startups founded by women, and women made up just 9% of the decision-makers at US venture capital firms.[17]

Still, we are seeing change.

The 2018 midterm elections in the United States were marked by the greatest number of women and the most racially and culturally diverse candidates in history. Ninety women were elected to Congress, including, at age 29, the youngest woman ever elected, along with the first transgender representative, the first openly bisexual representative, the first Native American representatives, and the first Muslim representatives. The US representation in government is coming closer to mirroring the populace it represents.

In corporations, gender equality may come more slowly but will accelerate as structural and policy changes take effect and the pipeline of talent becomes balanced. California passed a law requiring publicly traded companies headquartered in the state to have at least one female board member by the end of 2019. Moreover, the "Me Too" and "Time's Up" movements catalyzed an important dialogue about gender-based power dynamics. There still may be a far distance to travel, but we are taking solid steps toward equality.

Yet we must also acknowledge that the shift in the gender-based power dynamic in education, business, Congress, and beyond both threatens and empowers, and it has certainly left many men feeling adrift. Anne Case and Angus Deaton famously coined the term "deaths of despair" to capture the decline in life expectancy for largely non-college-educated, non-Hispanic white men who have been unable to participate in the modern economy, a demographic that has experienced a dramatic rise in deaths from opioids, alcohol abuse, suicide, homicide, and other mental health–related deaths.[18] This sad trend is one of the most challenging aspects of adaptation to the new economy. If you are not well prepared to participate in a changing labor market, and if your social status is being reshaped by changing demographic and gender norms, how can you be comfortable in the vulnerability required to learn and adapt?

Death of Distance Reshapes Human Relationships

Human populations have always aggregated in physical communities, city-states, and countries. Now, though, these geolocated populations are being eclipsed by a new form of association—online platforms. As we discussed in Chapter 1, the top 10 population "centers" in the world include only two countries. The other eight are social media platforms. With little friction to slow digital flows, this change occurred in the past five years.

Since societies are formed by a common language, culture, currency, and assets, we have to consider how new societies will be enabled by digital technology. Language can now be translated in real time by artificial intelligence. Cultures are forming and clustering in social media rather than IRL (the text messaging acronym for "in real life"). Currencies, once backed only by governments, are forming around a collective agreement of value exchange, and assets once backed by the gold standard are now understood as digital goods captured in intellectual property, algorithms, and artificial intelligence.

By some estimates, people in the developed world are spending 51% of their time online. Check your mobile device to see how many of your waking hours you spend on screen time on any given day. If your time looks like most people's, you are spending more than half your time in a "place" other than where we are physically located and engaging with people we may have never met in person. Yet, paradoxically, even as we are more connected, we are lonelier. In fact, according to the previously mentioned Cigna study, the most digitally connected generation, Generation Z, is also the loneliest. This epidemic of loneliness has serious consequences, impacting health and mortality to a degree equivalent to smoking 15 cigarettes a day.[19]

This formation of new, virtual societies reinforces the information and relationship filters that fortify our biases and beliefs. Our time online has changed how we socialize, shop, find jobs, and even find mates. Twenty-one percent of heterosexual couples and 70% of same-sex couples now say they met their partners online (Figure 2.7). These are some seriously solid filter bubbles.

So, Who Are You? Occupational Identity and Expertise

If so many facets of identity are being reshaped, the question "Who are you?" may be more rightly changed to "How do you define yourself?" Psychological security will be

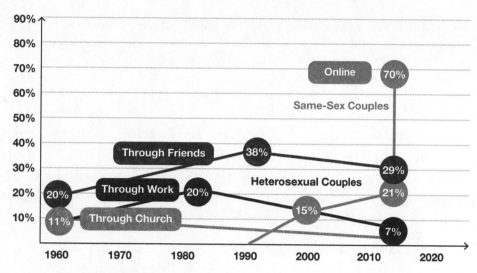

Figure 2.7: How We Meet Our Mates

Data source: Michael J. Rosenfeld and Reuben J. Thomas, "Searching for a Mate: The Rise of the Internet as a Social Intermediary," *American Sociological Review* 77, no. 4 (2012): 523–547.

dependent on our abilities to define, own, and embrace the fundamental aspects and values of our complex selves, especially in a world where we are not likely surrounded by people who look, eat, pray, or speak like we do. When our gender, family, and racial and cultural clans give way to diverse and global communities, we need to find new tethers for our complex identities.

Likewise, that ice-breaker question "What do you do?" loses its relevance when our job is no longer our primary identity. "Where do you find purpose?" may be the better question in a world where your career identity is fluid at best and more likely becoming a portfolio of self-expression. How do you express your professional expertise in a way that is nimble and adaptive? The trick is to root your sense of self to your purpose, passion, and curiosity. Work we love, work with purpose, is essential for every worker, not just the luxury of a few. Curiosity, purpose, and passion fuel lifelong learning and give us our adaptation advantage.

But to be clear, purpose is not some inner secret that is magically revealed. Rather it is carefully curated over a lifetime. As Annalie Killian with New York–based management consultancy sparks & honey puts it so well, "Purpose is not found but discovered through the editing process of life, trial and experimentation."

Finally, in this emerging digital era, how we connect and create community will supersede geographic and ancestral identities. The idea of being "from" a place will give way to a sense of belonging.

These cultural shifts find a common basis in technology's ability to move information at the speed of light. We see a wider landscape than ever before, and in that context, we begin to see ourselves differently and too often as different from the "other." As our cultural identity peels away, our instinct often is to retrench, to cling more tightly to what is left of our prior selves. It is our best and worst instinct. We are too confident in who we are to move in the direction of who we might become. As Dan Gilbert reminded us in our introduction, it is easier to remember than imagine.

Worse, these culture shifts have too often been politicized, skillfully used by politicians and manipulated through social media to divide our societies. According to Pew Research, the United States, for one, has long been evenly divided among Democratic, Republican, and Independent voters. Now, we are highly polarized between the right and the left, while 43% of the population finds no home at either pole; nowhere is this more true than with Millennials, 50 percent of whom now identify as Independents.[20]

Politically, socially, or geopolitically, we need to find a way back to belonging. That way relies on a secure sense of identity, being confident enough to admit the vulnerability that enables new ideas and knowledge to take root. Your adaptation advantage starts with a resilient and adaptive identity, even as the forces of globalization, diversity, and changing social and societal norms reshape your touchstones.

Notes

1. https://www.fya.org.au/wp-content/uploads/2016/11/The-New-Work-Mindset.pdf

2. https://www.afr.com/technology/business-must-change-for-the-ai-era-20191112-p539s9

3. https://www.brookings.edu/blog/the-avenue/2018/03/14/the-us-will-become-minority-white-in-2045-census-projects/

4. https://www.pewforum.org/2019/10/17/in-u-s-decline-of-christianity-continues-at-rapid-pace/

5. https://features.thecrimson.com/2015/freshman-survey/makeup/

6. https://www.pewresearch.org/fact-tank/2017/04/06/why-muslims-are-the-worlds-fastest-growing-religious-group/

7. http://www.genfkd.org/birth-rates-are-plummeting-all-over-the-developed-world

8. https://www.childtrends.org/publications/dramatic-increase-in-percentage-of-births-outside-marriage-among-whites-hispanics-and-women-with-higher-education-levels

9. https://www.pewsocialtrends.org/2019/01/17/generation-z-looks-a-lot-like-millennials-on-key-social-and-political-issues/

10. https://theweek.com/articles/815518/epidemic-loneliness

11. https://hbr.org/2019/06/research-women-score-higher-than-men-in-most-leadership-skills

12. https://pdfs.semanticscholar.org/f3e0/77a1ed80b10b7c07cd5782053821fe9fd412.pdf

13. https://nces.ed.gov/programs/digest/d17/tables/dt17_301.20.asp

14. https://www.wsj.com/articles/historic-rise-of-college-educated-women-in-labor-force-changes-workplace-11566303223

15. https://www.catalyst.org/research/women-ceos-of-the-sp-500/

16. https://fortune.com/2019/05/16/fortune-500-female-ceos/

17. https://www.fastcompany.com/40540948/91-of-decision-makers-at-u-s-venture-capital-firms-are-men

18. https://www.jec.senate.gov/public/index.cfm/republicans/2019/9/long-term-trends-in-deaths-of-despair

19. https://www.multivu.com/players/English/8294451-cigna-us-loneliness-survey/docs/IndexReport_1524069371598-173525450.pdf

20. https://www.pewsocialtrends.org/2014/03/07/chapter-1-political-trends/

3 You're Already Adapting and Not Even Noticing

Key Ideas

1. As we adopt new technologies, we are augmenting our human capabilities, often without even realizing it.

2. Technologies impact work in three ways—augmentation, atomization, and automation—and each of these has implications for the future of work and require that we upskill and reskill regularly as part of work.

3. We have already begun to adapt. Our ability to do so with agility and without fear is fundamental to our future productivity.

We've Already Begun to Outsource Our Memory

In the early days of 1996, Jeff Hawkins took the stage at the technology industry's DEMO Conference to introduce the PalmPilot to an audience of technophiles eager to see the future of mobile computing technology. This was the first widely adopted personal digital assistant (PDA) and the precursor to the smartphone, which Hawkins and his team at follow-on company Handspring would bring to market six years later. The PalmPilot included a contact list, datebook, calculator, to-do list, and notepad. By today's standards, this was a very simple device, yet it had a profound impact. The day the PalmPilot came to market was the day we began to outsource our memory to digital assistants.

In truth, though, this outsourcing began long, long ago. That's the way it is with "technology." The most rudimentary hand tools extended human potential.

The invention of written language meant humans could document their stories
to be remembered for generations. Computer technology was all that on steroids.
Most prosaically, Steve Jobs called the personal computer a "bicycle for the
mind," a machine profoundly extending human cognitive potential by storing
and retrieving information, executing calculations at the speed of light, processing
mountains of data in moments, and even orienting us in time and space. Hawkins'
handheld digital assistant was simply one more accelerant in a long train of human
augmentation.

Think about it: your mobile phone contains dozens, if not hundreds or maybe
thousands, of phone numbers. If you lost your phone right now, who could you call?
Maybe you remember your own number or the number that rang in your childhood,
or maybe that of your partner. Or maybe not. We no longer memorize phone
numbers because we don't have to. In fact, we send them from phone to phone
without them ever passing through our brains. Our phones contain hundreds of
photos and not just of our fabulous selves. We use the camera as a visual notepad to
remember everything from what we ate to the parts we need to buy at the hardware
store to the space where we parked our cars. Calendar and alarm functions remind
us where we need to be and by when, and weather apps tell us what we need to
wear when we get there. Calendar appointments synchronize with traffic data to tell
us when to leave to arrive on time. Social media platforms like Facebook remind
us of past experiences by resurfacing posts, and they never let us forget a friend or
loved one's birthday. Our apps count our steps, summon rides, find us a date, order
our groceries, and connect us to the biggest brain of all, the Internet. Estimates are
that, today, in the developed world, we spend 51% of our time online. That's more
than half our waking hours, and for many of us it means we are spending more
time nurturing our virtual communities than our physical ones. So much so that
we developed a text-message acronym—IRL, in real life—out of the necessity to
delineate between real and virtual events.

Ironically, few of us find any of these technology-enabled devices very scary, in
stark contrast to the ominous warnings that robots and AI are gunning for our jobs,
and maybe even our humanity. The fact is that new technologies have always had a
way of augmenting human capabilities. Steam engines augmented our ability to move
from place to place. Telecommunications augmented our ability to be in conversation
with people at a distance. Electricity extended our days beyond the hours of sunlight.

Computers augmented our ability to calculate numbers and quickly process standard tasks. The World Wide Web augmented our ability to publish and widely distribute our ideas. And so it goes.

Today technology has lowered the cost of labor for most physical tasks, and is now encroaching on high-level, professional cognitive work—law, medicine, and business—that was once thought to be safe from technology disruption. Artificial intelligence technologies coupled with lightning-fast processing and access to massive stores of data are eclipsing human cognitive abilities in narrow areas where tasks are specific and clearly defined. Consider these examples: Betterment is a low-cost robo-advising application that uses artificial intelligence to manage your financial portfolio at a fraction of the cost of a human investment manager. Ross is the first artificial intelligence–based legal research service. Each of these systems performs *specific* tasks more quickly than humans, but it is humans, ultimately, who make sense of these applications.

People Aren't Horses

When we describe the capabilities of a motor today, we talk about "horsepower"—a unit of measurement that compares the power of the machine to the organic assistance it replaces, a throwback to the time when these new engines needed a point of reference to the horses that previously did the job. Technology will continue to advance and assume many routine and predictable tasks at all skill levels. That idea strikes fear in many, but it shouldn't. Humans are far more adaptable than horses. We will do as we have always done in the wake of new "technology"; we will continually reskill, upskill, and reinvent ourselves in order to adapt. The only difference is that we have to adapt faster and more frequently now.

And adapt we must. Research by the National Bureau of Economic Research found that "on average, the arrival of one new industrial robot in a local labor market coincides with an employment drop of 5.6 workers."[1] What may be a frightening statistic, though, can also be an important reminder to make upskilling and reskilling an everyday activity. Why wait? By building the muscle to continuously adapt, we minimize the disruption caused by the way technology and globalization are changing work. We need to continuously adapt so disruptive technologies are not, in fact, so disruptive.

Atomization, Automation, and Augmentation

Three driving forces—atomization, automation, and augmentation—are dramatically reshaping work and will continue to do so for decades to come. By paying close attention to how these forces are reshaping work and our world, we can learn and adapt to maximize their transformative power, rather than fall victims to redundancy (Figure 3.1).

Today, the tasks of many jobs—particularly those at an entry level and increasingly those in the more advanced professions—can be broken into separate, discrete pieces. Those pieces, particularly if they are fully digital pieces, can be solved by the best and lowest-cost provider anywhere in the world. *This is the atomization of work.*

We saw the benefits of this type of unbundling of a single piece of work from the job that contained it in the mass manufacturing of products in the Second Industrial Revolution. The atomization of work occurred as "piecework"—components needed for a completed product were made by individuals in various workshops, then shipped to a central manufacturing site for final assembly.

In the digital age, as some tasks become certain and their outcomes clearly defined or at least predictable, they will be assigned in whole or in part to computerized labor. *This is the automation of work.*

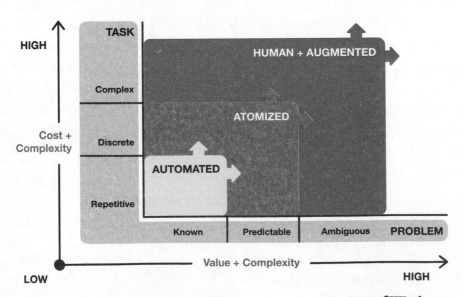

Figure 3.1: The Atomization, Automation, and Augmentation of Work

The robots that supported and often supplanted factory workers in physical labor are moving into the professional ranks and encroaching on knowledge labor.

Today, computer algorithms can analyze reams of data far faster than human workers can. Indeed, every job in the developed world is aided by some form of computer technology, from computation to scheduling to scanning to sensors to detecting patterns. IBM's Watson has shown some promising potential in its ability to scan and analyze legal briefs and early efforts to detect patterns in an MRI. *This is the augmentation of work.*

Atomization in Action

As we wrote this book, we needed to transform our PowerPoint graphics used in keynote talks to the vector graphics more suitable for print. Using the gig work platform Fiverr, we found Olga, a Serbian graphic designer at Josephine and Paul Designs. Olga has, working hours opposite of ours, transformed our graphic frameworks to the high-definition file formats required by our publisher. The work was done to specification efficiently and cost effectively. In this task, Olga was a part of our team. Where in your work can you identify tasks that can be handed to another provider to solve? Tapping into the global talent cloud allows you to find someone to do that work, perhaps even in another time zone, thereby extending your workday.

Automation in Action

Google is bringing automation to your Gmail inbox. By adjusting a few settings, Google can scan your email for event- and task-specific items, then automatically put the relevant information about an event in your calendar. If you travel as much as we do, you'll appreciate the reduction in time and frustration when you no longer need to search for information because the automation in Gmail has placed hotel addresses, flight confirmation codes, and other relevant information where you can easily find it. It even pops up a reminder when it's time to check in. Google Calendar also integrates with Google Maps and Waze to scan traffic and suggest a departure time so that you are not late to your next meeting due to a traffic delay. Gmail has also begun suggesting quick responses to routine emails, enabling you to dispense with your inbox in a fraction of the time it would take to draft replies on your own. Many routine and narrowly defined tasks like this can be automated today. Where in your work can you find tasks to automate?

Upskilling and Reskilling Exercise

One way to adapt to technical disruption in your work is to assess your job by scanning the marketplace for opportunities to outsource, upskill, and reskill. Upskilling is deepening your knowledge and skills in your current domain. Reskilling is extending your knowledge and skills to new domains. Consider which tasks can be handed off to atomization or automation, scan for new technologies that may augment your capabilities, and seek new skills and knowledge required to evolve the value you create today to a new business model. Doing so will allow you to adapt, reskill, and upskill ahead of the curve (Figure 3.2).

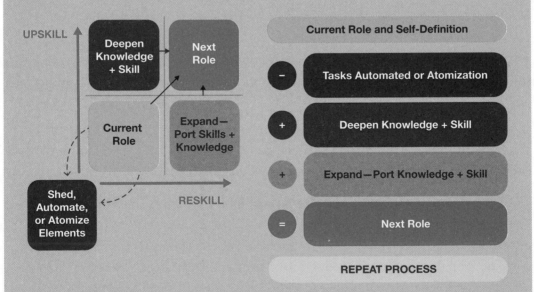

Figure 3.2: Upskill and Reskill Regularly

Augmentation in Action

As we began work on this book, Heather was struck with a rare and life-threatening health event: a massive gastrointestinal hemorrhage caused by a very, very rare condition called Dieulafoy's Lesion. Until recently, 80% of patients with this condition died from internal bleeding before the cause could be diagnosed. Advances in both interventional radiology and endoscopic procedures expanded the potential of her surgeon, who, with the help of these technologies, diagnosed and successfully treated her with only minimally invasive surgery. If you work in healthcare, you are surrounded by technological advances and experiments—from the da Vinci robot that extends the precision of a surgeon's hands to experiments with various forms of AI to detect patterns and diagnose conditions—that augment the quality of care delivered by human providers. Outside of healthcare, AI technology is augmenting all sorts of activities, from stock trading to legal work to sports strategy. You might even be driving a bit of AI technology if your vehicle alerts you to something in the blind spot, offers adaptive cruise control, or assists in parking your car.

Putting Atomization, Automation, and Augmentation Together

The forces of atomization, automation, and augmentation will continue to transform work and deliver new capabilities until, ultimately, most tightly defined tasks are captured in algorithms that execute jobs faster, more predictably, and more efficiently than any human worker, no matter how low cost *or* how intelligent. Algorithms augment until they replace many human tasks and skills. This is how atomization and augmentation of work interconnect to accelerate the transformation of work.

Once a job has been atomized and the routine and predictable components digitized, the atomic parts of a job can be parceled out to a global workforce willing to complete a task at the lowest cost with the highest quality. These workers are a resource in a human talent cloud in much the same way the software applications or data storage are now relegated to Internet-based systems, often referred to as "the cloud." In effect, the work to be done has been separated—unbundled—from the job itself, and workers from anywhere in the world can come together in a virtual workplace.

This transformation will continue until ultimately every clearly defined, objectively measured task is captured in an algorithm that can replace human work. Experts debate just how quickly these changes will fall into place, but the consensus is clear: work that can be replaced by an algorithm will be.

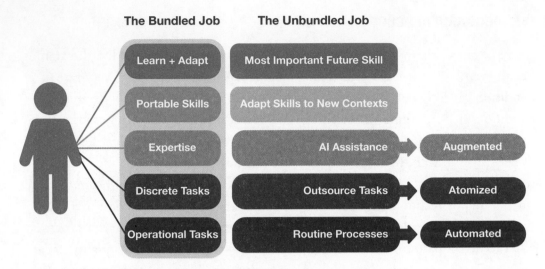

Figure 3.3: The Unbundling of a Job

Today's jobs, if they exist at all in the future, will have likely had the atomizable and automatable elements stripped out of them, with only computer-augmented expertise, portable skills, and learning agility remaining. But to be clear, the functions that can be captured in an algorithm are really only the tip of the capabilities iceberg. Many uniquely human attributes contribute to our work. They are fundamental to our ability to create and share value (Figure 3.3). By developing these uniquely human skills, we further build our adaptation advantage.

And even while technology is subsuming many job functions, there are many reasons to be optimistic. Aided by automation, we are producing goods and services at lower and lower costs, making even advanced products more affordable to more of the populations around the world. Consider, for example, an Apple iPad. Introduced in 2010 at a price of about $700, a lighter, brighter, more capable version of that iPad costs about $250 today, which is a superior product at 37% of the cost in under a decade. More importantly, rising machine intelligence advances our potential to solve the most complex and threatening problems, from disease to climate change to the efficient use of resources. Working in tandem with technology, people can create, solve, and shape the world for the benefit of all. In fact, we will need advancing machine capabilities to offset population declines in the developed world as our demographics shift dramatically, particularly in the United States.

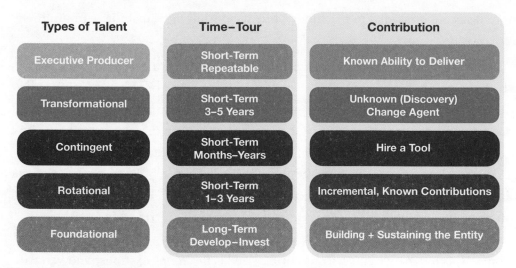

Figure 3.4: Five Types of Talent

Concept credit: Reid Hoffman (foundational, rotational, and transformational talent), Heather E. McGowan (contingent and executive producer talent).

The forces of atomization, automation, and augmentation are not just changing jobs; they are radically changing where and how people work. Companies that have been "containers" for jobs in which work was done will become "platforms" that leverage both technology and human talent to deliver productive outcomes (Figure 3.4). Employment itself will take various forms: foundational (those whose work is primary to the operation of the company), rotational (those whose work is periodically required), contingent (those whose often very specific skills are needed for a specific task), transformational (those brought in to navigate a change in organizational or product strategy), and executive producers (those who bring specific talent and networks to deliver a project or event). In his book *The Alliance,* founder and chairman of LinkedIn Reid Hoffman writes of people working in "tours of duty," wherein they cycle through specific projects, finishing one and moving on to the next, sometimes with a bit of respite or reskilling in between.

Coupled with the rise in computerized intelligence, this is a sea change not only in how work is done, but also in what humans do and how they gather the skills to do it. Gone will be the days of a straight-line path through college to work to promotion to career to retirement. (For more on this, please read the book's Introduction.) Instead, we are finding ourselves on a cyclical road where more and more tasks are offloaded to machines while we upskill our capabilities in uniquely human ways.

Many people find this prospect exhilarating, but there are as many who find it breathtakingly frightening. But keep in mind that we've been augmenting and adapting to new technologies and new ways of work for hundreds of years. Every time you embrace a new capability of a product or service that you already use or adopt a new product altogether, you've adapted. The difference now is speed. You can do it because you already *are* doing it. Think back over your lifetime. You have adapted to dozens of things you once found unthinkable. Depending on your age, you have likely adapted the way you bank, for example. A trip to the local bank became a stop at an available ATM, which became an app on your phone. And phones? From hard-wired devices to brick-sized cell phones to robust and versatile smartphones, we've adapted to so many aspects of communications that most of us have forgotten—if we ever knew—the sound of a dial tone. Television has transformed from programmed airwaves to cable to on-demand Internet, and so have our television watching habits. And few of us, we'd bet, would be willing to go back to typewriters and adding machines. Technologies deliver great convenience and advantage, even if they require adaptation. Now, as technologies change the face of work, we will adapt at a quickening pace. Change? Sure. But you've got this. You already have an adaptation advantage.

We have been told for decades that we have to "robot-proof" our careers, and that's the folly. There is nothing that can be taught to prevent any of us from having to adapt. The good news is that we are already adapting even if we don't sense it happening. Humans will continue to adapt to take on new roles, the ones that are not clearly defined or objectively measured. In other words, the automation and atomization of work *frees* human workers to do better and more fulfilling work by outsourcing the dull and routine tasks.

The same holds true for cognitively intensive work; human potential is enhanced through augmentation. Artificial intelligence systems such as IBM's Watson are being trained to detect cancer in MRIs and early prototypes show promise in their ability to do so. In a 2019 experiment, *Vice News* pitted the LawGeex AI against Tunji Williams, a graduate of one of the country's top law schools. The AI analyzed contracts with greater accuracy and greater speed than the human lawyer.

But here's the good news: these highly skilled humans can now focus on that which is uniquely human: applying that discovered knowledge and caring for patients and clients. When asked why he wasn't upset by the legal smackdown upset, lawyer Williams told *Vice News,* "I wasn't disappointed when the iPhone came out and I could do more things with this piece of technology, so this is exciting to me."[2] Williams understood that by embracing his adaptation advantage, he could do more, and even better, work.

Even jobs thought to be based in human creativity will benefit from augmentation. Renowned industrial designer Phillipe Starck, for example, created for Italian furniture maker Kartell a production-ready chair designed in collaboration with an artificial intelligence. Working with the computer-aided design company Autodesk, Starck taught the generative design software to understand design requirements—for example, the size, capacity, weight, and cost constraints—and the software offered hundreds of design options in return. Starck told editors at the design magazine *Dezeen* that the experience was "a lot like having a conversation."[3] Presented with hundreds of viable options, the designer can curate the computer-generated solutions and even 3D print samples using the software's specifications.

Cognitive automation is largely invisible because it happens in software. When Gmail interprets an invitation and puts a meeting on your calendar, that's adaptation. When that same application completes your sentences to make responding to and composing email messages quicker, that's adaptation. When you use the self-checkout lane at the supermarket, zip through a toll booth using a dashboard sensor, or ask Alexa to play your favorite song, that's adaptation. These are new, faster, cheaper, more efficient ways of doing things that once required at least some human intervention.

Automation will continue to develop gradually and is already happening in things you take for granted or even enjoy. And the fact is, companies have been using automation to redistribute workloads between systems and people. Still, there is plenty of work to do. If automation is the process of redistributing work between systems and people, people need to think about where they want to go once they've been relieved of the mundane tasks. And that's the tricky part. Every time you hand off something to an algorithm, you need to reach for something new. If you are handing your cognitive load to technology-enabled devices and services, what are you reaching up to learn? We are good at the handing off; we need to become better at the learning. And we have to become better at learning quickly and deliberately in order to "repace" evolution.

That is the adaptation advantage.

Notes

1. https://www.nber.org/digest/may17/w23285.shtml
2. https://blog.lawgeex.com/hbos-vice-news-features-lawgeex-in-the-future-of-work-and-lawgeex-beats-human-lawyer-again/
3. https://www.dezeen.com/2019/04/11/ai-chair-philippe-starck-kartell-autodesk-artificial-intelligence-video/

4 Getting Comfortable with Adaptation: The Slowest Rate of Change Is Happening Now

Key Ideas

1. The slowest pace of change you'll ever experience for the rest of your life is happening right now.

2. To gain advantage from change, organizations must make the shift from "scalable efficiency" to "scalable learning."

3. Effective learning requires organizations to tap into information flows, capturing the most emerging knowledge from sources inside and outside the company.

The Power of Pause

Stop. Breathe. Inhale deeply. Exhale slowly. Take a moment to experience slowness. Pause. As author and business strategist Dov Seidman says, "When you press the pause button on a computer, it stops. But when you press the pause button on a human being, it starts. It starts to rethink, reimagine, reflect." This is our unique, human, competitive advantage.

Feel refreshed? Great. Now get ready to leap into action. The speed with which technological, cultural, and social changes come at us is only accelerating. This exact moment in time, right now, is the slowest rate of change you will experience ever again. This speed of change makes it even more important to occasionally pause to reflect and focus on being human. Advances in technology allow machines to do many things, but they cannot dream, contemplate, or yet imagine our unseen future.

Both the acceleration in change and the need to pause may seem like frightening propositions to some. We, however, think this just might be the start of the most exciting ride of our lives. Why the optimism? Because the antidote to speed isn't slowness; it's learning and adapting. Do you remember what it was like to pack your lunch and get ready for the first days of a new school year? Those were exciting times in our childhood. Most everything about the days ahead was up in the air. Would we like the new teacher? Who would be in our class? What new subjects would be on the syllabus? Sure, there was anxiety, but there was also this one clear fact: the start of a new year was a clean slate.

Imagine what it might be like to tackle each workday as if it were the first day of school, but without the starchy new clothes. That idea—that every day is a new learning day—is at the heart of the adaptation advantage. Individuals and organizations best able to take in new data, read a situation, and pivot to a new opportunity are the ones best prepared to respond to—and even embrace—continuous change.

And here's the interesting thing: the same forces that are changing work as we know it are also providing the technology to help deal with that change. "Because we now have more access to data, and the ability to do more advanced workforce analytics, we tell someone where they can pivot to or what roles have good adjacency," says Joanna Daly, vice president of human resources at IBM. "We can deliver learning plans using automated recommendations. We have a digital learning platform, very Netflix-like. The technology five or six years ago might not have been there to run that kind of platform. So while on the one hand forces are at play creating the need for a much more agile learning culture, some of those same forces technologies are giving us the answer of how to respond."

From Scalable Efficiency to Scalable Learning

Management consultant John Hagel, co-chairman for Deloitte LLP's Center for the Edge, called this kind of continuous adaptation "scalable learning." Throughout history, industrial companies grew and thrived by embracing scalable efficiency.

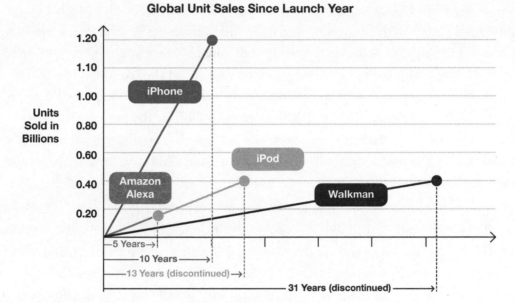

Figure 4.1: Speed-to-Product Peaks and Life Spans

Data sources: International Data Corporation and the product manufacturers.

Essentially, once a company figured out how to make something of value, it leveraged technology and process innovation to deliver the product more quickly and less expensively in order to make more profit. This model of scalable efficiency works well in an analog world where a company's performance is determined by how profitably it can deliver a product to more customers.

That model breaks in the digital era, however. Digital production at scale is virtually infinite and incremental costs are virtually zero. That's the upside. The downside is that products—digital and digitally enabled—have shorter life cycles than they once did. Consider the Sony Walkman, introduced to the market in 1979. For its time, the Walkman was an innovative personal, portable music machine. For the next 30 years, Sony continuously innovated the product line, altering styles and media from cassettes to compact discs to keep pace with fashion and technology innovation, ultimately selling 385 million units before discontinuing the Walkman brand in 2010.[1] By contrast, Apple introduced the iPod in 2001 and sold virtually the same volume—390 million units—before ending most production in 2014 (Figure 4.1). While the iPod Touch remains a product in the Apple lineup, it is a fraction what it was in the company's portfolio when the iPod held three or four spots in Apple's product lineup at once (Classic, Mini/Nano, Shuffle, Touch). Like Sony, Apple innovated iPod styling and capabilities, releasing new hardware models annually and software updates regularly, but despite these updates the market moved beyond a single-purpose personal media player and ended the iPod life cycle in less than half the time that Walkman products were in the market.[2] What killed the iPod? The iPhone. Apple killed its iPod cash cow in 2007 at the peak of iPod sales. The lesson here: if we disrupt ourselves at our peak, we'll be well prepared to surf the next wave of innovation and we'll own the timing of our transformation. That is the adaptation advantage in action.

Life spans of most digital media products are even shorter. Myspace launched in August 2003 and peaked five years later at just under 60 million users per month. Google Glass was all the rage, until it wasn't, going from darling to discontinued in just three years. RIM's early smartphone dominated the smartphone industry at the time; today, BlackBerry is little more than a footnote in the history of mobile device technology. The combined forces of social media and mobile photography enabled by smartphone cameras have all but killed the stand-alone camera business (Figure 4.2).

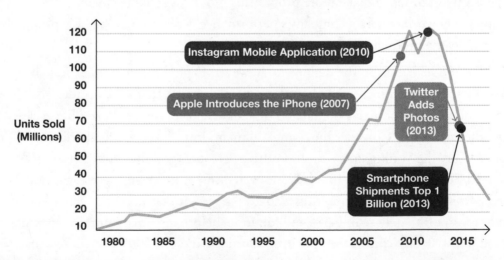

Figure 4.2: The Rise and Fall of the Camera

Data sources: The Camera and Imaging Product Association and International Data Corporation (smartphone shipments).

Surely, there are many reasons that these products could not sustain their market popularity, but at the risk of overgeneralizing internal business dynamics, one factor was crucial in determining whether the companies that created these short-lived products survived the bust: their ability to learn from the market and their mistakes, adapt to new opportunities, and move on. Research from the consulting firm Innosight, published in the *Harvard Business Review* in 2019, found that the companies that most successfully navigated the past decade of digital transformation did so by doing three things: identifying areas for new growth through novel products or services or markets, repositioning their core business, and improving financial performance. Essentially, this is our simple formula: learn, adapt, and perform. Consider Netflix, which launched in 1997 shipping DVDs by mail; they discovered new opportunity in streaming media and repositioned their core business to streaming media by 2007. In 2011 they started creating original programs, a pivot to new content that now comprises 44% of their revenue as of 2019.[3] In each of these strategic moves, Netflix flexed its adaptation advantage.

With that formula in mind, let's look at the history of the world's top five leading companies by market capitalization at 50-year increments, and the past trends become very clear (Figure 4.3).

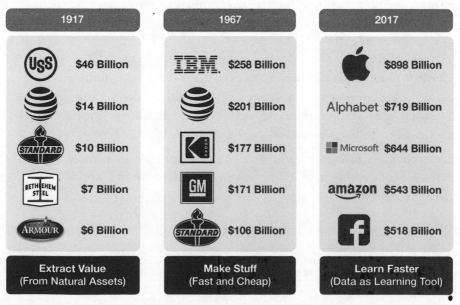

Figure 4.3: Top Five Companies by Market Capitalizations at 50-Year Increments

In 1917, four of the top five companies (US Steel, AT&T, Standard Oil, Bethlehem Steel, and Armour Meat Production) created value by extracting, processing, and packaging natural assets (oil, steel, meat). In 1967, four of the top five companies (IBM, AT&T, Kodak, GM, and Standard Oil) created value by optimizing the production (scalable efficiency by another name) of consumer goods. In 2017, all five of the top five companies (Amazon, Apple, Alphabet, Microsoft, and Facebook) were digital or digitally enabled. Technology and data makes these five companies thrive, for certain, but they are not just winning through technology. Digital technology enables flows of data, and data is an input to learning. These five companies created value by learning faster than their competition and easily adapting to new business models. Each company on this list has launched new products or services, repositioned its core business model, and continuously redefined itself. Amazon began as an online bookseller and now has reach into media, logistics, retail, grocery, and more. Every product Amazon offers is a vehicle to learn more about their customer; every interaction is a learning moment and a catalytic moment for new value creation. Every product offers feedback from customers, each and every one an input toward adaptation.

This is what Hagel calls scalable learning. Writing with renowned futurist John Seely Brown for *Deloitte Insights* in the Spring of 2013, Hagel was among the first management gurus to recognize the need to embrace a learning mentality.

> As the pace of change increases, many executives focus on product and service innovations to stay afloat. However, there is a deeper and more fundamental opportunity for *institutional innovation*—redefining the rationale for institutions and developing new relationship architectures within and across institutions to break existing performance trade-offs and expand the realm of what is possible.
>
> Institutional innovation requires embracing a new rationale of "scalable learning" with the goal of creating smarter institutions that can thrive in a world of exponential change.[4]

Scalable learning is what allows a company like Amazon to transform from online bookseller to global marketplace to web services provider to Academy Award–winning entertainment producer. Amazon seizes the opportunities that come like so much flotsam and jetsam of rapid market disruption.

From Stocks to Flows of Knowledge

But scalable learning is so much more than evaluating market turns and grasping at emerging fads. Principal to scalable learning is recognizing that information, which is the atomic stuff of learning, is changing. In a slow-moving world, we had time to codify information into curriculum, establish a pedagogy, conduct training sessions, memorize, test, and apply "stocks" of knowledge, quite like inventory stored in a supply closet for future use. When we stored those precious stocks of knowledge properly, we were granted a credential and deemed "educated." In a fast-moving world, the information comes at us not in packaged and digestible chunks but in continuous flows. To become scalable learners, we need to become adept at drinking in new information as it flows by (Figure 4.4).

Once more from Hagel and Seely Brown's 2013 essay:

> As the pace of change accelerates, the value of any stock of knowledge depreciates faster and faster. Today, competitive advantage is not based on stocks of knowledge, but having access to flows of knowledge to enable up-to-date information that enables adaptability.[5]

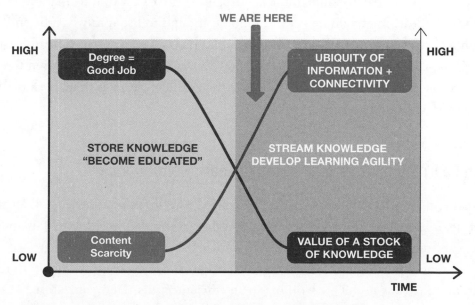

Figure 4.4: From Stocks of Knowledge to Flows of Knowledge

Credits: John Hagel (@Jhagel) for the stocks of knowledge concept and Laurence Van Elegem for the stream knowledge concept.

Flows come by opening ourselves and our organizations to new sources of information. Collaboration across organizational boundaries is one way of stepping into the flow. The payment-processing company PayPal, for example, offers a training program that rotates employees through short-term tours in the company's departments and business units. Employees are expected to learn the operations of each department and, more critically, to teach their colleagues about and provide insights into the other units they've experienced. In this way, everyone gets a broader view of the company and its capabilities. This model of learning-centric expeditions is what LinkedIn cofounder Reid Hoffman proposed in his seminal *Harvard Business Review* article "Tours of Duty: The New Employer-Employee Contract."[6]

Cisco Systems developed CHILL, Cisco Hyper Innovation Learning Labs, to bring customers from diverse industries together to "disrupt through the development of businesses and joint projects in 48 hours."[7] In 2018, a group of companies from industries as different as office equipment and oil refining gathered in San Jose for a two-day design sprint to learn how humans and machines might work and learn together in the future by prototyping product ideas. By working across corporate boundaries and making feedback from future users a critical part of the design process, participants in the lab expanded their flow of information. "The key factor in learning by doing is to be humble enough to listen to what the end user is telling you," says Kate O'Keeffe, director of CHILL. "People used to be interested in the innovations I was working on, and now they are far more interested in the curiosity and iterative approach that we take to get there." Why is that? Because that's where the learning happens.

From Learning to Work to Working to Learn Continuously

Fundamental in this shift from stocks of knowledge to flows of knowledge is letting go of the idea that we learn how to work and then apply that learning to a lifelong career. This thinking worked in the slower-moving industrial era. We progressed through school picking up and storing knowledge (and, let's acknowledge it, building discipline) that was useful for working in an efficient industrial organization. Along the way, we learned a lot about a specific function like accounting or supply chain management or mechanics. From time to time, we might have even refreshed our knowledge stocks with new information, taking professional and skills development courses to make our learning current. We exercised that knowledge on the job, every day, applying what we knew to the efficient processes that made an organization effective and, hopefully, profitable. Then, at the end of a long career, we retired. Learning to work to retirement was, for most folks, a pretty straight pipeline, and for way too many, a bit like living life as a component moving on a factory conveyor belt. (Revisit the book's Introduction if you are not familiar with these concepts.)

That conveyor belt not only prepared us for our jobs but also fixed our occupational identities in our minds. Work was more siloed by function and we tucked into those silos until business management gurus touted cross-functional teams and the notion of the "T-shaped" (team-based) thinker as a better alternative to the single discipline focus of the "I-shaped" (individual-based) worker.

That old conveyor belt of the past was a pretty effective system when business optimized for efficiency, but it's no kind of system at all when businesses optimize for learning, which they must do now to remain relevant.

Now, rather than learning how to work, we ought to work in order to learn. That is, we take learning *from* our work as the primary benefit *of* work. The products and services we create and sell deliver revenue to the company. More importantly, the individual and collective learning we take from the process of creating those products and services builds the capacity of the worker and the organization to learn, create, and produce even more. When the pace of change accelerates, the products and services we produce are evidence of our capacity and the result of our learning.

Further, this velocity of change requires that we abandon the discipline identity of both the I- and T-shaped theories and move to transdisciplinary "X-shaped thinking," wherein humans and machines collaborate from discipline-agnostic perspectives to find and frame emerging complex challenges (Figure 4.5). Working to learn requires that transdisciplinary mindset.

People have always learned on the job, but what they learned was *how* to perform the explicit aspects of the job; they acquired the skills to do the work. Now, we have to ask what the work has taught us. What did we learn from all the information that flows through the process of working? How were specific problems solved? Which approaches failed and why? How might those same approaches be effective in different circumstances? Who contributed and how well did they work as a team? What new skills and insights were developed in the course of the work? Where might we apply this new learning elsewhere in the organization? What did performing this work teach us about ourselves, our organization, and our abilities to do more

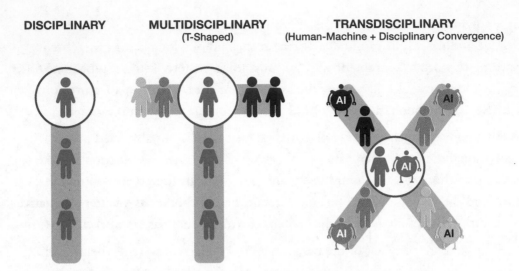

Figure 4.5: From I to T to X: The Transdisciplinary Imperative

and better work together? These questions are the tip of the iceberg of intentional learning, and they all start with the core questions: In what ways are we smarter now than before we started? How have we increased our capacity as individuals and as an organization? The answers to these questions get at another *how*, the tacit knowledge that underpins what we do in our organizations. Tacit knowledge flows around explicit skills, and both are needed to do a job well.

Identifying Patterns to Build Bridges

The same introspection that codifies workplace learning is essential for workers as they build bridges from one job to another. And it's the key to moving fast in the face of change. Rather than thinking about what you do *as* a job, inventory what you do *in* the job. That collection of capabilities and skills most certainly is widely applicable to many other, different kinds of work.

Consider the case of William. For nearly 30 years, he's made a career in education, first as a classroom teacher, then school principal, until finally he was hired as the superintendent of a regional school district. Along the way, he earned a doctorate in education. "I don't know what I would do if I weren't an educator," Will told us.

Frankly, we were stunned. Across his career, Will had exercised tremendous skills through a wide array of challenges. When an elementary school caught fire over a long holiday weekend, he successfully and swiftly managed the crisis, shifting hundreds of kids, teachers, bus schedules, and school staff to other locations and communicating complex logistics, so that students would not miss a beat when schools returned to session. When teachers went on strike, he negotiated the contentious relationship between the union and the school board, bringing everyone to the bargaining table and ultimately to agreement. He has overseen construction projects, mentored student teachers, managed public relations, and much more. Any of these skills are transferable to hundreds of jobs that would never have "educator" in the job description. But because Will attaches his professional identity to a singular kind of work, he fails to see that his pattern of experience might match that required for some other type of work.

Will is not alone. And this need to overcome the fixed occupational identity has created an opportunity for Michael Priddis, the CEO of Faethm.ai. Calling itself the "world's data source for the Fourth Industrial Revolution," Faethm has developed a software platform that uses payroll and HR records to analyze a company's workforce and, using predictive analytics and market data, identify opportunities to optimize through automation. Make no mistake, this optimization comes at the price of jobs. Automation of current work reduces headcount. But this foresight is a lot like fire: it can burn our homes down, but it also can cook our food and heat our homes. So Faethm's software also provides another, human-centric, view: it identifies opportunities to proactively upskill and reskill for the workers whose jobs are most at risk. Specifically, the platform can recognize which workers will be affected, and—most importantly—match those workers' skills to other needed roles within the organization. According to Faethm, the software calculates a "pivot score" that identifies the jobs that match an employee's capabilities and ranks them by the quality of the move, considering pay, location, and the shortest possible learning pathway (Figure 4.6).

For example, a bank might be shedding accountant jobs in favor of automation, yet that same bank may need to staff up on cybersecurity analysts. "The skill gap between the two is small," Priddis says. "The gap isn't a process gap, but a knowledge gap. The abilities and activities are almost the same, so you are really mostly retraining on domain knowledge."

By matching patterns, the Faethm software creates a "job corridor" from one role to another within the company, avoiding the expense and delays that are associated with the "spill and fill" approach to workforce management—laying off employees whose jobs are no longer needed and hiring new employees for newly created roles.

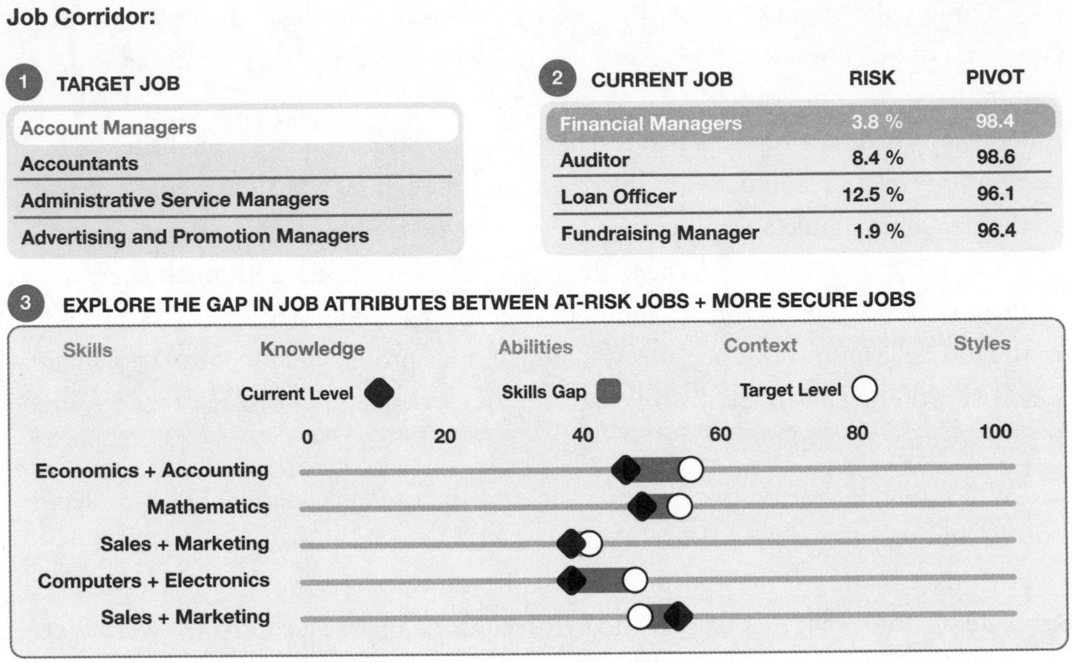

Job Corridor:

① TARGET JOB	② CURRENT JOB	RISK	PIVOT
Account Managers	Financial Managers	3.8 %	98.4
Accountants	Auditor	8.4 %	98.6
Administrative Service Managers	Loan Officer	12.5 %	96.1
Advertising and Promotion Managers	Fundraising Manager	1.9 %	96.4

③ **EXPLORE THE GAP IN JOB ATTRIBUTES BETWEEN AT-RISK JOBS + MORE SECURE JOBS**

| Skills | Knowledge | Abilities | Context | Styles |

Current Level ◆   Skills Gap ▪   Target Level ○

| 0 | 20 | 40 | 60 | 80 | 100 |

Economics + Accounting
Mathematics
Sales + Marketing
Computers + Electronics
Sales + Marketing

Figure 4.6: The Job Corridor and Pivot Score

Ironically, perhaps, because AI is often the basis of many job-disrupting technologies, this particular AI system is helping workers move to new jobs when technology takes the ones they currently have.

You don't need to be a highly tuned AI system to become an agile and adaptive pattern matcher, however. You simply need to think about your work more broadly than the narrow description that defines your occupational identity. What have you learned that gives you access to new opportunities?

A study by Willis Towers Watson found that 90% of maturing companies expect digital disruption, but only 44% are adequately preparing for it. AT&T saw changes coming to its business more than a decade ago when they realized that at least 100,000 of their 250,000 employees were in jobs that were unlikely to exist a decade later. They calculated that the median cost of replacing an employee was 21% of their salary and decided to take a different path. Those 100,000 people may have lacked the explicit knowledge in the skill areas of new positions, but they had tremendous tacit knowledge about the organization that would be hard to replicate. AT&T invested $1 billion in a massive learning infrastructure they called "Future Ready" with a companion employee guide called "Career Intelligence." Each employee can view the career intelligence dashboard that shows available jobs, required skills, salary range, and, most importantly, the job demand outlook—how long that job is expected to last. The company is explicit with employees that reskilling (learning new skills) or upskilling (going deeper on current skills) is not a one-time event but a continuous journey.[8] We spoke with Bill Blasé, senior executive vice president of human resources, about why AT&T started making these considerable investments more than a decade ago.

"As our company continues to evolve, we're working constantly to engage and reskill our employees, and to inspire a culture of continuous learning," he told us. "It's the right thing to do for many reasons, not the least of which is providing those who have helped to build AT&T an opportunity to grow and succeed along with the company. For us, the reskilling effort is about transparency and empowerment— creating learning content, tools and processes that help empower employees to take control of their own development and their own careers" (see Figure 4.7). While AT&T is not likely to retain every worker, the company's intent and process of training its existing workforce with new explicit knowledge has retained a tremendous amount of tacit knowledge, the know-how that enables the know-what.

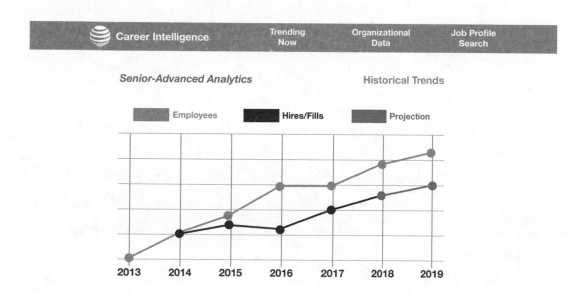

Figure 4.7: AT&T Career Intelligence Job Outlook

Data source: Information courtesy of AT&T.

By looking at skills and capabilities, rather than at specific jobs, much like AT&T and Faethm have done, the Foundation for Young Australians identified seven "job clusters" where common skills and capabilities are organized into a set of jobs.[9] It might not be surprising to learn that in the care-giving job (the "Carers") cluster, for example, physicians, social workers, and fitness instructors share similar sets of capabilities. Or that "Informers" such as teachers, economists, and accountants had overlapping skillsets. Hidden in that data, however, was a surprising and exciting discovery. By training for one job in a cluster, you acquire on average the skills for 13 other, different jobs. "This is profoundly important," says the organization's CEO Jan Owen. "The fact that you could unlock up to 13 other jobs by entering into one job in a cluster changes everything. It shows you that you can move."[10] The best organizations realize that talent mobility strengthens their adaptation advantage.

More importantly, Owen points out, these other jobs require relatively minor upskilling or retraining to move from one to another. You do not have to start over from scratch.

In this increasingly fast-moving, change-dominated world, the speed you need comes from matching the "how," rather than the "what," of what you do. Make that shift in perspective and identity, and you are well on your way to adapting to the emerging market.

Notes

1. https://www.sony.net/SonyInfo/CorporateInfo/History/SonyHistory/2-06.html#block2

2. https://www.cnet.com/pictures/the-complete-history-of-apples-ipod/

3. https://hbr.org/2019/09/the-top-20-business-transformations-of-the-last-decade

4. https://www2.deloitte.com/us/en/insights/topics/innovation/institutional-innovation.html

5. Ibid.

6. https://hbr.org/2013/06/tours-of-duty-the-new-employer-employee-compact

7. forbes.com/sites/westernbonime/2018/02/04/how-cisco-chill-turns-ideas-into-companies-in-48-hours/#35a85458cbb7

8. https://www.cnbc.com/2018/03/13/atts-1-billion-gambit-retraining-nearly-half-its-workforce.html?__source=twitter%7Cmain%7Ctext

9. https://www.fya.org.au/wp-content/uploads/2016/11/The-New-Work-Mindset.pdf

10. https://www.youtube.com/watch?v=fzI0gQyCiLI

Part II

Letting Go and Learning Fast to Thrive

Key Ideas

1. Our deep connection to our occupational identity challenges our ability to navigate change, but we can rewrite our narratives for a richer purpose.

2. Defining yourself, your skills, and your knowledge beyond the scope of your job is the first step to thriving in the future of your work.

3. To maximize human potential, we need to put humans at the center of every value proposition. If we focus on developing uniquely human skills, we'll continue to build value for ourselves and the organizations that engage us.

5 What Do You Do for a Living? The Question That Traps Us in the Past

Key Ideas

1. Whether voluntary or otherwise, people are changing jobs, and even industries, more frequently than ever before.

2. Our tight tether to occupational identity makes it even more challenging to adapt to a rapidly changing future.

3. To navigate change, we must rewrite the narratives that form our identities to avoid getting caught in an identity trap and to build our adaptation advantage.

The Questions That Limit Our Identity

Throughout our lives, we've gotten to know one another by asking three seemingly simple questions: "What do you do?" adults ask one another. "What's your major?" we inquire of university students. And who hasn't asked a child, "What do you want to be when you grow up?"

We use these questions to orient ourselves in the world, to describe and define ourselves and one another, and to give our academic pursuits a sense of direction. These questions, though inquisitive and well-meaning, might be just the thing that tethers us to a fixed identity and denies the fluidity that adaptation demands. Rather than giving us direction, purpose, and identity, these questions can become traps hindering personal growth and evolution.

What Do You Do?

In the United States, if not most places, it's the icebreaker at gatherings both professional and social. The answer is layered with social signals. "I am a lawyer," one person might say, and we imagine the intelligence and diligence required for the paper chase. We probe on the legal focus—corporate litigation, civil rights, malpractice, family law—and recalibrate assumptions. "I am an elementary school teacher," another person answers, and we envision the patience of the job required to mold young minds. Still another says, "I am an entrepreneur," and we make our assessment: a future Gates or a wide-eyed dreamer?

Doctor. Banker. Architect. Journalist. Account executive. Yoga instructor. Union steward. How we describe ourselves, the context we give our occupational identities, is fundamental to who we know ourselves to be. Take away that easy label and many of us become unmoored. Who are we, if we are not our jobs? In fact, studies have found that the loss of a job—and its associated identity—is more damaging to our emotional well-being and takes a longer recovery time than the loss of a loved one.[1]

Consider the implications of that finding when nearly 5 million people, voluntarily or not, separate from their jobs each month, according the US Bureau of Labor Statistics. Five million people! That's like everyone in the state of South Carolina wondering who they are now that their job is gone. Each and every month. And all signs indicate that this number will grow even bigger in the future. The professional social networking site LinkedIn found that people who graduated from universities in the United States between 1986 and 2000 averaged 1.6 jobs in the five years after graduation. That number jumped to an average of 2.85 for those who graduated between 2006 and 2010.[2]

The phenomenon is applicable to all developed countries. That data is reinforced by the Foundation for Young Australians, which projects that young people across the developed world and graduating from college can expect to have 17 different jobs across five different industries over the course of their careers.[3]

If job loss and change are the new normal—and they are—how will we ever learn to navigate our long career arc if we tether ourselves to a singular occupational identity? How do we let go of—or at least rethink—this obsession with career identity?

We have to start young.

What Do You Want to Be When You Grow Up?

Adults are always asking kids what they want to be when they grow up because they are looking for ideas.

—Comedian Paula Poundstone

It's no wonder that we ask adults "What do you do?" when we learned at an early age to connect with a future career identity. No doubt intended innocently enough to encourage a child's curiosity and aspiration, that question has become almost toxic as a device for focusing young children on realistic futures.

Not too long ago, Heather was talking to her then four-year-old niece Izzy about her day at preschool. The next day, Izzy told her, was career day and she was having trouble deciding what she would be because her teacher had told her that her idea about "being a unicorn" was not realistic.

Do we really need to ask children as young as four to decide on a realistic future self, especially when the world is changing so quickly that we may not yet even be able to imagine most of the future careers and even whole industries that will be options for today's preschoolers? Technological change will, in the words of IBM CEO Ginni Rometty, "reshape 100% of jobs."[4] Even if a youngster could tell you what she wanted to be when she grows up, it's likely that many tasks that job requires today will have been automated or re-formed completely by the time she's ready to earn her first paycheck.

Instead, we should be encouraging children's curiosity. Rather than asking what a child wants to be, let's ask what they like to *do*. Let's probe about the one thing they learned today and why that one thing was special or interesting. Let's free their imagination to envision a life and a planet that is full of possibility. What might that look like? What doors might open that we didn't even recognize were there? Let us simply ask children what they are curious about while encouraging them to develop their interests and areas of strengths.

So much of primary school in the United States focuses on the standardized tests that measure what a child does well—or worse, not so well—that children begin to form lifelong personal narratives long before they explore possibilities for their lives. Worse, early negative assessments cut off future exploration and limit individual and collective potential. "I am bad at math," for example, shuts down many career paths and now, especially, at a time when quantitative reasoning is essential. Encouraging curiosity, purpose, and passion will set young people on a path of lifelong learning. Such encouragement, more than test scores alone, will unlock potential and prepare children to learn and adapt across their now much longer career arcs. What we are really talking about here is agency, the capacity to act independently on one's own behalf. Agency is the opposite of hopelessness. Agency fuels the adaptation advantage.

Between "what do you do?" and "what do you want to be?" is one more question that we need to disrupt.

What Is Your Major?

Stop and think about your high school experience. How much of what you do today can you trace back to what you learned then or how you performed on some standardized tests? Now consider what young people today do in a world that is racing faster than the one you grew up in. We ask high school juniors and seniors to choose a focus of university study as part of the college application process. They step onto campus with the thinnest slice of experience and yet they are already tracked into coursework that is aimed at a specific, predetermined job that well might direct the remainder of their lives. Faced with the requirement to declare a major at the outset of post-secondary education, young people turn to familiar touchpoints to shape—and quite possibly limit—their future. Relying on high school experiences— "I'm bad at math" or "I love my French class" or "I hated my history teacher"—sends students looking for comfort, rather than challenges. Opting for areas of study that mimic the careers of parents' or parents' friends brings social acceptance. Falling prey to the influence of media provides a kind of endorsement of their choices. A 2009 study, for example, found the number of students majoring in forensic or crime scene science doubled over a five-year period and fully a third of those students were influenced by the popular *CSI: Crime Scene Investigation* television franchise.[5]

The social mobility implications of these influence-driven career choices are immense. Choosing a future self from the portfolio available in a child's family and social structure serves to replicate the conditions of that structure into adulthood. A child raised with high socioeconomic status will have a broader range of opportunity from which to select simply because they have been exposed to more options and had more aspirational and advanced professions modeled for them. Conversely, a child who grows up without socioeconomic advantages may see a much smaller world of opportunities. We can't break this cycle with a school system that screens students on a narrow set of skills and aptitudes, particularly when a child is the first in the family to attend university. How can these students see themselves in a field unfathomed by their family and community and unexplored in high school? Similarly, if you come from a long line of doctors or lawyers or fill-in-the-blank professions, it may be hard to imagine a self beyond the family business or the limits of the high school appraisal. Worse, following family footsteps has catastrophic potential as long-standing jobs and industries fall to automation and outsourcing. Imagine being the first in generations to reach for a career in an industry that has sustained your family for decades and longer only to find there is nothing to grasp.

University students commit to mortgage-level debt to pursue these monolithic degrees. A rigid curriculum, course sequencing, and class scheduling often push what was intended to be a four-year degree program to five or six years, increasing the cost of that degree by 25 or 50%. Recognizing this challenge, the National Center for Education Statistics now tracks graduation rates at six years for what has traditionally been a four-year degree. And what value is that degree? A study by the Federal Reserve Bank of New York found that only 27% of the people they surveyed work in the field of their undergraduate major.[6] Still, we myopically focus on the college major and push the decision earlier and earlier in the student's academic career, and with greater pressure. We tell students to pick a good major to get a good job in a good industry to climb a vertical career ladder. That ladder is gone. Good grades in high school may be an indicator of university completion rates, which itself might be an indicator of future earning potential. But let's be clear: good grades in a "good" major do not guarantee a "good" job.

Instead, shifting focus from a specific course of study or degree to a broadly applicable set of skills sets students up for success.

The Emerson Collective's XQ: Super Schools initiative is one of many emerging efforts to redesign the high school experience to better prepare students for a dynamic and rapidly shifting future. After a national listening tour, the Initiative established a set of "learner goals,"[7] including:

1. **Foundational knowledge**, the essential information you need to know to put new data in context, and

2. **Fundamental literacies**, the fluencies you need to operate effectively in the world. These include reading and quantitative skills, as you might expect, and to those add articulation, digital familiarity, collaboration skills, original and creative thinking, and lifelong learning.

Khan Academy, a nonprofit initially online-based learning company, launched the experimental Khan Lab School (K–12), where students are organized by independence level rather than age. They move through competencies rather than calendar years or standardized tests, and each student is required to teach as well as learn to reinforce their capabilities. Each student has a passion project in addition to their core coursework and teaching responsibilities. Collectively, these efforts communicate to students that they must have agency in life and specifically that lifelong learning is their responsibility. Connecting learning to purpose and passion is a means to self-fuel that learning. And, they establish an ideal foundation for lifelong adaptation.

The PAST Foundation takes a different approach by providing a place for experimentation outside the structure of a school system. Founder Annalies Corbin describes the PAST Innovation Lab, which opened in 2016, as an education R&D prototyping facility. "We opened the lab so that we could specifically test the boundaries of the work/school interface," she told us. "By fully embedding teaching and learning in industry R&D, startup, and launch, we saw exponential growth in students grasp of what is possible. Thus far, we have found when no longer constrained by the limits of traditional high school, students in the PAST lab excelled. They found the connections between industries and application and they are able to contribute to solving real-world challenges in real time as full active members of design teams. Our kids are only constrained by the limits of their own knowledge, which grows daily." The PAST lab has embedded the adaptation advantage into their learning platform.

These three examples are compelling experiments in creating the new foundational skills and abilities that will be necessary to navigate in this new world, and not just for high schoolers, but for everyone.

The Identity Trap

When we define ourselves by what we do, our childhood aspirations, and our academic study, we are constructing our identity from dangerous materials. These rigid building blocks fix in place who we are and, more importantly, who we are not. If these are the bricks of occupational identity, however, it is a deeper and long-running narrative that is the mortar between them. Our notion of who we are, our identity, is formed by our explorations and, so often, by what we are told to believe about ourselves.

As occupational and personal identity have become conflated, it's important, then, to take a step back and look at how personal identity is formed.

How Identity Is Formed

There are two predominant theories on how our personal identities are formed. The first is the identity status model, originally proposed by developmental psychologist Erik Erikson and later refined by psychologist James Marcia.[8] The second theory is the narrative identity theory proposed and developed by Dan P. McAdams.[9] Identity formation, notably personal identity formation, primarily begins in adolescence and likely continues throughout your life, identity experts say. Gender and racial identity formation already start in childhood.

Identity Status Model

The identity status model involves exploration of and commitment to one's sense of self. In this process of discovery, you pass through, and often land on, one of four distinct statuses:

1. Diffusion: Someone is not committed to an identity and not exploring options.
2. Moratorium: Someone is exploring but not committed.
3. Foreclosure: Someone has committed without exploration.
4. Achievement: Someone has explored and committed on an identity, the optimal status.

Maybe you accepted your parents' religious or political views without exploring your own values or you adopted their favorite sports teams without question. If so, these parts of your identity are foreclosed, according to the identity status model. Or maybe—as we have—you challenged your family's beliefs, causing them to shift from a foreclosure status to a moratorium or achievement status. As openly gay women and professional women often navigating male-dominated fields, we experienced not only our own change from moratorium to achievement, but also that of our parents, who reexamined their own religious (in Chris's case, her father was an ordained United Methodist minister) and social beliefs.

The point is this: identity needn't be set in concrete. New information can guide us from one status to another in this model of identity. In fact, Theo Klimstra, PhD, associate professor at the Tilburg School of Social and Behavioral Sciences at Tilburg University and an identity specialist, believes we are "never done with our identity formation," especially in today's society where so many factors are called into question by external changes. Indeed, our ability to navigate and reformulate our changing identity is core to our adaptability.

Narrative Identity Theory

The second major theory on the development of personal identity is the narrative approach, which McAdams cast as the life story model of identity. This theory proposes that we form our personal identity by creating our own narrative and memories of self. Those whose stories contain more references to meaning-making, research suggests, have higher levels of happiness. And while there is no commonly accepted research to prove the point, we can't help but wonder if this meaning-making might also lead to more satisfaction and engagement with work. Narrative experts do, however, believe that more and deeper reflection helps us make connections to meaning.

Considering all these facets of narrative identity theory, we have an obligation to ourselves to identify the source of the stories that shape us. And as organizational leaders, we have the opportunity to make self-reflection an important tool as we support our workers as they develop and adjust their occupational identities. We will take a closer look at these concepts in Chapter 9, including the ideas of managing the impression others have of us as leaders and vulnerability as strength in leadership identity.

Narratives Can Trap Us in the Past and Limit Our Future

Identity need not be static. Yet how often do we cling to a story of our past self at the expense of our future selves? Once again we recall Dan Gilbert's insight that we remember more easily than we imagine. How often do we hear our work and social cohorts brag about now long-gone glory days? Do they go on about their successes in high school or college sports? Are they still glowing in the early praise that they were smarter, better looking, or more charming than others, even as those attributes have faded or the competition against which we were judged has become so much greater? That is an identity trap, the formulation of a self-image based on a moment in time. As we consider the speed of change coupled with the lengthening of our life spans, we will be devoured by these traps if we don't learn to recognize and avoid them. We don't have to get stuck, though; instead, we can learn and adapt to reinvent ourselves time and again.

Our identities begin to take hold when we believe the narrative we are told—directly and indirectly—about ourselves. Dr. Klimstra told us a story of his early career to make this point. As one of the only men in a cohort working in developmental psychology, he was often asked by both fellow (usually female) students and professors to be a study partner on quantitative subjects like statistics. Professor Klimstra had no particular quantitative prowess. He was just the lone male student, who others assumed would be skilled in this learning. Professor Klimstra admits now that he worked harder on those subjects so that he wouldn't fall short of the expectation that others had of him. As a result, he did well in those subjects, and it redirected his career from practice to research.

Chances are good that something like this has happened to you. Somewhere along the way someone told you that you were good at something and you worked hard to realize that expectation. Or worse, you were told that you could not do something, so you never even tried. Identity traps begin in narrative, then take on many different forms. These traps hinder adaptation.

Gender, Narratives, and Identity

Much like Professors Klimstra's experience, perhaps the most influential narrative given to us is our understanding of gender roles. Yet there is a profound disconnect between competence and confidence. Dozens of studies from organizations as diverse as Goldman Sachs to Columbia University have found that companies that employ women in large numbers outperform their competitors on every measure of profitability. At nearly every level of academic achievement, women outpace men. Women now far outnumber men among recent university students in most industrialized countries.[10] For the ninth straight year, the Council of Graduate Schools (CGS) reports that for every 100 men who earn a doctoral degree at US universities, 137 doctoral degrees are awarded to women.[11] Since 1981, more women have earned master's degrees than men. For every 100 master's degrees granted men, 167 go to women. For every 100 bachelor's degrees going to men, 120 are awarded to women.

You might think that after decades of academic acceleration, women would make headway in achieving leadership positions in the workforce. Women now compose 47%[12] of the US workforce in general and 50% of the workforce with at least a bachelor's degree.[13] Still, women account for just 5% of the CEOs of S&P 500 companies and 6.6% of *Fortune* 500 companies. Women are achieving professional credentials at higher rates than men *and* studies prove that having more women in the workforce leads to better company performance. Still, the proportion of women in leadership roles is abysmal. So, where's the disconnect? Slow social change is one answer, but there's likely something else: the way we socialize gender.

The Confidence Gap

For nearly 50 years, girls have outperformed boys in academics. In "Leaving Boys Behind: Gender Disparities in High Academic Achievement" (National Bureau of Economic Research 2013), researchers identified a gender gap in GPAs among high school seniors of about 0.2 between 1976 and 2009.[14] Then, girls began earning even higher grades, pushing the trendline up as more young women reported plans to attend not only university but, specifically, to pursue advanced degrees.[15] Perhaps one way to account for this difference is the guidance we give to boys and girls. Boys are often praised for their performance as is. Girls are told they need to be better, perfect even, if they are to compete with boys. It's a narrative that creates a persistent insecurity. A 2015 report by the Organisation for Economic Co-operation and Development (OECD) entitled *The ABC of Gender Inequality in Education* found that boys spend one hour less per week on homework than do girls, resulting in a Programme for International Student Assessment (PISA) score that is, on average, four points lower for boys than girls.[16]

At a recent talk, Heather shared this research and hypothesis with senior executives for a large international hotel chain. After the talk, a female executive took her aside. "I do this," she said. "I don't know why I do this, and I never realized I am part of the problem. I have two children close in age. When my son brings home a test score of an 85 (out of 100), I figure that is good enough considering he was probably tired. When my daughter brings home an 85, or even a 95, I ask her why she did not study more. I know how hard I had to fight to make it up the career ladder as a woman in this industry. I guess I am figuring my daughter will have to fight as hard, but I did not realize I was eroding her confidence in the process while bolstering my son's." Confidence is key to adaptation.

In the summer of 2019, 24 people—six women and 18 men—launched campaigns to become the Democratic nominee for the 2020 presidential race. By almost all measures, former vice president Joe Biden was the early frontrunner and considered the most electable candidate, even though he had twice lost his prior bids for the nomination. Of the six female candidates, all but one had been elected repeatedly and often in hotly contested districts. The other 17 male candidates offered a mixed bag of political success, yet most of these were considered viable candidates. The constant refrain among pundits of all political stripes was consistent: "Is she electable?" "Can a woman win?" Maybe these comments are echoes of Hillary Clinton's loss in 2016. Or maybe we simply continue to believe an ancient narrative. Let's consider what happens at work.

A Hewlett-Packard internal report, quoted in *Lean In*, *The Confidence Code*, and dozens of articles, looked at the rates of promotion between men and women throughout its organization. Men, they found, put themselves forward for promotion when they had 50 to 60% of the skills required for the job. By contrast, women waited until they had a full 100% of the skills. Or, to summarize another corporate study by the Catalyst Foundation, "We promote men for potential and women for accomplishments."[17]

Still, we have to ask: Why the confidence gap?

Writing for *The Atlantic* in May 2014, journalists Katty Kay and Claire Shipman explored what they called "The Confidence Gap." An extensive review of research into perceptions of competence and confidence, the article posited that women are encouraged to gain competency, whereas men are encouraged to gain confidence. Further, for women to succeed in jobs and careers, they must fill the confidence gap. In short, school systems are competence factories for females and confidence foundries for males, resulting in unequal foundations for adaptation.

To make their point, Kay and Shipman leaned on the 2003 study by Cornell psychologist David Dunning and Washington State University psychologist Joyce Ehrlinger,[18] who looked at both confidence and competence in professional women to correlate the relationship between one's perceived competence and one's confidence in a job was well done. The researchers asked male and female students to rate their perception of their scientific skills before taking a quiz on scientific reasoning. Perhaps not surprisingly to many, women rated their skills more modestly than did men, rating themselves 6.5 on average on a 10-point scale, while men rated themselves on average at 7.6. Asked how well they thought they did on the quiz, women thought they scored 5.8 of 10; men thought they got 7.1 answers correct. In fact, their test scores were almost the same: women answered 7.5 questions correctly and men scored slightly better at 7.9 correct answers on average.

The lack of confidence extended beyond the quiz-taking for women. When offered the opportunity to compete for prizes in a science quiz prior to knowing their results, the women passed on the opportunity 51% of the time, compared with men, who declined only 29% of the time even though their scores were almost identical.

Dunning and Ehrlinger are not alone in their findings. The *Atlantic* article goes on to highlight the work of Brenda Major, a psychologist at the University of California at Santa Barbara. Major's findings were consistent with those of Dunning and Ehrlinger. When presented with a series of tasks and asked to predict how they would perform on them, women regularly underestimated their ability and their performance. The opposite was true for men. "It's one of the most consistent finding you can have," Major tells the article's authors.

If you consider these research studies together, you'll see the systematic challenge: differing expectations and standards for males and females are quite literally coding the confidence gap—and, by extension, the adaptation potential—inequitably by gender from cradle through career (Figure 5.1).

Not surprisingly, inequity cuts across race and is pervasive in hiring standards, too, as Dr. Vivienne Ming found in her research. Ming mined data from 122 million LinkedIn profiles to isolate two names—Joe and José—that, while similar-sounding, are commonly associated with White and Latino men, respectively. She then zeroed

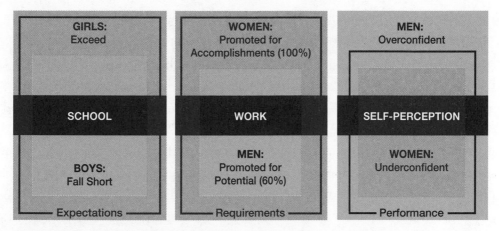

Figure 5.1: How We Build Competence and Close the Confidence Gap for Girls and Women

Data sources: "Leaving Boys Behind: Gender Disparities in High Academic Achievement" (National Bureau of Economic Research 2013); Katty Kay and Claire Shipman, "The Confidence Gap"; 2003 study by David Dunning and Joyce Ehrlinger; Hewlett-Packard internal employment study.

in on a single job function, "software developer." With a final data set of 7,105 Joes and 4,896 Josés, she found that to hold the same job, José most often needed a master's degree and that Joe did not require even a bachelor's degree. The difference in standards is quite literally what Ming calls the tax on being different.[19]

If, as the Narrative Identity Study suggests, we embrace identity through the stories we are told about ourselves and others, then collectively we are socializing a confidence gap in women and the achievement gap in minorities to the detriment of business and social benefit. We believe what we hear, and it becomes a self-fulfilling prophecy. And it is a tragic loss of human potential.

Identity Is Never Done

If Professor Klimstra is right that our identity formation is never really complete, we ought to become more intentional about our explorations and narratives as more and more external factors are called into question. As we spoke to Klimstra for this book, he mused that white males, who in most Western societies enjoy the highest privilege and status, may have never explored many aspects of their personal identity because their status based on race and gender was more likely to be assumed than challenged.

White males are often channeled into higher-paying, higher-status jobs, while women are steered toward higher-caregiving, often lower-paying, jobs.

Identity formation, Klimstra notes, is a negotiation between internal beliefs and observations on one side and on the other, external narratives, notably what people—including the media—tell you about yourself and others. The cultural and societal normative changes we talked about in Chapter 2 demand a continuous renegotiation of identity, and that will be particularly difficult for people who believe their status and privilege is slipping away. It is very difficult to learn and adapt when you feel your core identity is under threat. Learning and adapting requires a certain vulnerability and a comfort with not knowing. When long-given status is called into question by other races, other genders, and even by technology, it is very difficult to be vulnerable in order to adapt to a new profession or occupation.

An Occupational Identity Crisis Isn't Limited to Job Loss

In a review of research on the effects of job loss, the What Works Wellbeing Centre in London found that job loss can take longer to recover from than the loss—through death or divorce—of a primary relationship. Job loss has financial implications, of course, but the greater effect on wellbeing is the impact of the loss on one's social and personal identity. Men, they discovered, are more impacted than women, and many folks never fully recover from the loss of a job.

Consider where we started this chapter. Who are you if you are no longer a banker or a lawyer? How does your social status—real or perceived—change if you no longer work for that Fortune 50 company or blue-ribbon firm? What if the career path you chose is a dead end rather than a long road? These aren't just hypothetical questions, and they each point to a potential crisis in identity. In fact, the authors have seen the effects up close among their friends.

Marie[20] worked for nearly two decades as an investigative journalist for what she viewed as among the handful of prestige print outlets. Of her own accord, Marie left the organization to join a well-established broadcast news organization. The new job came with a very substantial bump in pay and the ability to shape the investigative news unit she had joined. But just two weeks into the job, Marie was in full-blown panic, thinking *What if this fails? What if I cannot find my way back into the prestige print world? My new colleagues don't work at my pace. What have I done with my life? I should see this like a sabbatical or a learning tour, but if it fails, what will I do?* These questions pour out of a job change–driven identity crisis.

Charlotte,[21] on the other hand, is a rare female in the male-dominated broadcasting industry. Her career has spanned nearly three decades with a major network. Like her peers who have spent their entire career with the likes of ESPN, ABC, and CBS, she has focused on rising in the ranks. These days, Amazon is actively buying the rights to sports broadcasts, so it is only a matter of time before Charlotte has to adapt to a change in her home base. But Charlotte gives sports production a broad definition. She's not concerned about who owns or licenses the production because, at the end of the day, an investment in good content is an investment in her production. Amazon has shown through their investment in entertainment media that they are willing to invest in quality. Charlotte has no qualms about working for Amazon.

Between us, we know dozens of people who intended to make their careers in academia. Each was nurtured through a system of higher education that said their academic achievement and the ultimate award—a doctoral degree—would give them entry into an elite class of professionals. Our friends trod the path that promised a tenure track position and lifetime employment. Some were successful. Many others realized that dream wouldn't happen for them and successfully segued to other industries, adapting their skills and knowledge to adjacent markets from sales to marketing to educational product development to educational technology. Still others, unable to obtain the academic appointments their studies assured, have spent their careers stringing together adjunct teaching incomes. These friends so closely identify as college and university professors that they haven't been able to adapt their skills and knowledge to another context.

These stories are not unique. No matter what your identity, your chosen path, your "what do you do," you will one day need to learn and adapt. Whatever you do now, unless you are closing in on your target retirement years, is unlikely to be your last job. If you have been at the same job for five to seven years without a change, brace yourself; change is coming. If you lean into the change, follow your curiosity, continually update your skills, nurture your network, and with a market mind continually assess the landscape for an opening for your abilities, you will be just fine. You've found your adaptation advantage.

Notes

1. What Works Wellbeing Center, London. https://whatworkswellbeing.org.

2. https://blog.linkedin.com/2016/04/12/will-this-year_s-college-grads-job-hop-more-than-previous-grads

3. https://www.fya.org.au/report/the-new-work-mindset-report/

4. https://www.cnbc.com/2019/04/02/ibm-ceo-ginni-romettys-solution-to-closing-the-skills-gap-in-america.html

5. https://www.telegraph.co.uk/education/6348107/CSI-fuels-forensic-science-degree-rise.html

6. https://libertystreeteconomics.newyorkfed.org/2013/05/do-big-cities-help-college-graduates-find-better-jobs.html

7. https://xqsuperschool.org/xq-schools/xq-learner-goals

8. J. E. Marcia, "Development and Validation of Ego-identity Status," *Journal of Personality and Social Psychology* 3 (1966): 551–558.

9. D. P. McAdams, "The Psychology of Life Stories," *Review of General Psychology* 5 (2001): 100–122.

10. https://www.studyinternational.com/news/record-high-numbers-women-outnumbering-men-university-globally/

11. http://www.aei.org/publication/women-earned-majority-of-doctoral-degrees-in-2017-for-9th-straight-year-and-outnumber-men-in-grad-school-137-to-100-2/

12. https://www.dol.gov/wb/factsheets/qf-laborforce-10.htm

13. https://www.pewresearch.org/fact-tank/2019/06/20/u-s-women-near-milestone-in-the-college-educated-labor-force/

14. David Autor and Melanie Wasserman, "Wayward Sons: The Emerging Gender Gap in Labor Markets and Education." Washington, DC: Third Way.

15. https://pdfs.semanticscholar.org/f3e0/77a1ed80b10b7c07cd5782053821fe9fd412.pdf

16. https://www.oecd.org/pisa/keyfindings/pisa-2012-results-gender-eng.pdf

17. https://www.catalyst.org/research/the-myth-of-the-ideal-worker-does-doing-all-the-right-things-really-get-women-ahead/

18. https://pdfs.semanticscholar.org/1f54/81ffac7c9495782c423b3de8034d8d2ac ba5.pdf

19. https://www.ft.com/content/1929cd86-3eb6-11e6-8716-a4a71e8140b0

20. Name changed.

21. Name changed.

6 Finding the Courage to Let Go of Occupational Identity

Key Ideas

1. Know why: Understanding what you do, or even how you do it, pales in comparison to knowing why you do what you do.

2. Let go: Defining yourself, your skills, and your knowledge beyond the scope of your job is the first step to gaining your adaptation advantage.

3. Embrace failure: Sometimes your "worst" setbacks are your best career boosts.

What Does the Parable of the Three Stonecutters Have to Do with You?

In his seminal book *The Practice of Management*, Peter Drucker describes the parable of the three stonecutters:

> An old story tells of three stonecutters who were asked what they were doing. The first replied, "I am making a living." The second kept on hammering while he said, "I am doing the best job of stonecutting in the entire country." The third one looked up with a visionary gleam in his eyes and said, "I am building a cathedral."[1]

Before you read on, think about your own work, then jot down which stonecutter sounds most like you.

Drucker used the stonecutter parable to illustrate the importance of managers who see the bigger picture, are driven by a vision, and are not distracted by the means to that end. Drucker identified the first stonecutter as a highly manageable individual seeking a "fair day's work for a fair day's pay." The third stonecutter, he wrote, was the true manager. The second stonecutter, he lamented, was the real problem. "The majority of managers in any business enterprise, are, like the second man, concerned with specialized work."

When Drucker's book was first published in 1954, managers believed that the best workers did not think, but instead just did what they were told. In that old economy, management wanted workers who did not think. Today, we need a different kind of workforce, one in which everyone is able to think, adapt, learn, and create new value for their organizations and themselves.

In fact, that's what makes this parable—and its many retellings—even more relevant today. In one version of the story, the third stonecutter declares, "I am building a cathedral to bring people together." In that version of the parable, the stonecutter reveals not just a vision—to build a cathedral—but also a purpose—to bring people together. And the first stonecutter, today, may be in the best position to adapt. His focus on "making a living" is untethered from any particular occupational identity. Even so, however, that worker's lack of connection to his work means he may not have the necessary motivational drive to traverse from one occupation or industry to the next unless the pull of making a living itself is strong enough. The second stonecutter, though, is in a world of hurt in the emerging world of work. He is entirely defined by the material, the job, the business model, and the industry. As we discussed in Chapter 5, identity tightly tied to a current job or an application of current and specific skills and knowledge is very dangerous when the world is moving rapidly around us.

Instead, a purpose-driven identity—a sense of self that transcends job title and skillsets—is the best defense against work-related obsolescence. Yet, building that identity is not easy, because to have a sense of purpose, you must first discover your purpose.

Annalie Killian, vice president of human networks at New York management consulting firm sparks & honey, described finding your purpose as "a lifelong process of experimentation and editing." Amazon CEO Jeff Bezos famously signs his annual shareholder letters "two decades later, still in Day 1." His point is that it is very easy to fall into routine. "Day 2," he wrote in his 2017 letter to shareholders, "is stasis. Followed by irrelevance. Followed by excruciating, painful decline. Followed by death. And *that* is why it is *always* Day 1."[2]

The Day 1 Mindset: You Are a Prototype; Start with Why

How do we avoid falling prey to occupational identity traps? We start with Why.

A decade ago, at a TEDx event in Puget Sound,[3] leadership guru Simon Sinek put forth a concept he called the "Golden Circle" in his talk "How Great Leaders Inspire Action," This talk has been viewed by over 46 million people and is the third most watched TED Talk of all time. Sinek codified his observations in his best-selling book *Start with Why*,[4] in which he posits that people do not buy What you do, they buy Why you do it. We are attracted to things, he says, but we are even more connected to shared purpose.

At the outer ring of his Golden Circle, Sinek proposes that every organization—and, we would add, every individual—can tell you what they do. Companies offer some sort of unit of value, like a product or service. We define ourselves by what we do in our jobs, readily connecting to a title, industry, or set of responsibilities. Every company answers the What question easily.

One ring closer to the center, though, the question gets trickier. Good companies, Sinek says, can also answer the How question. How do you create your unit of value? The answer is generally the special process, whether technical patents or human capabilities, that enables a company to deliver its What. Our How, as individual contributors, is our set of unique capabilities, something most of us are able to describe.

Truly great companies, Sinek says, reach the center of the Golden Circle: the Why. These companies can tell you why they exist. They can explain their purpose and what they believe, at their core, to be true. They have a sense of mission that enables customers and employees to connect across shared values.

In the age of accelerated change, every company needs to define themselves not just by their What or How, but also by their Why. The Why is the principle that guides organizations through rapidly transforming market requirements, product and services opportunities, and business model adaptation. The Why is every company's unique advantage.

Consider Amazon and Barnes & Noble, both booksellers, but with different Whys. In response to Amazon's market entry, Barnes & Noble began selling books online as well as in its brick-and-mortar stores. Amazon determined its Why "to be Earth's most customer-centric company, where customers can find and discover anything they might want to buy online, and endeavors to offer its customers the

Figure 6.1: Amazon's Why, How, What

lowest possible prices."[5] Amazon became a massive retail presence with offerings that span streaming media, entertainment content, drones, consumer technology, healthcare, and industrial cloud services. Barnes & Noble, focusing its Why on serving book lovers, remains largely a brick-and-mortar retailer with some online presence and modest forays into adjacent markets such as toys, games, and stationery products. Where you shop for books likely depends on your specific needs, but you can be pretty sure that Barnes & Noble won't be winning an Academy Award or providing your healthcare (Figure 6.1).

As technological and social change unmoor us from our professional identities, we must connect to our Why as well. If the research reported in the Foundation for Young Australians' seminal paper "A New Work Mindset" is correct, young people in the developed world graduating today will likely hold 17 jobs across five different industries in the course of their careers.[6] To navigate that trajectory, you cannot define yourself by what you do. Instead, you must take your definition from how and why you do it (Figure 6.2). This search for meaning is a lifelong process of negotiation and experimentation. Experimentation allows you to try out versions of you and edit until you zero in on things that matter most to you. These versions will change over time, each being a chapter in the book that is your career. We loved the way Kate O'Keeffe, founder of the Cisco Hyperinnovation Living Labs (CHILL), expressed that idea to us: "We need to stop thinking about ourselves as forming a finished product and we need to start thinking of ourselves and our careers as a

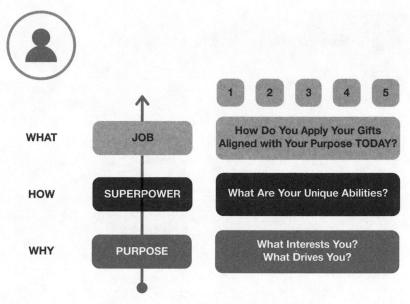

Figure 6.2: Purpose First, Job Last: Your Why, How, What

prototype in continual states of change and improvement." That continual state of change is the adaptation advantage at work.

By thinking of your career as a continual "beta," you will develop your relationship to purpose, better understand and develop your superpowers, and come to recognize that your job is merely the application of your skills and a connection to your purpose at a moment in time. This is how you move from "a fair day's work for a fair day's pay" (stonecutter 1) or a fixation on your current tasks (stonecutter 2) to a greater purpose-driven vision (stonecutter 3), "building a cathedral to bring people together."

Exercise 1: Your What, How, Why

Describe your career in the What, How, and Why framework. Consider all your Whats or at least the most import ones—the jobs that were most meaningful to you, the ones where you felt like you were firing on all cylinders, expressing your true self. Then, try to capture your Hows—consider the things you believe you do well and ask yourself what your unique abilities and aptitudes are that make you good at what you do. Finally, think about your Why. Your Why is what drives you. You do not necessarily need alignment between your Why and your employer's Why, but it does help. (If you need help with your Why, go to Exercise 2.)

Exercise 2: Passion and Curiosity Inventory

Finding your passion sounds simple but figuring out what motivates you and aligning that motivation with market opportunity may be one of the hardest, and most important, tasks in navigating your career. Try starting with a simple exercise: journaling. Keep a journal for at least a week or two and maybe a month if you can manage it. Enter your activities for the day every day. Once you have finished your list of things you've done that day, review the list and circle the things that gave you energy. Note the tasks, meetings, conversations, or anything else that you could not wait to tackle. Capture the thoughts and ideas that entered your mind as you woke in the morning and would not leave your mind as you sought to sleep at the end of the day—not the things that haunted you and stressed you out, but the things that you generally enjoyed doing. Can you aggregate these things and synthesize them into a single statement or two?

This can be a daunting exercise, so it's only fair that we take you through our own experiences as examples.

Heather has a background in industrial design (product design, design thinking) and an MBA with a concentration in entrepreneurship. She likes finding a pathway through ambiguity by researching, asking questions, synthesizing information, and visualizing the resulting complexity to provide a clear plan of action. She currently applies her design and business skills (her How) by crafting keynote talks (her What) that allow her to realize her Why of continuous learning. Heather does not want routine. She does not want to go into an office and do the same thing every day. Her job as a keynote speaker takes her all over the world to all sorts of companies and organizations, keeping her on a continuous and steep learning curve with frequent opportunities to experience and adapt to new and different cultures. That work energizes her. The rapid rate of change means business leaders, educators, investors, policy makers, corporate governors, and many more folks are trying to make sense of the shifting opportunities for their organizations. That's a rich market opportunity for Heather. Prior to this work she engaged in consulting, ranging through product design and design strategy, socially responsible investing, educational consulting, and corporate consulting—each also providing a continuous and steep learning curve with a high need for adaptation.

Chris has always seen her work through the eyes of a journalist. She is an observer, a reporter, an analyst of situations, and a communicator of ideas. Early in her career, she jumped into the tech sector, applying her craft as an editor, largely focusing on new personal computing products and, specifically, on the sector's startup companies. She quickly understood that technology had tremendous potential to transform society and wanted to champion its use for good (her Why). By listening to and interviewing more than 20,000 startups, Chris discovered that her superpower is connecting the dots among people and ideas, seeing patterns that others often miss (her How). Today, she consults with select startups, curates a community of journalists, and writes about emerging ideas (her What).

How Job Loss Can Be a Gain

The US Bureau of Labor Statistics reports that 1.5 million involuntary and 3 million voluntary job "separations" occur each month. The problem is not limited to the United States. In just about every part of the world, job loss and job change are the new normal. It helps no one to act as if they're not.

Losing a job is hard. It can be devastating financially, socially, and personally to lose your place, your status, your sense of self, and the financial stability that supports your primary relationships. As Chapter 5 discussed, overcoming job loss can be more difficult than getting past the loss of a primary personal relationship. Sometimes, though, job loss and change can be a gift. You can, if you allow yourself, learn the most in these hard moments and find ways in the end to liberate yourself from the constraints of your past occupational identities.

Although he was asked many times, Steve Jobs (Figure 6.3) only gave one commencement speech in his life. In his speech to the Stanford graduating class of 2005, his honesty and vulnerability provided great insights into the gift of job loss. The world's most famous CEO, the modern Ben Franklin, had been fired. What he said about that experience is remarkable.[7]

In what is widely recognized as one of the best commencement speeches ever given, Jobs talked of the early success of Apple, growing the company from a workshop in his family's garage to a $2 billion enterprise in just 10 years. At about that time, Jobs recruited former Pepsi-Cola CEO John Sculley to work with him as Apple's CEO. What started as a great collaboration turned into a greater conflict. The Apple board took Sculley's side, and Jobs was out of the company he created. "So at 30 I was out. And very publicly out. What had been the focus of my entire adult life was gone, and it was devastating," Jobs told the Stanford graduates.

Figure 6.3: Steve Jobs

Photo © Asa Mathat.

"I didn't see it then," he said, "but it turned out that getting fired from Apple was the best thing that could have ever happened to me. The heaviness of being successful was replaced by the lightness of being a beginner again, less sure about everything. It freed me to enter one of the most creative periods of my life."

Jobs's story is the stuff of legend. In addition to NeXT, he started the animated movie company Pixar, which created the first fully computer-generated animated film, *Toy Story*, now one of the top-grossing animated film franchises ever. In a twist of fate, Apple bought NeXT, and Jobs returned to Apple, ultimately reclaimed the CEO's office, disrupted the music industry by bringing the iTunes and iPod products to market, and supercharged the smartphone market by introducing the iPhone.

"I'm pretty sure none of this would have happened if I hadn't been fired from Apple," Jobs recounts in his speech, adding later, "I'm convinced that the only thing that kept me going was that I loved what I did."

His advice for the Stanford graduates is excellent advice for anyone: "Your work is going to fill a large part of your life, and the only way to be truly satisfied is to do what you believe is great work. And the only way to do great work is to love what you do."

Modeling Vulnerability: We Share Our Hard Lessons

Like most of our readers, we authors have both experienced the tough love that comes from disconnecting with occupational identity. We want to share our stories in the hopes that you might learn from them. What's more, it's reassuring for all of us to recognize that this is a shared experience that we are growing through together.

Chris

Recently, I was asked what metaphorical mountain I had climbed in my career. I was stumped. For much of my career, I didn't see mountains; I just forged ahead, doing the work and taking on challenges that, in aggregate, looked like a well-intentioned career as a technology journalist turned startup guru turned author. I began my career almost accidentally, taking a job in a publishing company while waiting to begin graduate school. Soon, the job was much more interesting than the prospect of more school and I surrendered my fellowship to dive into work. Over time, I rose to editorial leadership positions at the top technology publishing company, ran the industry-leading startup showcase that ushered some 1,500 startups to market, and launched my own startup event and advisory firm. For nearly 30 years, my professional identity was wrapped up in that work and I was widely recognized for it. But the underpinnings of my company weren't as strong as they needed to be. In the parlance of the startup world, we pivoted from event producer to software platform to a co-working space, and we never got enough lift to really soar. At the end of 2012, I closed the business, and without realizing it, largely closed a chapter of my career without knowing the plot of the next one.

What unfolded over the next five years is truly the biggest mountain of my career. Actually, "quest" might be the better word. In that time, I had to face the question "Who am I if not who I was?" I needed to be brave enough to shed an identity that no longer fit and to find comfort in a new self-definition. I grabbed at new experiences like a sailor hugs a mast in a storm, anything to find safety in the midst of deep change. I took a turn at seafaring (literally), where I mentored social-impact entrepreneurs aboard a ship circumnavigating the globe. I spent an academic year in a journalism fellowship, then got and then lost a job at a world-class academic institution. On a lark, I even tried bartending school and experimented with the gig economy, driving for Uber and working through UpWork and Thumbtack to better understand the experience of all three. None of it made answering the question "What do you do?" any easier, but all of it got me closer to articulating the Why of how I spent my working capital.

Each of those experiences taught me something about myself, and collectively they taught me the value of intentionality, about doing work not because it was something to do, but rather because it was *the* thing to do. I learned which work gave me purpose, which did not, and most importantly, how to say no to work that took more than it gave in satisfaction and learning.

Learning to work with purpose and intention sounds like it should be the simplest thing in the world. It is not. In fact, it's been the hardest work of my long career.

Heather

I have three hard lesson stories: rejection, a firing, and feedback. All three have informed my life every day since.

In my twenties, I had somehow managed to avoid failure. Somehow everything I had truly wanted had materialized. In high school sports, I had been varsity, captain, and all-star. I was accepted into the college of my dreams, Rhode Island School of Design. After a couple of professional jobs in design, I was repeatedly told I was asking inappropriate questions about why we were pursuing certain products or markets. That, I was told, was the domain of "business" and if I wanted to ask those questions I ought to get an MBA. Okay, roger that. I figured I would just go to an Ivy League school and pick up an MBA. My presumption of privilege was off the charts. I took the required standardized tests and got hard lesson number 1: I scored 440 out of a possible 800. I buckled down, studied endlessly, tested again, and received a 700. Good enough. I applied to all the top business schools. To my surprise, rejection after rejection arrived. One admissions counselor told me, "Frankly, we do not have any idea why you want to study business if you studied art and you work in design. Maybe this just isn't for you." Finally, after admissions season, I applied to Babson College and was accepted. The funny thing was that I received a rejection letter from a school I had not applied to that year. It was like they wanted to send the message: "Seriously, Heather, it is never going to happen, so we are now sending you a 'don't even think about it' preemptive rejection." I went to Babson, which turned out to be the exact right place for me. Entrepreneurial thinking is a perfect complement to design thinking. Design thinking helps you find and frame problems; entrepreneurial thinking helps you scale solutions and create value. This is my first hard lesson story.

Hard lesson number 2, unfortunately, came around the same time as the first hard lesson. I was fired. I was treading water at that large sporting goods company and they decided I was far more trouble than I was worth. I was arrogant, angry, and lacked the maturity to process the business school rejections I had been receiving. Frankly, I also was not very good at this kind of design and I cared little about it. Technically, I lost my job in a downsizing, but I made myself an easy target for cost savings. Still, I was stunned. I was deemed no longer relevant. Making sense of this took some time. On the one hand, I was lucky, because I transitioned immediately into consulting work and fairly quickly and easily picked up enough consulting work to keep myself afloat. On the other hand, design was my job. How did they get to decide I was suddenly no longer needed with no notice and little financial runway? Suddenly I lost my daily routine, work identity, and face-to-face interaction with my work friends. It took me a few years to fully appreciate this experience, but losing my job and then building a consulting practice taught me to create new value every day, for myself and for any organization that engages me as a consultant or a speaker. Every moment of every day, I strive to provide maximum value to the organization. I never take that for granted. I only work for places that share my values, which makes it easier to concentrate on creating value for those organizations.

Hard lesson number 3 was simpler, but no less impactful. As a young consultant, I joined forces with another much more seasoned and successful consultant who had his own well-established firm. I had an idea for a product for the medical industry, which was his specialty. Together, we pitched my idea to a very large company. After the pitch meeting, the senior consultant took me aside and offered me advice. I was young and not nearly as self-aware as I should have been. I was not expecting a critique. In fact, I might even have been expecting a compliment. I had run much of the meeting and thought I had done a pretty good job. He said, "You are smart, and you have some really great ideas, but you have absolutely zero idea when people are no longer listening to you. You are clueless about your audience. It would benefit you to pay much closer attention to your audience and cater your message, rather than focus on telling every detail you deem important." I was a bit stunned but pretty quickly realized that this was really valuable feedback I could do something with. I have thought about that feedback frequently over the 20 years since it was offered. I have written a few times to my senior colleague, now long retired, telling him how much his candor meant to me because it quite literally changed my life. I make a living now as a speaker, which I am quite certain would not have happened if I had not learned how to connect and communicate rather than simply spew my talking points on whatever poor souls landed in front of me.

So for me, hard lesson number 1, rejection, taught me that to find my fit is far more important than prestige lists. Hard lesson number 2, the firing, taught me to create new value for my clients every day. When I can no longer create new value, I should move on to my next challenge. And hard lesson number 3, feedback, taught me to speak to my audience's interest, not my own. I am very thankful to the person who fired me, the many admissions counselors who rejected me (as well as the one who accepted me), and Jack, my consultant friend who was generous enough to give me a hard and much-needed message.

Exercise 3: Learning from Hard Lessons

What are your hard lessons? What are the most difficult things you have experienced or endured and how have you learned from them? If you need more inspiration than our or Steve Jobs's stories, we suggest a couple of TED Talks. No matter what you might think about her now-infamous White House internship, Monica Lewinsky's life has been defined by a very public lapse of judgment in her early twenties, and for it, Lewinsky has been a target of cyberbullies and unflattering press. Few others have faced such harsh and public repercussions for their errors in judgment. And few have had to do the work Lewinsky has done to process that experience. We highly recommend her TED Talk in which she gives a clear path forward to anyone who's suffered deep shame.

In another recommended TED Talk, the mother of Columbine High School shooter Dylan Klebold shares her struggle to make sense of raising a son who becomes a murderer. Sue Klebold has become involved in medical research and brain science to try and help prevent future tragedies.

If these two women can emerge from their experiences you may be able to as well. Think about this exercise as creating a TED Talk about your hard lesson. How do you make sense of it? What did you learn from it? What lessons or gifts were contained in the bad-tasting medicine you received?

What Do You Do Now?

So now it is up to you. What kind of stonecutter are you? How do you define your Why and How? How does your What manifest your Why and How? What is your purpose? Pay attention to what interests you; that is the fuel source for your lifelong learning and the basis for your adaptation advantage. In fact, the answers to these questions will give you the courage to let go and thrive.

Notes

1. Peter Drucker, *The Practice of Management* (New York: Harper & Row, 1954), p. 122.

2. https://www.geekwire.com/2017/full-text-annual-letter-amazon-ceo-jeff-bezos-explains-avoid-becoming-day-2-company/

3. https://www.ted.com/talks/simon_sinek_how_great_leaders_inspire_action?language=en

4. https://www.amazon.com/Start-Why-Leaders-Inspire-Everyone/dp/1591846447

5. https://www.amazon.jobs/en/working/working-amazon

6. https://www.fya.org.au/wp-content/uploads/2016/11/The-New-Work-Mindset.pdf

7. https://news.stanford.edu/2005/06/14/jobs-061505/

7 Learning Fast: Why an Agile Learning Mindset Is Essential

Key Ideas

1. To thrive in the future of work, we must be agile and resilient, adept at both learning and unlearning to continuously adapt to change.

2. Skills alone are not enough to adapt in the future of work. We must also work to build resilient and adaptable identities, develop an agile learning mindset, and focus on the uniquely human skills that enable us to collaborate effectively.

3. In the midst of accelerated change, businesses must shift focus from extracting value with limited resources to creating new value by scaling organizational learning.

Learn Fast—What Does That Even Mean?

We are in the greatest velocity of change in human history, and somehow we've got to keep up. The thing is, we will never keep pace by doing the same things faster. In fact, that will only get us farther behind. Why? Because it is the modality of the past. To keep up with this quickening pace, we need to focus not on speed and efficiency, but on agility and adaptability.

We are emerging from decades of work formed around what Deloitte's Center for the Edge founder John Hagel calls "scalable efficiency." In this model, a company triumphed in the marketplace by making goods faster, cheaper, and overall more efficiently. They extracted the greatest value by optimizing every aspect of the production process. That method worked when business models and product lifecycles lasted a long time. Workers could perform similar tasks over longer periods of time and focus on refining their processes to improve efficiency.

Not so in the digital economy we now find ourselves squarely in. Old ways of doing things are quickly becoming obsolete and sending businesses off course in a race to the future. As the *New York Times*'s Thomas Friedman says, "When you are in accelerated change, small errors in navigation can get you off track very quickly." It is critical, then, to remain open and attentive to the signals that recommend course corrections, lest you quickly go too far astray.

What's the answer? To keep up with change, we must foster learning and adaptive organizations, ones that are able to see and interpret change as it comes at them. As Friedman notes, "The most open and connected systems allow you to get the signals first."

Those signals enable you to sense and respond to changes in technology or the market. Those signals require new learning.

What Do We Mean by Learning? First-, Second-, and Third-Generation Learning Organizations

To understand what it means to be a learning organization, it's instructive to consider the evolution of organizational learning. Global management consulting firm Boston Consulting Group (BCG) defined "generations" of learning organizations in its 2018 paper, "Competing on the Rate of Learning."

- "In first-generation learning organizations, businesses learned how to execute existing processes more efficiently—best exemplified by the 'experience curve.'"[1] In other words, first-generation learning companies acquired knowledge and stored expertise.

Second-generation learning companies eye the current product life cycle and optimize for efficiency while simultaneously seeking the next product introduction. They operate in two modes of learning at once, modes we call efficiency and exploration. BCG notes that a second-generation learning company is increasingly important today because "technological innovation has compressed product life cycles, so new learning curves appear before old ones have fully played out—and firms must balance both dimensions of learning at the same time."

The third-generation learning company is the most advanced. It uses what the BCG calls the "autonomous learning loop." In this scenario, sensors, platforms, and artificial intelligence rapidly accelerate the rates of learning by generating, gathering, and processing data in real time. In this third scenario, the company becomes self-tuning around its processes. Humans focus on complementing the technology by leveraging their uniquely human skills to add value to and make meaning from automated data processes.

The S-Curve of Learning: Explore, Experiment, Execute, Expand

Regardless of how we work, we all do so within the context of a business, and a business is merely the ability to identify and solve a problem and provide a solution at scale. By this definition, every organization is a business, whether it is a for-profit corporation, a nonprofit religious or social group, a government bureaucracy, or an academic institution. A business is simply a container for work, no matter what its purpose.

The process of finding that problem and solving it at scale follows a classic S-curve. The classic S-curve of any technology or business model begins with an investment in time, money, or both, then scales quickly as users adopt the offering, before leveling off as the offering reaches maturity and is replaced, ultimately, by a better solution.

The S-curve is a macro process in two phases: exploration followed by exploitation or, in other words, value creation followed by value extraction. Within these two macro phases are four stages, not unlike many design thinking processes (Figure 7.1):

1. *Explore.* Begin by exploring the problem or opportunity space to frame the challenge.
2. *Experiment.* Then experiment with possible solutions to the framed challenge.
3. *Execute.* Once a viable solution is identified, introduce the solution to market.
4. *Expand.* Then, finally, expand the market and extract the maximum value until this solution is replaced with a new and better one.

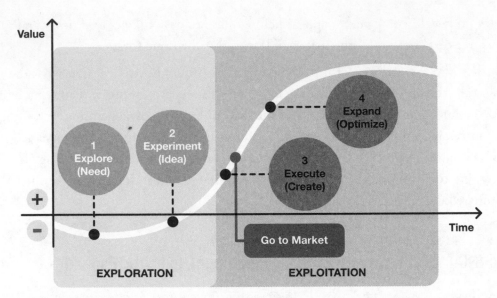

Figure 7.1: The Value Creation S-Curve: Explore, Experiment, Execute, Expand

These phases are iterative and each progression from one phase to the next may circle back to check assumptions and make sure the right question is being answered by the value created.

When the world was slower and products, services, and business models lasted longer, much of a company's activity lived in stages 3 (execute) and 4 (expand), during which time the product went to market. The bulk of the effort was spent creating greater efficiencies in production while driving demand through promotion. Now, because the rate of change has accelerated, the S-curves are shorter and closer together, so we must become more comfortable working in stages 1 and 2 (exploration and experimentation) (Figure 7.2).

And there is advantage in it, too. So many skills can and will be replaced with AI, neuroscientist Dr. Vivienne Ming reminds us. "If you want something that grows, changes, explores, pushes boundaries, there's just nothing in the fields of AI that does anything like that right now," she told us. "There's no machine learning I can build that can explore. That's the unique value proposition of humans."

That view is reinforced in BCG's third-generation "Autonomous Learning Loop" report. Product and business model lifespans shorten and technologies better address efficiency, leaving humans to look past the expertise of the exploitation phase and refocus efforts and abilities on the exploration phase of value creation. This shift

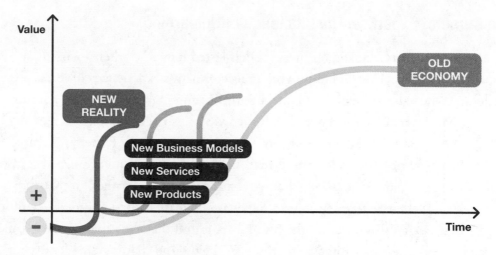

Figure 7.2: Old Economy S-Curve Gives Way to Shorter and More Frequent S Curves

has driven the popularity of Design Thinking, a set of exploratory practices that deliver deep investigation into problem understanding, user empathy, and solution matching. In recent years, Design Thinking has been a popular buzz phrase, and is often used narrowly to describe only one of several applications, such as customer-centric innovation, iterative prototyping, continuous improvement, or broad and freeform brainstorming. Design Thinking can be all of those things.

Originating in industrial design, Design Thinking places the user or customer at the center as the primary focus of the product, service, or system development efforts. Design Thinking begins by looking carefully at the challenge to make sure the problem to be solved is correctly identified and understood, then framing the challenge in a way that reflects that deep understanding, and finally developing, testing, and iterating on proposed solutions. It's relatively easy to come up with new forms of existing solutions. Design Thinking comes into play when we consider the challenge the original product was created to solve. That's the difference, for example, between creating a new kind of drill bit and designing new ways to make holes. In the context of our four-stage S-curve, we need Design Thinking for the "explore" stage. Design Thinking helps find the right problem to be solved by framing the success criteria of the solution, not just the symptoms of the problem. Understanding these success criteria is as important as the problem-solving phase of development, and the agile mindset is the primary tool to do this work.

The Curse of Expertise: The Challenge of Unlearning

When products, services, and business models lasted longer, workers focused on deepening their expertise and improving their company's experience curve. As change accelerates, the value of that experience diminishes and may even become a hindrance because that expertise may prevent you from adapting to new methods of creating and delivering value. A 2015 study by Yale researchers Matthew Fisher and Frank Keil, "The Curse of Expertise,"[2] found that the more we learn and acquire expertise, the less willing we are to question what we assume we know. Further, in the study discussed in "When Self-Perceptions of Expertise Increase Closed-Minded Cognition: The Earned Dogmatism Effect,"[3] the researchers found that the expertise curse can strike nonexperts as well. In their experiments, they found that merely identifying oneself as an expert, regardless of their abilities or knowledge in the area, can create closed-mindedness to new information. In essence, we lose our beginner's mind and create a dangerous blind spot for ourselves.

In conversations with business leaders who hold a steadfast commitment to tried-and-true business practices and who have failed to evolve, the reaction is always the same: we did not see the change coming, or, more often, we didn't think it would come that quickly. In some cases, those executives saw a competitor gaining on them. They just could not stop doing what they were doing. They did not know how to change course. In almost every instance, these leaders say they were overconfident in their way of doing things such that they could not pivot even when the end was, upon reflection, obvious. You'll recall from Chapter 4 that Apple took the decision to launch the iPhone at the height of iPod's success. The company anticipated the next wave and took measures to capture it, even at the expense of its then-flagship product. That's incredibly difficult to do, particularly when all instincts are telling you to hold on to current success. We'll talk more about this challenge in Chapter 9 when we introduce you to telecom executive David Walsh.

To avoid this trap, leaders need to cultivate mindsets that are predisposed to adaptation. Specifically, they need to become adept at unlearning that which they believe is paramount in order to learn what is new.

The Iceberg: The Substance Beneath the Surface

To understand how to set the conditions for learning that is predisposed to adaptation amidst changing culture, identity threats, and a coming shift in skill

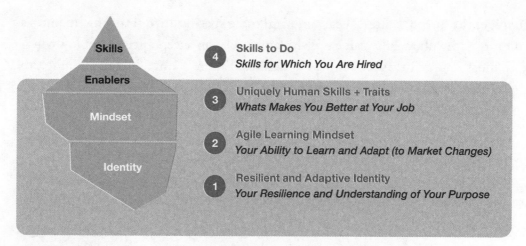

Figure 7.3: The Iceberg: Layers Required for Learning and Adaptation

demands from technical to social, consider the iceberg (Figure 7.3). We embrace the skills we see and in which we have been trained, while ignoring the underlying fundamentals necessary for a resilient workforce—notably, those skills that enable the adaptation advantage. Those underlying capabilities are what make both learning and unlearning possible.

Our Iceberg Model has four basic layers. Explicit skills and knowledge rise above the surface, are visible, and are understood. Enablers, sometimes called soft skills, sit at the water line; they are those things that make us better at our job and relationships but are rarely the abilities for which we are explicitly hired. An agile learning mindset lies below the surface and enables us to continuously learn and adapt. At the base of the iceberg, a resilient and adaptive identity connects our motivation and our purpose. Like an iceberg afloat in the ocean, it's easy to see the explicit skills once learned and often employed. If we are to become adept at learning and adaptation, we will need the whole stack—not just what is easily seen or certified, but the layers deep beneath the surface that support us through the long arc of our careers. As we discussed in Chapter 2, the rapid changes in social and cultural norms cause many people to feel they have lost their status or place. This identity threat at the base of the iceberg makes the entire stack harder to manage.

Identity: The Core of the Adaptive Mind

The ability to learn and adapt continuously requires both an agile learning mindset and a resilient and adaptive identity. It is nearly impossible to learn and adapt if your core identity is under threat. Learning, and more specifically unlearning, requires a comfort with vulnerability, an ease with ambiguity, an acceptance of not knowing, and, most importantly, an openness to failure. "Failure is not a bug of learning, it's the feature," according to Rachel Simmons, a leadership development specialist at Smith College's Wurtele Center for Work and Life.[4]

In her pivotal book *Daring Greatly,* renowned sociologist Brené Brown writes, "Vulnerability is the birthplace of love, belonging, joy, courage, empathy, and creativity. It is the source of hope, empathy, accountability, and authenticity. If we want greater clarity in our purpose or deeper and more meaningful spiritual lives, vulnerability is the path."[5]

Adaptive workers must tap into this vulnerability and dare to say "I don't know." These three simple yet difficult words are the first step to developing an adaptive mind. It is the letting go of knowing, it is the foregoing of expertise, it is the bypassing of ego in order to be open to newness, and it is the willingness to shun conventional wisdom to embrace your own internal understanding. Yet to do this, you must first have some security in answering for yourself the fundamental questions: "How do I define myself?" (personal identity), "How do I express myself?" (occupational identity), and "Where do I belong?" (community identity). The deepest level of the iceberg is identity.

The Agile Learning Mindset

In order to operate in an accelerating world that demands continual adaptation, we need a mindset outfitted to navigate change. We need an agile learning mindset.

The agile learning mindset is separate and distinct from the agile methodologies of software and product development, although it shares similarities with those practices. Susan McIntosh, attempting to define what the agile mindset means in the world of agile methodologies, wrote on infoq.com, "An agile mindset is the set of attitudes supporting an agile working environment. These include respect, collaboration, improvement and learning cycles, pride in ownership, focus on delivering value, and the ability to adapt to change. This mindset is necessary to cultivate high-performing teams, who in turn deliver amazing value for their customers."[6]

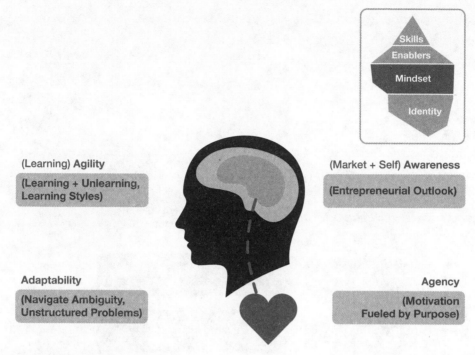

Figure 7.4: The Agile Mindset

The agile learning mindset, as we define it (Figure 7.4), contains four components: *agency, agility, adaptability,* and *awareness.*

Agency

Agency, in social science parlance, is the capacity to act independently and to make choices for oneself. Some describe agency as the opposite of powerlessness. Navigating a rapidly shifting future of work will require the agency to learn and adapt quickly, understanding explicitly that learning is your responsibility. Connect that agency with purpose, curiosity, or motivational drive to fuel your learning and exploration. Agency connects the What, How, and Why that were discussed in Chapter 6 (Figure 7.5).

Agility

Agility, and specifically learning agility, is the ability to both learn and unlearn. It is founded in your own learning style to optimize how you take in new information, form new knowledge, and let go of information that is no longer useful. It is

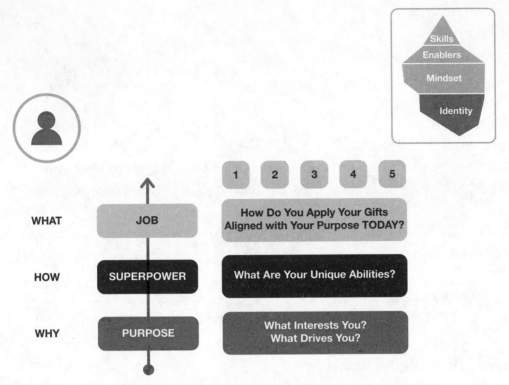

Figure 7.5: Agency Is Rooted in Understanding Your Purpose and Superpowers

flexibility, nimbleness, and responsiveness. Agility includes your ability to pivot not only to take in new information, but also to deliver value when old processes and business models begin to fail, and new ones are required.

We very much like how executive recruiting firm Korn Ferry describes learning agility:[7]

- *Mental agility*—embracing complexity, examining problems in unique ways, making fresh connections, and staying inquisitive.

- *People agility*—being open-minded toward others, enjoying interaction with diverse groups, bringing out the best in others.

- *Change agility*—willingness to lead transformation efforts, continuously exploring new options.

- *Results agility*—delivering results in tough situations, responding to challenge, inspiring others to achieve more than they thought possible.

- *Self-awareness*—being reflective, understanding strengths and weaknesses, seeking feedback and personal insight.

Adaptability

Adaptability is so central to the agile mindset that we made it the centerpiece of this book's title. Charles Darwin is thought to have said, "It is not the strongest of the species that survives, but the most adaptable." (While Darwin gets the credit for this idea, there's no conclusive evidence to tie him to those words.) In work as in life, then, evolutionary success belongs to those who can most readily adapt. Adaptability enables us to navigate ambiguous situations and work through challenges even when not all the information is clear or even known. In the introduction to this book we shared Professor Jeff LePine's distinction between adaptability and flexibility and it bears repeating here: "Flexibility is the ability to pivot from one tool in your toolbox to another or from one approach to another. Adaptability requires you add something. Adaptability may require you to drop that tool and forge a new one or drop that method, unlearn it and develop an entirely new one."

Awareness

Awareness starts with an understanding of self. Self-awareness and your sense of personal identity are essential to engage meaningfully in work. Writing in "Collaboration Overload" for *Harvard Business Review*, researchers Rob Cross, Reb Rebele, and Adam Grant identified an increase of 50% or more in collaborative activities at work over the past two decades. Their conclusion: work is now conclusively a social act.[8]

Awareness, though, extends beyond the self and your social environment. One must also have a keen market awareness. When the pace of change was slower and, as a result, business models lasted longer, you could successfully hold a job without fully understanding the business model of the organization for which they engaged because your work was, in effect, hardwired into it. That's no longer the case. Change is coming so quickly now that organizations are in a constant dance, pivoting from one business model to the next. In fact, one might argue that the pivot *is* the business model. As a result, all workers—and most certainly every leader—need to understand how the organization creates value and how they contribute individually and collaboratively to that value creating. And no doubt about it, self-awareness and market awareness are the most important and difficult to master aspects of the agile mindset.

Agile Mindset in Action

Search-engine giant Google set out to discover what made for a high-performing team, hoping they might even be able to create an algorithm to optimize future teams. What they found surprised them. The researchers originally thought that the best teams would be those comprised of the most outstanding individuals. Instead, they learned that "who is on a team matters much less than how team members interact, structure their work, and view their contributions."[9] We discuss this research in greater detail in Chapter 9.

To perform well in the collaborative workplace, then, we need the high levels of self-awareness that enable us to productively contribute in teams.

We also need great situational or market awareness. You will no longer have a job processing just a piece of work; you will need to know how that work fits into the broader organization, from product through business model. You will need to understand how your organization creates and captures value, and how your activities contribute to that value creation. If you understand this and can continually learn and adapt to contribute meaningfully to that value creation, you will never have to look for a job because you will continually make opportunities happen for yourself.

The Enablers: Uniquely Human Skills

What many people describe—and often discount—as soft skills are the uniquely human skills that are the positive enablers throughout your life and work. These good human skills make life and work far easier. As technological capability advances and encroaches on human cognitive tasks, our uniquely human skills become increasingly valuable. A 2019 research study at Swinburne University's Centre for The New Workforce in Australia titled "Peak Human Potential" found that "the more an industry is disrupted by digital technologies, the more that workers in those industries value uniquely human 'social competencies.' From collaboration, empathy, and social skills to entrepreneurial skills, these social competencies are less vulnerable to being displaced by AI and automation."[10]

Organizations from the World Economic Forum[11] to the Institute for the Future[12] enumerate these skills and their value in the future of work. Ultimately, these skills all center on social and emotional intelligence, creativity, communication, judgment, sensemaking, and empathy. And they are all fundamental to the adaptation advantage. We place these skills at the waterline in the Iceberg Model because while they are sometimes evident and explicit on the job, they are also quite often the invisible enablers of your best work.

And here's the thing: these so very important skills get better with age, setting up a paradox in a modern culture that tends to value the cognitive skills and rapid learning ability of the so-called "born digital" generation over the experience and uniquely human skills of workers who have developed beyond the sponge-like learning years of the late teens and early twenties. This is a substantial argument for lifelong learning and investment in a multigenerational workforce (Figure 7.6).

The psychologist Raymond Cattell noted this distinction in his 1971 book *Abilities: Their Structure, Growth and Action*.[13] Cattell separated what he called fluid intelligence (the ability to solve novel problems independent of past experience) and crystallized intelligence (the ability to tap experience to address new challenges). Both, it turns out, are a valuable combination in an adaptive learning organization. Our collective understanding of these cognitive peaks has grown more nuanced

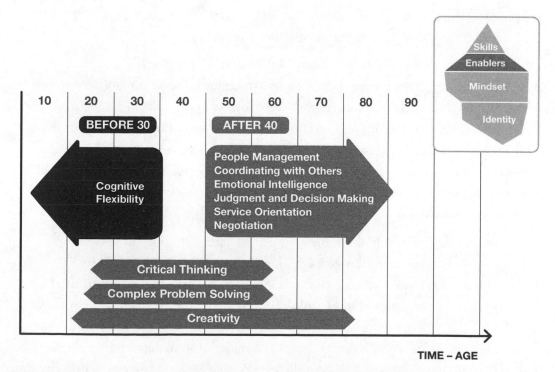

Figure 7.6: Future of Work Skills Peak with Age and Wisdom

Data source: Future of Work Skills from the Future Jobs Report, World Economic Forum.

with time. Researchers Joshua Hartshorne, a postdoc in MIT's Department of
Brain and Cognitive Sciences, and Laura Germine, a postdoc in psychiatric and
neurodevelopmental genetics at Massachusetts General Hospital, address this in their
paper "When Does Cognitive Functioning Peak? The Asynchronous Rise and Fall
of Different Cognitive Abilities Across the Life Span."[14] Their research points to a
broader range of peaks between fluid and crystallized intelligence. "We were mapping
when these cognitive abilities were peaking, and we saw there was no single peak for
all abilities. The peaks were all over the place," Hartshorne told *MIT News*. "This was
the smoking gun."[15]

"It paints a different picture of the way we change over the lifespan than
psychology and neuroscience have traditionally painted," adds Germine. Vocabulary,
comprehension, arithmetic, and reading all peak later in life, supporting the
argument that lifelong learning and adaptation is always possible.

We asked Dr. Germine for more insight into these emerging discoveries. "The
world has changed so much in terms of how we live and how we work that we cannot
rely on results from older studies of lifespan cognitive performance to be necessarily
true today," she told us. "Studies from the 1970s on when cognitive abilities peak
may not be relevant to today's human cognitive function."

She went on to explain this in a broader context: "Consider the longer view of
how humans have adapted over time. We live in regions once uninhabitable to our
ancestors. We make use of resources that were useless to our ancestors. We make tools
that augment our limitations and extend our longevity and the quality of our lives.
Our brains are capable of continual adaptation to new environments, which may
explain the many peaks of different cognitive abilities between the old markers of
fluid and crystallized intelligence. There is a difference between the time in your life
when a particular cognitive ability peaks and brain health."

Brain development, Dr. Germine told us, is a "constant tension between
specialization and flexibility." As we age, our brains tend toward specificity,
discarding information that the brain deems irrelevant. To better envision this
move toward specialization, Dr. Germine constructed a useful analogy. "A piece of
wood can be anything, but once you start the process of whittling it down to make
a spear, that piece of wood is not as useful as a material to make a chair. A lot of
research about development, aging, and the brain suggests that exposing ourselves to
a broad range of meaningful experiences for as long as possible—to continue to try

new things and learn new things—might counteract the brain's natural tendency to overspecialize at the expense of flexibility."

That last comment struck us as especially important now. An obsession with hyperspecialization and expertise may actually limit our ability to adapt. Remaining open to new learning, on the other hand, may be the secret to successful intergenerational work forces.

We talked with Robert Burnside, former chief learning officer (CLO) at Ketchum, a 96-year-old global public relations firm, about how his firm drew on the longevity advantage while upskilling and reskilling the workforce for digital capabilities. In 2014, Burnside was tapped by the company's CEO to implement a new digital strategy with the firm's 2,000 account services professionals. His approach: team older, often senior employees who lacked digital skills but had deep business experience with younger workers who were digital savvy but hadn't yet learned how public relations can best serve clients. The resulting learning groups included people of all levels, ages, and geographies to maximize diversity, with the explicit goal of bringing everyone's digital and business skills to par. "This was engaging for everyone," Burnside told us. "In the end, it is a 'both/and,' not an 'either/or.' We need all the skills, which vary by generation and life phase, and we need to find a way for our people to engage and inform each other."

The example Ketcham set may be useful not just in filling skills gaps; it may also address the growing gap in social and behavioral skills. Both PricewaterhouseCoopers Annual CEO surveys and IBM Institute for Business Ventures Global Surveys are finding that the social or behavioral skills gap is now greater than the technical skills gap. Specifically, the IBM surveys saw a shift in concern about a shortage of technical skills in 2016 to worry about a lack of social skills in 2018. The number-one skill in demand? Adaptability (Figure 7.7).

Why We Need the Agile Mindset: The Broken Education-to-Work Pipeline

In the Second Industrial Revolution, we began to embrace skillsets and build careers around them. We created a pathway from apprentice to journeyman to master craftsman based on the acquisition and perfection of certain skills. As we moved from the Second to the Third Industrial Revolution, we identified a growing need for a skilled and trained labor force beyond the trades. It demanded education

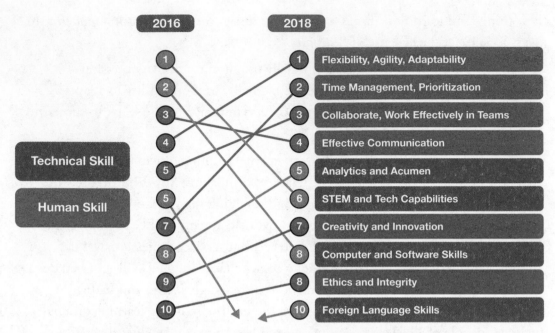

Figure 7.7: Technology Skills Slip as Behavioral Skills Rise (IBM)

Sources: 2016 IBM Institute for Business Value Global Skills Survey; 2018 IBM Institute for Business Value Global Country Survey.

that extended beyond high school, and stimulated demand for a higher educated workforce. (If you are unfamiliar with the four industrial revolutions, check out the book's introduction where we explain them.)

Following World War II, interest in and demand for post-secondary graduates took hold, driving a greater demand for specifically educated college and university graduates. From 1960 to 1990, the number of higher education institutions in the United States doubled, in a period that might best be described as the massification of higher education. Increasingly, hiring companies, and indeed society, became focused on monolithic degrees. Students were told to "pick a good major" to guarantee a path to a good, stable ride up the career escalator. The university trained you in a single skill set, in a single industry, and if you had a decent starting salary, the academy could declare success.

Now, while we have unmet needs for a highly educated workforce in fields like data analytics and cybersecurity, we have a huge number of students graduating with debt and degrees they cannot monetize because the skills they were taught were

Exercise: Your Workplace Thinking Style

Mark Boncheck, CEO of Shift Thinking, and Elisa Steele, Chairman of the Board of Cornerstone on Demand, developed an elegant yet simple tool to understand your workplace thinking style (Figure 7.8).

First, select a focus area from the following: ideas, process, action, or relationships. Once you have narrowed your focus, look at your orientation: Are you a big picture person or a detail person? The simple two-question assessment can tell you where you like to play on a team.

Boncheck and Steele describe eight types that result from the four-by-two matrix. (You can read more about this work in their 2015 *Harvard Business Review* article "What Kind of Thinker Are You?"[16])

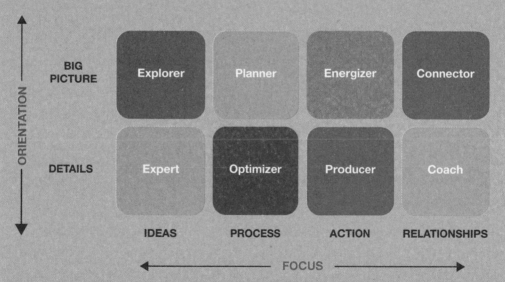

Figure 7.8: Bonchek and Steele: What Kind of Thinker Are You?

Source: Mark Bonchek and Elisa Steele.

- **Explorer** thinking is about generating creative ideas.
- **Planner** thinking is about designing effective systems.
- **Energizer** thinking is about mobilizing people into action.
- **Connector** thinking is about building and strengthening relationships.
- **Expert** thinking is about achieving objectivity and insight.
- **Optimizer** thinking is about improving productivity and efficiency.
- **Producer** thinking is about achieving completion and momentum.
- **Coach** thinking is about cultivating people and potential.

outdated or irrelevant even before they began their studies. To be clear, we neither discredit nor devalue the experience of higher education; we're believers! It's the myopic focus on monolithic degrees for workforce preparation with which we take issue. Higher education has focused almost exclusively on training people in technical skills by offering the false promise that these students could leverage that training for their entire career rather than as a starting point in a long arc of lifelong learning.

ABL: Always Be Learning

In the cult classic film *Glengarry Glen Ross*, Alec Baldwin exhorts his salesmen to "always be closing." In today's world of work, we think organizations should "always be learning" because, as business theorist Peter Senge wrote in *The Fifth Discipline* and Royal Dutch Shell business executive Arie de Gues echoed in book, *The Living Company*, "The ability to learn faster than your competitors may be the only sustainable competitive advantage."

Notes

1. https://www.bcg.com/publications/2018/competing-rate-learning.aspx

2. https://onlinelibrary.wiley.com/doi/full/10.1111/cogs.12280

3. https://www.sciencedirect.com/science/article/pii/S0022103115001006

4. https://www.nytimes.com/2017/06/24/fashion/fear-of-failure.html

5. Brené Brown, *Daring Greatly: How the Courage to Be Vulnerable Transforms the Way We Live, Love, Parent, and Lead* (New York: Penguin Random House, 2015).

6. https://www.infoq.com/articles/what-agile-mindset/

7. Robert Cattell, *Abilities: Their Structure, Growth, and Action* (New York: Houghton-Mifflin, 1971); definitions for the five faces of learning agility from https://focus.kornferry.com/leadership-and-talent/the-organisational-x-factor-learning-agility/

8. https://hbr.org/2016/01/collaborative-overload

9. https://www.thinkwithgoogle.com/intl/en-gb/marketing-resources/content-marketing/five-dynamics-effective-team/

10. https://www.swinburne.edu.au/media/swinburneeduau/centre-for-the-new-workforce/cnew-national-survey-report.pdf

11. https://www.weforum.org/agenda/2016/01/the-10-skills-you-need-to-thrive-in-the-fourth-industrial-revolution/

12. http://www.iftf.org/futureworkskills/

13. Cattell, *Abilities*.

14. Joshua K. Hartshorne and Laura T. Germine, "When Does Cognitive Functioning Peak? The Asynchronous Rise and Fall of Different Cognitive Abilities Across the Life Span," *Psychological Science* 26, no. 4 (2015): 433–443.

15. http://news.mit.edu/2015/brain-peaks-at-different-ages-0306

16. https://hbr.org/2015/11/what-kind-of-thinker-are-you

8 Rise of the Humans: Developing Your Creativity, Empathy, and Other Uniquely Human Capabilities

Key Ideas

1. We need to value our own intelligence—the uniquely human ways we learn, adapt, and create new value that we call organic cognition—over artificial intelligence—what we call silicon cognition.

2. As technology advances and consumes more routine work, the value of work requiring organic cognition increases. If we focus on developing uniquely human skills, we'll continue to build value for ourselves and the organizations that engage us.

3. To maximize human potential, we need to put humans at the center of every value proposition, augmenting human capacity with ever more capable tools and staying mindful of those most vulnerable to technological unemployment.

Play Is the Way Forward

The future of work is often presented as a binary choice: a hunger game between organic and silicon cognition that results in either a dystopian nightmare in which humans fight for the last jobs not taken by robots or an nearly inconceivable utopia

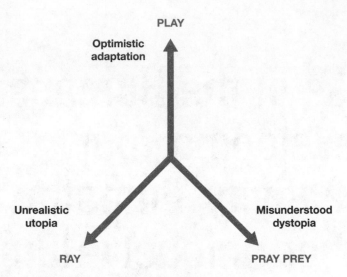

Figure 8.1: Mickey McManus's Ray-Pray-Play

Concept credit: Mickey McManus.

where artificial intelligence surpasses human intelligence, yet we bask in the leisure and self-expression afforded our newfound time free from work. Autodesk fellow Mickey McManus describes this choice as the "Ray-Pray-Play" model that perfectly captures our perspective (Figure 8.1).

Futurist Ray Kurzweil, director of engineering at Google and cofounder of Singularity University, leads the utopian charge. In his vision, we will create a massive, common, organic–silicon hybrid cognition called the singularity. While Kurzweil has proven to be prescient about many things (he enjoys an 87% accuracy rate with predictions to date), his big vision of this singularity is fraught with challenges, the most glaring of which is bias. Everyone has biases; they are the imperfect human shortcuts that allow us to quickly and even unconsciously interpret the world around us. These biases get incorporated into constructed silicon cognition, not necessarily for any malevolent purpose, but more simply because program designers don't even realize they hold a particular point of view.

Take, for example, facial recognition software. Some facial recognition software has failed spectacularly at recognizing nonwhite, nonmale faces because the algorithms and databases upon which it was based are biased by the world view of their largely white male developers.[1] Biases are not necessarily racist, sexist, or otherwise bad, at least not intentionally so. They are, in all their complexity, a reflection of the experiences and perspectives of those who hold them. They are unwelcome, though, if they become codified in the systems that are meant to fairly and ubiquitously navigate the world. Biases run in every direction, but it's fair to say that we run the risk of magnifying our blind spots if we encode bias at scale.

Still, Kurzweil's utopia is the "Ray" in McManus's model.

McManus dubs the dystopian "technology eats the humans" perspective "Pray." Indeed, there is a crowd of catastrophists predicting a future where technology consumes the majority of jobs, leaving humans scraping by on meager universal income supplements, leaving us to *pray* that we survive or, worse, that we don't become *prey* to one another and the machine.

McManus, though, adds a third perspective: "Play." McManus and his colleagues at Autodesk believe, as do we, that humans are driven to create, explore, communicate, and learn through the acts of making and play. When we putter around making things without a clear and direct utilitarian need, often we are learning. Jazz, improvisation, analogy, metaphor, synthesis, interpretation—all of these types of creative play and learning are unique to human beings.

The idea of playful learning is especially intriguing when we think of it in the context of what makes us uniquely human. As it turns out, today's machine learning is more analogous to that of a four-legged species than it is to the human species. Let us explain.

The Uniqueness of the Human Drive to Learn and Create

Is pedagogy, the method and practice of teaching, innate to humans? Some psychologists say yes, although many biologists reject that idea. The answer, however, may lie in the definition of "teaching." All animals learn, some through mimicry and some through guidance or behavior modification. In all species, behaviors are learned through repetition, usually for a utilitarian purpose, such as finding food rather than becoming it. Humans, though, seem special in the drive to create, explore, and synthesize information purely to expand our body of knowledge. Knowing that Zimbabwe has the most official languages—16!—may not help you secure your dinner, but it might win you a bar bet. And more than just stockpiling facts, humans seem to be distinct in their penchant to reflect on how we learn in order to improve our ability to teach others.

We turned to our stable of educators and scientists to validate or reject our theory, and we found ourselves in a long, learning-filled debate that itself validated the thesis. Lisa Rioles Collins is both a scientist and a voracious learner. When asked for her take on learning in humans versus other species, she shared these insights:

> There is evidence that birds teach their young songs and that birds can learn the songs of other birds as well as other sounds. There is also evidence that birds with elaborate nests teach their young how to make those nests. There is lots of other evidence regarding "teaching" in nature. Cheetahs will bring live prey back to their cubs for them to practice killing their own prey. What I really think separates us from animals has more to do with our ability to reflect on our learning and on the learning process. We have the unique position and, thanks to modern technology, the time to sit and reflect on what we are learning, how we are learning, how we would like to learn, and how to better teach our students.

Dr. Maria Calkins, a university professor of psychology, summarizes it this way:

> I think what makes us human is our ability to gain "wisdom" as well as being able to generalize learnings to new applications, which takes creativity. Human creativity involves generating original ideas, making nonlinear connections between things that are seemingly unrelated, looking at things from a variety of viewpoints, and putting ideas together in various ways to come up with something new. All of those, in my view, are unique to the human species.

Hungarian developmental psychologists György Gergely and Gergely Csibra hypothesize that humans have what they call the *pedagogical learning stance*, which allows an infant to retain generic information. According to their theory, human babies are able to learn information in a given instructional setting, through communication, that they can later apply to a wide range of potential new situations. "Natural pedagogy is not only the product but also one of the sources of the rich cultural heritage of our species," Gergely and Csibra write in their 2011 paper "Natural Pedagogy as Evolutionary Adaptation."[2] They believe it is our ability as humans to accommodate that knowledge for future application that differentiates us from other animals.

With these scientists, psychologists, and educators informing our thinking, it seems that it may be our ability and inclination to continuously learn and disrupt ourselves that makes us uniquely human. No other animal species disrupts themselves by creating new innovations and new, more complex tools, and certainly not ones that threaten their very survival as a species.

Interestingly, some of what separates us from other animals is also similar to what separates us from today's artificial intelligence (AI) technologies. Silicon cognition has not been able to replicate or demonstrate innateness, that inherent sense of awareness, sentience, or wisdom found in humans. It struggles to apply learned skills and knowledge to new contexts. It simply lacks common sense. Paul Allen, cofounder of Microsoft, recently announced a $125 million investment in his AI lab called Project Alexandria with the goal of exploring how to develop "commonsense AI" because, as Oren Etzioni, a former University of Washington professor who oversees the Allen Institute for Artificial Intelligence, says, "AI recognizes objects, but can't explain what it sees. It can't read a textbook and understand the questions in the back of the book. It is devoid of common sense."[3]

DARPA has a similar initiative underway called The Machine Common Sense Program. "The absence of common sense prevents an intelligent system from understanding its world, communicating naturally with people, behaving reasonably in unforeseen situations, and learning from new experiences," said Dave Gunning, a program manager in DARPA's Information Innovation Office (I2O). "This absence is perhaps the most significant barrier between the narrowly focused AI applications we have today and the more general AI applications we would like to create in the future."[4]

In late 2019, Microsoft announced a $1 billion investment in Elon Musk's OpenAI to support building artificial general intelligence (AGI) because they believe "Modern AI systems work well for the specific problem on which they've been trained, but getting AI systems to help address some of the hardest problems facing the world today will require generalization and deep mastery of multiple AI technologies."[5]

While there are many parlor tricks and even more practical examples of narrow artificial intelligence, we are a long way from achieving generalized AI despite mind-boggling investments by the likes of Microsoft to make it so. In a June 20, 2019, article for *Wired,* reporter Gregory Barber wrote that even as AI becomes increasingly capable of handling specific tasks, the lofty goal of general AI that easily switches among diverse tasks is still a long way off. How far? "Please don't hold your breath," Barber wrote. "Preserve those brain cells; you'll need them to out-think the machines."[6]

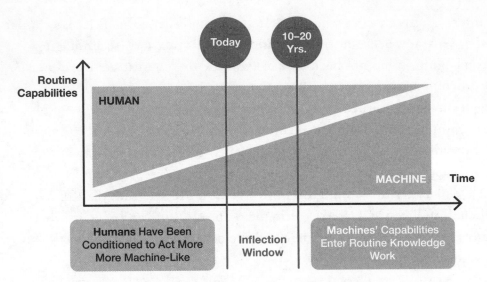

Figure 8.2: Routine Tasks—Human versus Machine Abilities

Or, as biologist Janine Benyus says, human cognition has benefited from "3.8 billion years of evolutionary R&D."

We are so focused on developing machine capabilities to perform cognitive work that we nearly fail to develop our uniquely human skills, and paradoxically we have trained humans to act more like machines. We are conditioned, for example, to respond to the stimulus of a smartphone alert and have trained ourselves to structure data in ways computers can understand. We test people on tasks that machines can do (retrieve information), rather than asking people to act more like humans (creating and collaborating). We ponder just how powerful silicon cognition can become and yet we don't even know what humans are capable of doing (Figure 8.2).

The Predictive Markets Declare Future Skills Favor Humans

Will this uniquely human ingenuity drive us into the future? Check any list of future skills from the World Economic Forum to the Institute for the Future (Figure 8.3) and you will find one particularly intriguing similarity: none of them are specifically technical skills. The skills most needed in the future of work all center on uniquely human skills and our ability to think about our own thought processes and how we operate, and, more specifically, to collaborate with rising technology capabilities. To those we would add the ability to adapt fluidly as new data informs our

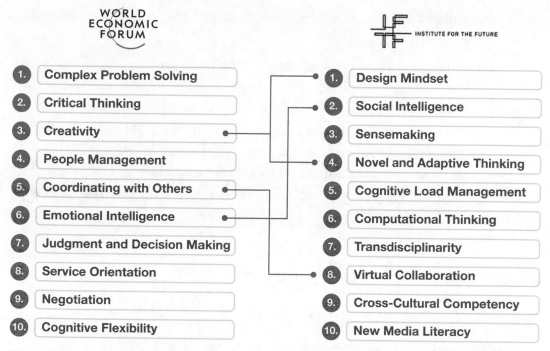

Figure 8.3: Future Work Skills: Institute of the Future and World Economic Forum

Data sources: Institute for the Future and World Economic Forum

surroundings. So why are so many people grasping at technology and sounding the alarm that schools need to teach more and better STEM skills, insisting that every kid must learn to code?

Without a doubt, digital skills are important. They are, in fact, now a fundamental literacy just as are reading, writing, and the quantitative skills that involve the manipulation of numbers from math to statistics to economics to data analysis. Knowing how to code may help you get a job in coding, but, more importantly, it will help improve your logical reasoning. And, much more importantly, it will help you understand what can be coded and automated. That skill, says Dr. Randy Swearer, vice president of learning futures at Autodesk, is critical. "Humans need to understand what's computable. They don't need to understand a code, or to code, but they need to understand what's computable."

The real advantage to digital fluency is that it enables uniquely human skills to be seamlessly augmented with technological capabilities. That empowers individuals to see what can, and perhaps should, be automated. It empowers you to see that your real value comes from your uniquely human skills—your ability to leverage the technology tool and provide the wisdom, judgment, and common sense to maximize the value you create.

Uniquely human skills. Soft skills. Nontechnical skills. Power skills. Noncognitive skills. Enablers. Whatever you decide to call them, these are the skills that are, at this point in technology's evolution, difficult for machines to achieve. In Chapter 7, we looked at the World Economic Forum's skills list focusing on individual skills. By comparison, we divide the Institute for the Future (ITF)'s Future Skills 2020 list into two camps: individual performance skills and the aptitudes that enable better human-to-human and human-to-machine collaborations. Let's take a closer look at each of these.

Individual Skills

We recognize these ITF skills to be foundational for every worker.

- *Design mindset.* ITF defines design mindset as the "ability to represent and develop tasks and work processes for desired outcomes." Leaning on Heather's background and experience in design, we would extend this definition to include the ability to deal with ambiguity, focus on finding and framing challenges, and placing the human at the center in seeking novel solutions.

- *Novel and adaptive thinking.* ITF defines novel and adaptive thinking as "proficiency at thinking and coming up with solutions and responses beyond that which is rote or rule-based."

- *Cognitive load management.* ITF defines cognitive load management as the "ability to discriminate and filter information for importance, and to understand how to maximize cognitive functioning using a variety of tools and techniques." We can more effectively leverage these technology tools, including finding insights in data, when our own cognitive processes are not overwhelmed. And here, there is genuine reason or concern. Researcher Dr. Martin Hilbert at the University of Southern California calculated that the amount of data coming at us every day from sources as diverse as television to smartphones exploded from the equivalent of 40 newspapers a day in 1986 to as many as 174 in 2007. It's not surprising, considering the rise of social media and smartphone apps, that the number leaped to the equivalent of 280 newspapers in 2012. Imagine how high that pile of papers reaches today! Our ability to sift and filter through this data deluge will be essential for our ability to continuously adapt.

- *Sensemaking.* ITF defines sensemaking as the "ability to determine the deeper meaning or significance of what is being expressed." While this is just one application of sensemaking, finding insights in analyzed data is an enormous opportunity. Soon every company will be both a data company and a learning company. To learn from data requires sensemaking to extract insights from observations that become transparent in data. According to IBM, in 2013 the world created more data than ever in human history.[7] This trend in data creation is following an exponential growth curve as every connected person, every connected device, and every interaction leaves a data trail. The networking giant Cisco projected that every person will have four Internet-connected devices by 2020, up from two in 2010.[8] The leading technology market research firms punctuate this projection—and the problem it creates. IDC projects growth rates for data to exceed 61% compounded annually,[9] while Forrester reports that 60–73% of data is ignored today,[10] presumably because we just can't process it. These trends are huge opportunities for future insights to be found by applying both data analytic skills and sensemaking.

Collaborative Skills

To be well prepared for human interaction and lay the groundwork for human-to-machine collaboration, IFT recommends we develop these skills:

- *Social intelligence.* ITF defines social intelligence as the "ability to connect to others in a deep and direct way, to sense and stimulate reactions and desired interactions." We add "emotional" intelligence to this definition, adopting the guidance of author and science journalist Daniel Goleman, who believes that social and emotional intelligence comprises both self and social awareness and self- and social management. In short, his framework states that you must be aware of your own emotional reactions and responses as well as those of others before you can manage your own social responses or those of others. Social intelligence is essential for effective collaboration.

- *Transdisciplinarity.* ITF defines transdisciplinarity as "literacy in and ability to understand concepts across multiple disciplines." We broaden the definition just a bit to include, specifically, the ability to set aside the tunnel vision of one discipline in order to assess the situation and fully understand the challenge from a fresh perspective. Only then can you integrate disciplines and technologies to optimally address the challenge. (See Figure 4.5 in Chapter 4 to review the I to T to X evolution toward trandisciplinarity.)

- *Cross-cultural competency.* ITF defines cross-cultural competency as the "ability to operate in different cultural settings." Put another way, we need to develop a fluency of culture, much as one would a fluency of language, in order to adapt appropriately to different cultural settings. Cross-cultural competency is essential to successfully adapt in our hyperconnected and interdependent global economy in which no one culture dominates.

- *Computational thinking.* ITF defines computational thinking as the "ability to translate vast amounts of data into abstract concepts and to understand data-based reasoning." Autodesk's Randy Swearer describes this skill as "not necessarily the ability to code, but the capacity to understand what can be coded or what

Stripping Stereotypes from Skills Categories

As we were writing this book, we needed to decide what language we wanted to use to describe uniquely human skills. We opted not to use the term "soft skills" because for many generations, the idea of "soft" and "hard" skills broke down along gender lines. Women were discouraged from pursuing the "hard" sciences thought to be the territory of men who dominated careers in mathematics, engineering, chemistry, and the like. Instead, women were ushered into the "soft" sciences such as psychology or sociology, or perhaps encouraged to skip science altogether. Perhaps worse, the "soft" skills of listening, empathy, compassion, and collaboration were relegated to women, while men did the heavy lifting of "hard" skills like competition and leadership.

These gender stereotypes have little place in the modern workforce, and not just as a matter of workforce equality. Study after study shows that a well-integrated mix of so-called hard and soft skills leads to greater professional and personal success.

For these reasons, we eschew the term "soft skills" in favor of "uniquely human skills" to capture those capabilities that enable better work and stronger relationships.

can be computed." Computational thinking, in the context of collaboration, is a tool to support your adoption and use of—your collaboration with—technology tools.

- *New media literacy.* ITF defines new media literacy as the "ability to critically assess and develop content that uses new media forms, and to leverage these media for persuasive communication." Like computational thinking, new media literacy describes collaboration with technology tools.

- *Virtual collaboration.* ITF defines virtual collaboration as the "ability to work productively, drive engagement, and demonstrate presence as a member of a virtual team." As we increasingly work on global and often virtual teams, we must hone our ability to forge new relationships with, and perhaps even lead, people we may never meet in person.

Understanding Uniquely Human Skills

In the emerging world of work, collaboration is king. According to data collected by the *Harvard Business Review*, in the past two decades time spent on collaborative activities at work by both managers and employees has increased by more than 50%.[11] In writing this book, we spoke with Donna Patricia Eiby, creative director for the Future Work Skills Academy, a learning solutions provider formed by a global coalition of skills experts who came together to create the Future of Work Skills Academy based on the groundbreaking work by the Institute for the Future. Eiby highlighted the importance of the ITF skills:

> Collaboration is the agency to deliver value through other humans or in concert with technology or a blend of both. Given the growth in both human-to-human and human-to-technology collaboration, it is not surprising that 50% of the IFTF's skills relate to collaboration. Skills requirements now move so fast in work that mastery may be a thing of the past. Instead the Generalist, as described in David Epstein's book *Range*, is the new normal by which we deliver value as transdisciplinary team. Therefore, effective team collaboration is mandatory in the Future or Evolution of Work.
>
> Humans need to understand what is computable or codable for automation and the list of IFTF skills are not, at this point, automatable. I believe that the nonroutine work of humans is essentially managing friction. What does this mean? Friction

is the space between you and your goals—whether that be greater sales, better solutions, happier workers, happier customers. Anything. Every organization operates in an ecosystem where the primary purpose is to identify friction between actors and their desires and then determine how to manage it. Managing doesn't mean reducing [friction]; in some cases an increase in friction, for example FOMO or Fear of Missing Out, can be a desired state. This is the work of humans and in the past, this has been the domain of only creatives, research and development, and marketing. I believe, in the evolution of work, we should see all human workers first and foremost managing friction. It is the heart and soul of nonroutine work. Can machines identify points of friction? Absolutely, if they are optimized to that goal. And in fact, AI (big data/machine learning) is a fabulous tool for identifying friction points. But it's humans who frame the problem and imagine the solution. And therein lies the heart of the matter: humans imagine and machines don't.

Eiby's work, with its emphasis on learning and uniquely human skills, reinforces our own theory that our uniquely human ability to create and explore at points of friction is also our uniquely human adaptation advantage. Still, it's difficult for many to stop chasing new skills.

Chasing STEM at Our Peril

Human skills are clearly important, but what about STEM? Society is currently obsessed with STEM skills, valuing science, technology, engineering, and math over humanities and social sciences and rewarding STEM practitioners with higher starting salaries. But when you look beyond entry-level jobs, something interesting happens.

David Deming and Kadeem Noray at Harvard University joined with the employment analytics company Burning Glass Technologies on research that found that "the earnings premium for STEM majors is highest at labor market entry and declines by more than 50% in the first decade of working life."[12] The reasoning for this decline, they say, is that STEM jobs experience the highest rate of technological change, and those in STEM jobs tend, over time, to learn new STEM skills more slowly than new graduates who have dedicated their full-time attention to learning the latest technologies. They also found that 58% of STEM graduates leave the field within a decade.

In another, earlier study, Deming looked at STEM-based jobs, specifically those requiring math skills, and coupled them with required social skills. He found

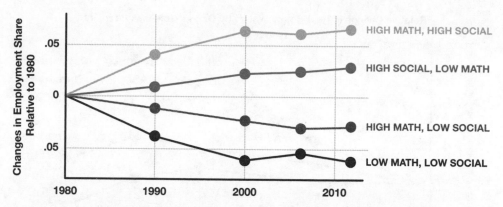

Figure 8.4: Deming: Changes to Employment Based on Task Intensity

Data source: David Deming, Occupational Task Intensity based on 1998 O*NET (source: 1980–2000 Census, 2005–2013 ACS), in "The Growing Importance of Social Skills in the Labor Market," May 2017.

that demand to fill jobs requiring high math *and* high social skills has surged and exceeded the supply of capable applicants. Conversely, demand for talent to fill jobs that require high math but low social skills and jobs requiring neither high math nor high social skills has been on the decline since the 1980s (Figure 8.4). Even more interestingly, jobs that required high social skills *but not* high math skills have risen in inverse correlation to jobs requiring high math skills but not high social skills. Accompanying the rise and fall of these coupled skills is the relative compensation for those roles (Figure 8.5). "Specifically, today's job market favors those who have the skills to be good team players. Social skills reduce the cost of coordinating with others," Deming said. "Each time there's a new set of people, they have to figure out anew what their roles are."

Despite the clear advantage of uniquely human skills, we are gutting them from our educational programs globally. Following the 2002 education reform law known as No Child Left Behind, a law hyperfocused on improving math and reading competencies, 22% of surveyed schools reported that they had reduce or eliminated music and arts instruction.[13] The 2008 global financial crisis further slashed education budgets, and arts and music programs fell victim to so-called cost savings. Paradoxically, investment in arts and music results in higher levels of both student engagement and persistence.[14] Eighteen years after No Child Left Behind became law, these students are entering our workforce en masse.

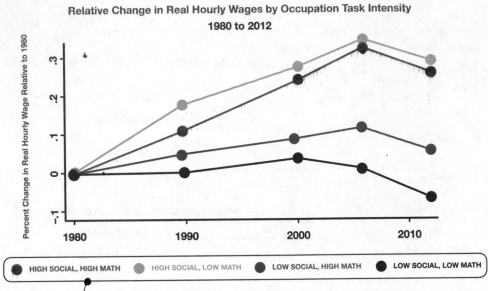

Figure 8.5: Deming: Changes in Hourly Income Based on Task Intensity

Data source: David Deming, Occupational Task Intensity based on 1998 O*NET (source: 1980–2000 Census, 2005–2013 ACS), in "The Growing Importance of Social Skills in the Labor Market," May 2017.

Perhaps worse, a 2016 Gallup survey of 3,000 schoolchildren found 74% of fifth graders reported that they are engaged in learning. That number drops to 45% by grade 8 and plummets to 34% by grade 12.[15] Can we really afford to have our kids disengaged from learning when learning itself is the foundational skill for the future? Clearly not, as evidenced by Gallup's State of the American Workplace study that found only 30% of workers are engaged at work, a scenario that costs $450 to $550 billion a year in the United States[16] (Figure 8.6).

This trend in cutting arts and music and hyperfocusing on technology is a global phenomenon. A recent BBC report found that "in China, the government has unveiled plans to turn 42 universities into 'world class' institutions of science and technology. In the United Kingdom, government focus on STEM has led to a nearly 20% drop in students taking A-levels in English and a 15% decline in the arts."[17]

In the debate of STEM versus uniquely human skills, we spoke with Matt Sigelman, CEO and founder of Burning Glass Technologies. Burning Glass is an analytics software company that provides real-time data on job growth, skills in demand, and labor market trends. Sigelman shared this:

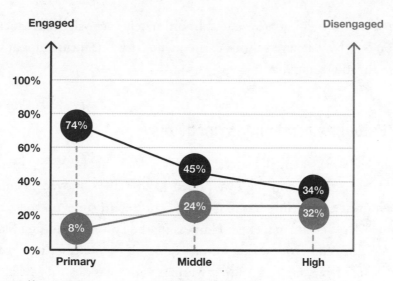

Figure 8.6: Gallup: Engagement and Disengagement in Education

Data source: Gallup 2016 survey of 3,000 schools in the United States (https://news.gallup.com/opinion/gallup/211631/student-enthusiasm-falls-high-school-graduation-nears.aspx).

One of the most important trends for jobs in the future is the rise of hybrid jobs. In these roles, you need both technology fluency and human skills to be successful, and perhaps more importantly, to adapt to changes in your work and navigate your career trajectory. I have seen the recent reports that suggest that human skills are now more important and showing more unmet market demand than technology skills. Research from Burning Glass Technologies makes it clear that it is important to have balance: this is not a choice between either technology skills or human skills, but rather a combination of both.

One of the most interesting things we found in our research is that as jobs require more technology skills and knowledge, the intensity of human skills to be successful in the role also increases. That's particularly true for collaboration, research skills, and communication skills. For example, software development roles may be technical jobs, but those jobs are as likely to demand good writing skills as any other job we track. Jobs like these also now require business skills, like project management and data visualization, which are crucial to getting things done and yet haven't traditionally been found in technical roles. What we think may be happening is in our rush and focus on getting everyone to acquire technology skills, we are leaving the human skills behind at a time they are growing in demand.

In other words, a well-intentioned—but ultimately short-sighted—focus on exclusively on STEM will have serious consequences for our future global workforce. In fact, we're already seeing that it does.

The Skills Battleground: Humans Need Apply

PricewaterhouseCoopers annually surveys CEOs worldwide. In 2019, for their 20th annual survey, the accounting firm polled 1,300 CEOs in over 75 countries to ascertain their greatest priorities looking ahead. This report sums up these concerns in the title alone: "The Talent Challenge: Harnessing the Power of Human Skills in the Machine Age." The report found that human capital is the number-two concern, with 77% of CEOs reporting that not finding workers with the skills they need is a threat to their business. What is most interesting is that those skills are neither technical nor digital; they are uniquely human (Figure 8.7). Specifically, the skills CEOs found both most important to their business and the most difficult to find were problem solving, leadership, creativity, innovation, and, very notably, *adaptability.*

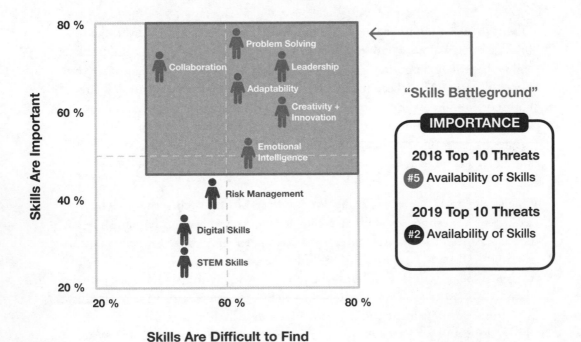

Figure 8.7: PricewaterhouseCoopers: Skills Battleground

Data source: PwC 20th Anniversary CEO Survey.

The Return on Being Human

Uniquely human skills will not only be valued in the future, but they are also having an impact today as we straddle the Third and Fourth Industrial Revolutions. As machines strip away routine and predictable work, the complex work that remains requires people who can think across disciplines. No wonder transdisciplinarity is high on ITF's list of valuable future skills. Having an undergraduate degree in one discipline and a graduate degree in another yields higher compensation than a concentration in a single discipline (Figure 8.8). Again, from the BBC report:

> In the US, an undergraduate student who took the seemingly most direct route to becoming a lawyer, judge, or magistrate—majoring in a pre-law or legal studies degree—can expect to earn an average of $94,000 a year. But those who majored in philosophy or religious studies make an average of $110,000. Graduates who studied area, ethnic and civilisations studies earn $124,000, US history majors earn $143,000, and those who studied foreign languages earn $148,000, a stunning $54,000 a year above their pre-law counterparts.[18]

Ironically, many of those undergraduate majors are often dismissed as useless for securing future jobs, even as they provide the key critical thinking and, more importantly, uniquely human skills needed for stable, long-term career success.

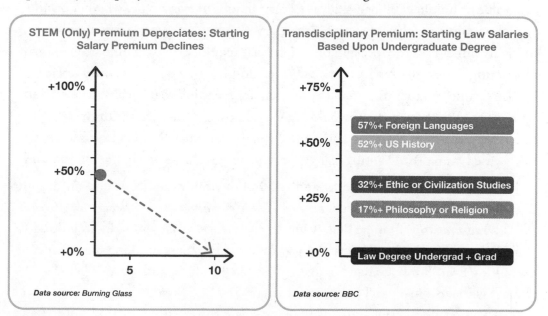

Figure 8.8: The Premium of a Liberal Arts Undergraduate Degree in the Legal Profession

Burning Glass has found that if you graduate from a STEM program you get your highest premium in your first starting salary. Over 10 years, unless you infuse your STEM education with other skills, notably uniquely human ones, that premium drops dramatically. Placed in the context of the BBC research, it's reasonable to conclude that technology skills depreciate while human skills appreciate (Figure 8.8).

In their book *The Future Computed*, Brad Smith and Harry Shum put it this way: "As computers behave more like humans, the social sciences and humanities will become even more important. Languages, art, history, economics, ethics, philosophy, psychology, and human development courses can teach critical, philosophical, and ethics-based skills that will be instrumental in the development and management of AI solutions." Further, a 2015 study by the British Council that surveyed 1,700 people in 30 countries across a variety of industries found that more than half the people in management and leadership positions had bachelor's degrees in either humanities or social sciences.[19] We expect that number to grow even higher in the future as uniquely human skills continue to grow in importance for leadership.

Return on Humans for All Jobs: The Special Power of Empathy

The value of uniquely human skills is evident in jobs of every type, whether or not the job requires a higher education degree. Every job today experiences a return on uniquely human skills, especially those jobs that require extensive human-to-human interaction. Customer service. Personal care. Hospitality. Sales. The entire service industry, from restaurants to retail. This includes every job that involves interaction with other humans, which we would argue is almost 100% of work. In these high-touch jobs, the most powerful and underestimated uniquely human skill is empathy. Or, to use Donna Patricia Eiby's language, empathy is the key to removing friction.

In 2009, Dev Patnaik, founder and CEO of the innovation consulting firm Jump Associates, wrote the book *Wired to Care: How Companies Prosper When They Create Widespread Empathy*. In it, he details Jump's experiences using empathy to unlock creativity and innovation. Describing itself as a total systems thinking management consulting firm, Jump leverages empathy to create products and services better aligned with customers' real needs and desires. "The best organizations and the ones that survive economic tsunamis," Patnaik says, "are those with empathic cultures and managers who are able to step outside themselves and walk in someone else's shoes."

The power of empathy isn't limited to the creation of commercial goods, however. It is the heart and soul of healthcare, education, and governmental reform. For example, an Italian study of more than 20,000 patients with diabetes looked at the power of empathy in wellness. Patients were divided among three groups of physicians. All physicians were prescreened for their levels of empathy. The patients treated by the physicians with higher levels of empathy had statistically significant lower levels of diabetic complications than those served by the physicians with lower levels of empathy.[20]

Evolving Beyond Shareholder Value: The Purpose of a Company

On September 13, 1970, in an article in the *New York Times* titled "The Social Responsibility of a Company Is to Increase Profits," economist Milton Friedman argued that the sole purpose of a company was to generate returns for shareholders.[21] For nearly 50 years now, companies have done precisely that. According to the Economic Policy Institute, from 1979 to 2018, productivity grew almost 70% while wages increased less than 12%.[22] Friedman's declaration launched the shareholder value era. Companies merged, downsized, right-sized. They reduced the size of their workforces and treated our natural resources as unending. They prioritized shareholder value over employee value, and often even over customer value. Once a by-product of overall value creation, shareholder value became the guiding principle for companies. Where human workers were once considered an asset to develop, they instead became a cost to contain. The Business Roundtable, a collection of America's most influential CEOs and leaders, shared that corporate shareholder priority from 1997 to 2019.

Until something changed.

In 2019, the Business Roundtable released its "Statement on the Purpose of a Corporation,"[23] signed by nearly 200 CEOs, which reads, in part, as follows:

> Americans deserve an economy that allows each person to succeed through hard work and creativity and to lead a life of meaning and dignity. We believe the free-market system is the best means of generating good jobs, a strong and sustainable economy, innovation, a healthy environment, and economic opportunity for all.
>
> Businesses play a vital role in the economy by creating jobs, fostering innovation, and providing essential goods and services. Businesses make and sell consumer

products; manufacture equipment and vehicles; support the national defense; grow and produce food; provide health care; generate and deliver energy; and offer financial, communications, and other services that underpin economic growth.

While each of our individual companies serves its own corporate purpose, we share a fundamental commitment to all of our stakeholders. We commit to:

- Delivering value to our customers. We will further the tradition of American companies leading the way in meeting or exceeding customer expectations.

- Investing in our employees. This starts with compensating them fairly and providing important benefits. It also includes supporting them through training and education that help develop new skills for a rapidly changing world. We foster diversity and inclusion, dignity and respect.

- Dealing fairly and ethically with our suppliers. We are dedicated to serving as good partners to the other companies, large and small, that help us meet our missions.

- Supporting the communities in which we work. We respect the people in our communities and protect the environment by embracing sustainable practices across our businesses.

- Generating long-term value for shareholders, who provide the capital that allows companies to invest, grow and innovate. We are committed to transparency and effective engagement with shareholders.

Each of our stakeholders is essential. We commit to deliver value to all of them, for the future success of our companies, our communities and our country.

Reflecting on this profound shift, Paul Polman, CEO of Unilever from 2009 to 2019, said in a *New York Times* interview, "You cannot solve issues like poverty or climate change or food security with the myopic focus on quarterly reporting. We have to move the financial markets to the long term as systems change. We need to decarbonize this global economy if we want to keep it livable. We need to find an economic system that is more inclusive."[24]

This sea change in corporate culture, at least in language, comes at a critical time as human and technology assets vie for their place in the corporate value chain. By acknowledging the value of human workers as an essential link in that chain, these CEOs are, in effect, embracing the power of the adaptation advantage and the potential of uniquely human skills, giving those skills and the humans who possess them renewed stature in the corporation (Figure 8.9).

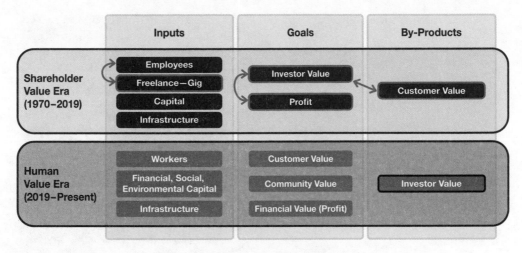

Figure 8.9: Shareholder Value and Human Value Eras

To Maximize Human Potential, Place the Human in the Center

We've said it many times in many ways: technological capability is growing at an incomprehensible rate. We will soon experience automation and niche artificial intelligence, or, as we prefer to call it, silicon cognition, as reliable collaborative tools. What we can't say often enough, though, is this: every time we hand something off to a technology actor—whether to automation or niche silicon cognition—we must reach up and learn new skills that enhance and evolve our own capabilities. It is this awareness and ability to reach and learn that lies at the heart of the adaptation advantage.

Terms like upskilling and reskilling are used without explanation, so let's give them a definition. Reskilling is acquiring new skills to expand your abilities to new industries or contexts; by reskilling, you are often replacing one set of skills or applications with another. Upskilling is deepening your knowledge or abilities in the domains where you currently operate. To navigate the evolution of work, we will need to do both. But rather than continuously grasping for the newest technology, focus on nurturing your uniquely human skills alongside your technical literacy. That will enable you to reach greater levels of human potential. Your job is moving, and if you are not moving with it, it may be moving away from you (Figure 8.10).

We have only begun this journey. In 2015, the McKinsey Global Institute estimated that only 18% of the US economy had been digitized.[25] Of those digital

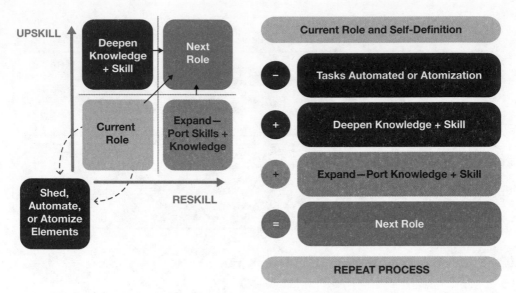

Figure 8.10: Your Job Is Moving: Reskill and Upskill Every Day

transformations, McKinsey claims, less than 30% are successful. Given these numbers, it's clear that most of the digital transformation is yet to come. This digital transformation is the necessary first step toward leveraging silicon cognition, automation, and augmentation, and so it is now that we must be mindful to place humans at the center of that transformation. Have no doubt about it: when we use phrases like "digital transformation," we are really talking about "human transformation."

While no one is insulated from the changes ahead, McKinsey reports that "Routine predictable physical and cognitive tasks will be the most vulnerable to automation in the coming years."[26] In some areas of our economy, early phases have already occurred. A recent study by Ball State, "The Myth and the Reality of Manufacturing in America," found that the majority of the 5 million manufacturing jobs lost since 2000 were outsourced to history and replaced by technology.[27] We had no plans for either upskilling or reskilling those 5 million Americans, so we lost them as a valuable resource to the industries to which they were contributing. This is a profound loss of human potential to our economy and our society.

Looking ahead, it will be our least educated workers, especially those in routine or predictable work, who will be most vulnerable to automation. Indeed, they already have been. We must proactively plan for a productive and engaged workforce by

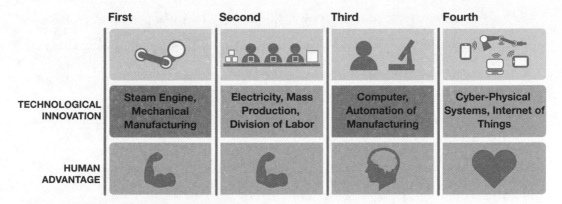

Figure 8.11: The Fourth Industrial Revolution Requires Heart

Concept credit: Dame Minouche Shafik, director, London School of Economics and Political Science, and Dov Seidman, CEO, LRN and author of *How.*

placing the human at the center of our transformation plans (Figure 8.11). As Dame Minouche Shafik, director of the London School of Economics and Political Science, noted in a recent interview, "In the past jobs were about muscles, now they're about brains, but in future they'll be about the heart. We need to invest to make sure that both young people and current workers have access to the kind of training they'll need to adjust to this new labor market. That is what we should be thinking about."[28]

Rise of the humans indeed.

Notes

1. https://www.nytimes.com/2018/02/09/technology/facial-recognition-race-artificial-intelligence.html

2. https://www.ncbi.nlm.nih.gov/pmc/articles/PMC3049090

3. https://www.nytimes.com/2018/02/28/technology/paul-allen-ai-common-sense.html

4. https://www.darpa.mil/news-events/2018-10-11

5. https://news.microsoft.com/2019/07/22/openai-forms-exclusive-computing-partnership-with-microsoft-to-build-new-azure-ai-supercomputing-technologies/

6. https://www.wired.com/story/power-limits-artificial-intelligence/

7. http://bigdata-madesimple.com/exciting-facts-and-findings-about-big-data/

8. https://www.cisco.com/c/dam/en_us/about/ac79/docs/innov/IoT_IBSG_0411FINAL.pdf

9. https://www.networkworld.com/article/3325397/idc-expect-175-zettabytes-of-data-worldwide-by-2025.html

10. https://go.forrester.com/blogs/hadoop-is-datas-darling-for-a-reason/

11. https://hbr.org/2016/01/collaborative-overload

12. https://scholar.harvard.edu/files/ddeming/files/demingnoray_stem_sept2018.pdf

13. https://thehill.com/opinion/op-ed/7275-no-child-left-behind-act-wrongly-left-the-arts-behind

14. https://www.lawstreetmedia.com/issues/education/cutting-art-programs-schools-solution-part-problem/

15. https://news.gallup.com/opinion/gallup/211631/student-enthusiasm-falls-high-school-graduation-nears.aspx

16. https://news.gallup.com/businessjournal/162953/tackle-employees-stagnating-engagement.aspx

17. https://www.bbc.com/worklife/article/20190401-why-worthless-humanities-degrees-may-set-you-up-for-life

18. https://www.bbc.com/worklife/article/20190401-why-worthless-humanities-degrees-may-set-you-up-for-life

19. https://www.britishcouncil.org/voices-magazine/what-do-worlds-most-successful-people-study

20. https://journals.lww.com/academicmedicine/Fulltext/2012/09000/The_Relationship_Between_Physician_Empathy_and.27.aspx

21. http://umich.edu/⊠thecore/doc/Friedman.pdf

22. https://www.epi.org/productivity-pay-gap/

23. https://www.businessroundtable.org/business-roundtable-redefines-the-purpose-of-a-corporation-to-promote-an-economy-that-serves-all-americans

24. https://www-nytimes-com.cdn.ampproject.org/c/s/www.nytimes.com/2019/08/29/business/paul-polman-unilever-corner-office.amp.html

25. https://www.mckinsey.com/industries/high-tech/our-insights/digital-america-a-tale-of-the-haves-and-have-mores

26. https://www.mckinsey.com/business-functions/organization/our-insights/unlocking-success-in-digital-transformations

27. https://conexus.cberdata.org/files/MfgReality.pdf

28. http://www.alainelkanninterviews.com/minouche-shafik/?fbclid=IwAR3HF3bB

Part III

Leading People and Organizations in the Evolution of Work

Key Ideas

1. New times call for a new approach to leadership. The best leaders are constant learners unafraid to be vulnerable in pursuit of increasing their capacity.

2. Culture is the most important tool of an adaptable company. It is the context in which a company exercises and expands its capacity to learn, grow, and identify and capture new opportunity.

3. To build the adaptation advantage into their teams, leaders must break the narrow definitions of jobs and organizational structure.

9 Leading in Continuous Change: Modeling Vulnerability, Learning from Failure, and Providing the Psychological Safety that Builds Trusting Teams

Key Ideas

1. New times call for a new approach to leadership. Let your team know who you are and what you care about to establish your moral authority and to make clear why your team is following you.

2. The best leaders are constant learners unafraid not to know and open to being wrong in pursuit of increasing their capacity.

3. Psychological safety is the greatest determinant of high-performing teams. That safety starts with the leader and their willingness to be vulnerable and build trust.

You Are at the Wheel

We are driving faster and faster toward a horizon that none of us can see with perfect vision, and we're doing it with one eye on the rear-view mirror. Virtually all of our understanding of leadership was derived from Third Industrial Revolution practices. Many of those leadership theories remain relevant, yet so many other ideas, language, and analogies can be downright dangerous in accelerated change. As we wade into the Fourth Industrial Revolution, we have to be more thoughtful about who we are leading and where we are taking them. We were reminded of that truth when we spoke with leadership guru Jim Kouzes, coauthor with Barry Posner of the seminal book *The Leadership Challenge.* For nearly 40 years, Kouzes and Posner have studied the best practices of effective leaders, and we wanted to hear his views about what accelerated change means to leadership. "The context of leadership has changed in some very dramatic ways since Barry Posner and I started researching and writing on the topic, but the content of leadership has not changed much at all," he told us. "The most self-evident and stable truth is that, at its heart, leadership is a relationship between those who aspire to lead and those who choose to follow. It is the quality of the relationship that makes the difference, not the rapidly advancing technology, or the fact that there are more human beings on the planet, or that organizations are more diverse, or that the economy is more global. We've gathered data from over 70 different countries for over four decades, and we continue to find the same results. The more frequently leaders exhibit exemplary behaviors, the more likely it is people will feel engaged, be more productive, deliver higher-quality work, and all the other measurable outcomes you would expect from exemplary leadership."

What, then, are those "exemplary behaviors" that deliver exemplary leadership in the context of accelerated change? How can we drive, eyes forward, to lead the future of work?

Oddly enough, we found some answers in cookies and chickens.

Leadership, Power, Cookies, and Chickens

Emboldened by Milton Friedman's shareholder-value era, corporations embraced the view that leadership should drive productivity to extract maximum value from processes and people. That concept does not apply so well in today's world. As we enter the Fourth Industrial Revolution, the hyperfocus on productivity and value extraction shifts to embrace creativity, innovation, and value created by adapting faster and learning more than your competition. This shift from scalable efficiency that ruled the Second and Third Industrial Revolutions (go back to Chapter 7 if we're losing you here) to scalable learning that is at the heart of the Fourth Industrial Revolution requires a new leadership style, one that inspires human potential (Figure 9.1). Two experiments, one involving cookies and the other using— you guessed it—chickens, best exemplify the old style of leadership that we most need to rethink.

A look at those two experiments helps us make the point.

Emotional Intelligence and the Cookie Monster

In his 2015 study of power, Dr. Dacher Kelter, professor of psychology at University of California, Berkeley, and director of the Berkeley Social Interaction Lab, conducted an experiment to illustrate the famous thesis of nineteenth-century historian and politician Sir John Dalberg-Acton: "Power tends to corrupt and absolute power corrupts *absolutely*."

Kelter's so-called cookie monster experiment brought together three people, chosen arbitrarily, to work together to complete a routine task. One of the three was randomly selected to be in charge of the team. Midway through the task, researchers

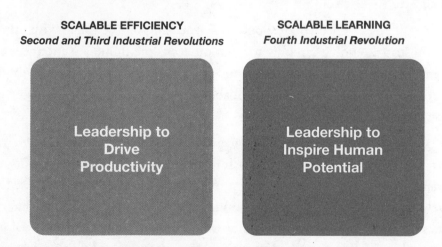

Figure 9.1: Leadership Shift from Driving Productivity to Inspiring Human Potential

Sources: John Hagel (scalable efficiency and scalable learning) and Heather E. McGowan (leadership for productivity or potential)

Figure 9.2: Who Gets the Extra Cookie?

Source: Photo by Wendy Rueter on Unsplash.

put a plate of four warm chocolate chip cookies on the table (Figure 9.2). One cookie remained after each participant took a cookie. Almost always, that last cookie was taken by the person who had been placed in charge. Not only did they take the cookie, but consistently, they ate that extra cookie with gusto, mouth open, dropping crumbs all over themselves.

Kelter explains, "When you feel powerful, you kind of lose touch with other people. You stop attending carefully to what other people think."[1] Kelter goes on to explain that in most work environments, the very qualities that earned you the position of power—notably empathy, collaboration, and fairness—fade once you begin to feel power and prestige.

The cookie monster experiment is one grotesque illustration of what Dr. Travis Bradberry found in his analysis of over 1 million workers. Bradberry is coauthor of *Emotional Intelligence 2.0* and president of TalentSmart, a company focused exclusively on emotional intelligence assessments and training. He found that the highest levels of emotional intelligence were found in those in managerial or supervisor roles; the lowest were in those in senior executive and CEO roles (Figure 9.3).

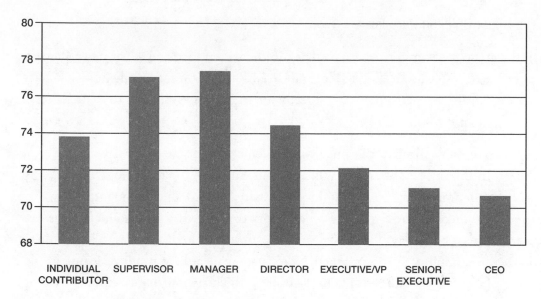

Figure 9.3: Emotional Intelligence and Job Title

Source: Travis Bradberry, PhD, president, TalentSmart, Inc., coauthor, *Emotional Intelligence 2.0.*

This glide path—from growing emotional intelligence as an individual contributor up through the position of supervisor, then declining to the lowest levels in CEOs—might suggest that you need to ditch the empathy to succeed in business. However, Bradberry paradoxically found that the most *successful* senior executives and CEOs are those with the highest levels of emotional intelligence; they are able to obtain power and maintain compassion and self-awareness.[2]

Since nearly any work that is mentally routine or predictable can or soon will be addressed by an algorithm, the work that remains is some combination of labor that is volatile, uncertain, complex, or ambiguous, often referred to by the military term *VUCA*. VUCA work is all the stuff that technology cannot handle (at least yet) without human engagement. To maximize human engagement and really tap into our adaptation advantage, we need to be more human ourselves, and that means we have to work harder as leaders to develop the empathy, compassion, and even vulnerability that establishes the trust necessary so teams can let go, learn, and adapt to the emerging challenges.

The Super Chicken Paradox

In the chase for ever greater productivity, leaders often focus on super performers to carry the day. On its face, this Third Industrial Revolution management style makes sense: identify top performers and direct your energy and resources to their success.

Not so fast.

A second experiment, this one involving chickens, discovered a flaw in that theory. In the early eighties, Dr. William Muir, an evolutionary biologist and professor of animal sciences at Purdue University, created an experiment in an attempt to increase the egg-laying productivity of hens. Chicken productivity is easy to measure; she that lays the most eggs is the most productive. To test his hypothesis on the inheritability of this productivity to thereby be able to produce a superior breed of egg-layers, Muir created flocks of nine chickens, putting each flock in a cage and selecting the most productive hen from each flock to breed the next generations of ever more productive hens (Figure 9.4).

Figure 9.4: In Search of Super Chickens

Source: Photo by William Moreland on Unsplash.

Interestingly, that's not what happened. Having placed the nine most productive hens into their own flock, Muir noticed something rather awful. The flock quickly dwindled from nine to three chickens. The other six were killed by the survivors, which continued to attack one another incessantly. In reality those prolific hens—or super chickens, as Margaret Heffernan referred to them in her TED Talk "Forget the Pecking Order at Work" (a video very much worth the 15 minutes to view)—only reached that status by subduing the yield of the rest of the flock. It turns out, in hens at least, that bullying behavior is heritable and several generations were sufficient to produce a strain of psychopathic chickens.

And what was happening in the other cages? In a parallel experiment, Muir monitored the productivity of the flocks and selected *all of the hens* from the best-producing cages to breed the next generation of hens. All nine hens survived, fully feathered. Egg productivity increased 160% in only a few generations, "an almost unheard-of response to artificial selection in animal breeding experiments,"[3] Muir's research found.

Interestingly, Muir repeated this research across varying species over much of the past 30 years and verified the robustness of the method and showed it could be applied to any species.

What do super chickens have to do with the future of work, learning, and adaptation? Simply put, when we focus on the "star performers" who come from the "best" schools, giving them the "best" jobs at the "best" companies, we create a sort of Hunger Games, pitting teammates in hypercompetition with one another. It is a practice that is failing us. We are pecking each other to death. Annual reviews, for example, are great for feedback, but they almost always include a ranking—are you a number 1 or a number 5? To be number 1, someone else has to be number 2. No doubt, metric rankings assist management in distributing raises and bonuses, but we need to ensure that ranking doesn't pit our talent against one another.

In fact, our obsession with star performers may be our Achilles' heel. Collaborative research from INSEAD, Columbia University, and VU University Amsterdam found that "talent facilitates performance—but only up to a point, after which the benefits of more talent decrease and eventually become detrimental as intrateam coordination suffers."[4] In the paper "The Too-Much-Talent Effect: Team Interdependence Determines When More Talent Is Too Much or Not Enough," they looked at three team sports—basketball, baseball, and football—which "revealed that the too-much-talent effect emerged when team members were interdependent (football and basketball) but not independent (baseball)." Football (soccer, for us Americans) and basketball require tight interdependence between players in order to win (Figure 9.5).

Team play is not essential in just sports. "As business becomes increasingly global and cross-functional, silos are breaking down, connectivity is increasing, and teamwork is seen as a key to organizational success," write Rob Cross, Reb Rebele, and Adam Grant about their 2016 paper in the *Harvard Business Review.* "According to data we have collected over the past two decades, the time spent by managers and employees in collaborative activities has ballooned by 50% or more."[5] In short, more of work is interdependent.

Or, as Margaret Heffernan noted in her TED Talk, "Companies don't have ideas; only people do. And what motivates people are the bonds and loyalty and trust they develop between each other. What matters is the mortar, not just the bricks."

It's time to think about your super chickens very carefully. Are you pitting your talent against one another or are you creating the conditions, like the cages of the best hens, for optimal human potential?

Figure 9.5: Soccer: An Interdependence Sport

Source: Photo by Jannik Skorna on Unsplash.

TED Talk Signals Leadership

The now-ubiquitous TED Talks are often an early indicator of emerging ideas in culture and business. People say things on the TED stage often long before they become mainstream ideas. It's interesting to note, then, that in 2019, four of the five most-watched talks of all time gave insight into the shifting future of work, and two of those talks tackled the changing nature of leadership. (No. 5 on the list was "Ten Things You Did Not Know about an Orgasm." We'll leave it to you to decide what, if any, relevance that may have in your future of work.) The five most-watched TED Talks as of 2019 were:

1. "Do Schools Kill Creativity?" Sir Ken Robinson
2. "Your Body Language May Shape Who You Are," Amy Cuddy
3. "How Great Leaders Inspire Action," Simon Sinek
4. "The Power of Vulnerability," Brené Brown
5. "Ten Things You Didn't Know About an Orgasm," Mary Roach

What Makes a Modern Leader?

Jim Kouzes and Barry Posner first published *The Leadership Challenge* in 1987. Now, more than 30 years later, they have produced a suite of leadership books and training programs that focus on five essential leadership practices that have not changed since they began their work together. This, they believe, is the essence of leadership:

1. *Model the way*: Establish principles around how others should be treated and how goals should be obtained and create interim milestones when a goal is too far out or too complex.

2. *Inspire a shared vision:* Create a future state that others both believe in and desire to help realize.

3. *Challenge the process*: Change the status quo by including experimentation and learning from failure.

4. *Enable others to act*: Foster collaboration and build spirited teams based on mutual respect and trust.

5. *Encourage the heart*: Celebrate accomplishments, and make team members feel like heroes.

We would not do them justice to attempt to summarize their decades of research in leadership, but we will shine a light on two ideas that we think have particular applicability at this unique moment in time. If you take nothing else from Kouzes's and Posner's work, let it be this: model the way and enable others to act in order to lead adaptive teams. By embracing these two ideas, you will set the conditions for rapid learning, unlearning, and build the transformational teams at the heart of your adaptation advantage.

Model the Way: Introduce Yourself and Share Your Values

While you may assume your team knows who you are, you may be surprised to find they actually do not know what you value. Kouzes told us this story: "In some leadership seminars we conducted at Northrop Grumman Corporation, Ron Sugar, CEO and chairman at the time, came to speak to the executives at his company. His immediate questions to them were, 'Do the people you lead know who you are, what you care about, and why they ought to be following you?' These are three wonderful questions, and every leader must be able to answer them. But it's that first question— 'Do the people you lead know who you are?'—that requires every leader to do some serious soul searching." Who are you as a leader now? What kind of leader do you want to become? What's the gap between who you are and who you want to be? What do you need to do to become your best self?"

We wanted to test this concept, so we spoke with Carol Leaman, president and CEO of Axonify. Axonify is a micro learning platform used in corporate environments to help frontline employees learn in the flow of work. Leaman was previously CEO of PostRank Inc., a social engagement analytics platform she sold to Google, and prior to that she was CEO at several other technology firms, including RSS Solutions and Fakespace Systems. Besides her remarkable track record as an entrepreneur, Leaman has a 97% employee approval rating on Glass Door, a virtually perfect rating. Based on her multiple tours in the CEO suite and her unusually high employee approval rating, we wanted to know how she does it. She told us that while business may be incredibly complex, she models her leadership on simple tenets:

I want every single person at Axonify, when they leave us at whatever point they leave us, to look back and think that this was the best place they ever worked. In order to achieve that, I set out every day to create an environment of openness, and complete transparency. I make mistakes. I own them and then I try to fix them.

With the exception of payroll, everyone who works at Axonify knows everything. There is not a single person in this company that has an excuse to say that they don't know who our customers are, or that they don't know what our revenue is, or that they don't know what our targets are, or that they don't know how we're doing against those targets. Every single person sees all the gory details because I fundamentally believe that if people don't know, they make stuff up. People interpret stuff always negatively, not positively.

I host a session called AMA for Ask Me Anything. Employees can anonymously submit questions and no matter the question, I have to answer it on the spot. This is a really important session because it tells me what is on folks' minds. One of the questions I often get is how I stay so calm. I may be stressed but I know there is always a way. If I model calmness and focus while leading with authenticity and transparency, I find people do their best work and that is my goal: to inspire the best in our employees.

When Heather spoke at Axonify's annual summit of their top clients, she was intrigued that the company didn't talk about its technology platform at all. Instead, they spoke about how their clients could create an atmosphere where people do their best work. This is a passion for Leaman, and when she speaks, she shows great vulnerability and authenticity that establishes trust. Trust is the cornerstone of great leadership and essential to the formation of great teams. What if instead of driving productivity you focused on "creating the best place to work" and the atmosphere that inspires optimal human potential and adaptation?

Model the Way: Be Vulnerable

Vulnerability in leadership is tremendously challenging. It requires that you leave yourself exposed and, potentially, susceptible to harm. It takes courage and strength to be a vulnerable leader. When Leaman admitted her errors and opened herself to be asked anything, she demonstrated strength in vulnerability.

Too often, we think of vulnerability as a weakness, but University of Houston research professor and best-selling author Dr. Brené Brown has convinced millions over nearly 10 years that vulnerability can also be the basis of strength and connection. We say it often enough to be a mantra: as machines do more and more routine and predictable work, humans need to be, well—more human. More of our work is knowledge based, rooted in ideas, ideas come from humans, not technology tools. In Chapter 8, we highlighted recent global surveys of corporations that found an increase in unmet demand for individuals with uniquely human skills, skills from empathy to compassion to judgment to creativity. This is not just true for workers, but it is now especially true for leaders. At the base of all these skills is vulnerability. And vulnerability is anything but weakness.

In her work with the military, Brown noted that there is no courage without vulnerability. "Vulnerability is the birthplace of innovation, creativity and change," she writes.[6] If that is true, where is leadership on this? One of Brown's latest books is called *Dare to Lead.* In it, she examines how and why vulnerability is essential to modern leadership. Vulnerability establishes trust and the safety to share what you know (ideas) as well as what you do not know (gaps). When we do not hear all the ideas that come from our team, we experience the loss of human potential. When we do not hear when our teams need help (gaps), that is a loss of opportunity. It is an unfilled capability gap.

According to Brown, a leader is "anyone who takes the responsibility to find the potential in people and processes and has the courage to develop that potential." That leadership can come from surprising places. In recent years, a number of young people have stepped up to take that responsibility with courage. Greta Thunberg, who was nominated for a Nobel Prize at the age of 16 and honored as *Time Magazine*'s 2019 Person of the Year, led rallies across the globe and spoke passionately to world leaders at the United Nations, demanding they take action on climate change in 2019. Malala Yousafzai has become an outspoken advocate for girls' education in the Middle East and the youngest recipient ever of the Nobel Peace Prize. The survivors of the Parkland School shooting are speaking out on gun safety and leading the fight for legislative reform. All of these leaders assumed the responsibility and showed the courage to voice their concerns for their peers and their generation, often when their lives were literally at stake. Agree with them or do not, but you cannot deny that they are stepping up and showing incredible vulnerability and courage.

What they display is what Dov Seidman, CEO of global consultancy LRN Corporation, refers to as moral leadership. Moral leadership, he says, is "focusing on human progress and improving the world, having the courage to speak out for principles and being willing to ask tough questions about right and wrong."[7]

Moral leadership, Seidman's research suggests, is both in short supply in business and could offer a path to performance improvement. From LRN's survey of 500 business executives:

> Sixty-two percent of employees believe their colleagues' performances would improve if their managers relied more on their moral authority than on their formal power and 59% say their organizations would be more successful in taking on their biggest challenges if their leadership had more moral authority.[8]

We see moral leadership in business every day. In 2018, Nike decided to celebrate the 30-year anniversary of their "Just Do It" campaign with an ad featuring controversial former San Francisco 49ers quarterback Colin Kaepernick. Kaepernick was, and remains, at the center of controversy when he decided to "take a knee" during the playing of the National Anthem to protest the deaths of African Americans at the hands of police. While the response to the ad from social media was mixed, Nike stock reached an all-time high the week they released the ad, a bump of $6 billion in market capitalization.

Hobby Lobby, a chain of arts and crafts stores, believed a mandate in the Affordable Care Act that required employers' insurance to cover contraception, including access to the morning-after pill, violated the founders' religious beliefs. The company took its case all the way to the Supreme Court, which found in 2014's *Burwell v. Hobby Lobby* that the mandate did, in fact, violate a privately held company's right to religious freedom. Publicly expressing its values hasn't been bad for Hobby Lobby's business. The private company continues to successfully operate more than 800 stores across the United States.

We wondered how the concept of vulnerability played with *Leadership Challenge*'s Kouzes. He told us this story:

> One of my friends owns a coffee farm, and when he was first starting out his agronomist offered him some advice. He said that they needed to build a *buena casa*—a good house—in order to provide the right kind of environment in which the coffee plants could thrive. They could dig a shallow hole, put a coffee plant in it, and it would produce for a short while, but it wouldn't have the flavor and the longevity that it would have if they dug a deep hole filled with nutrient-rich soil. We

have been digging shallow holes around all of these human issues, and we haven't yet built a nutrient-rich environment in which it is possible to have conversations about vulnerability, compassion, empathy, and emotional intelligence. While we've begun to build a *buena casa* in some organizations in which these kinds of relationships are more likely to thrive, we have a long way to go. More so than before the need is there for us to develop and sustain a richer and deeper human connection."

Throughout this book, we have aimed to model vulnerability by sharing our own failures and challenges. Vulnerability does not mean oversharing personal details, but rather revealing information that demonstrates what you, as a leader, believe and why you believe it so that your team can connect with you authentically, feel safe to share with you, and engage with you in pursuit of company missions based upon shared values.

Model the Way: Trust Is Essential at Speed

Vulnerability and trust are not new ideas, but they take on new meaning when accelerated change enters the scene. In order to learn and adapt to new technologies, new roles, and new business models, we have to think like a trapeze artist and let go of one bar so we can grab the next. If you are asking your team members to leap, you have to assure them there is a net to catch them should they fall (Figure 9.6). This process of letting go of who you are (role) and how you did things (technology and business model) requires both vulnerability and courage in an environment of trust.

When we asked Kouzes about this concept, he had another story for us:

I was talking to a friend of mine who's a race car driver by avocation. He will tell you that when you are driving fast, you have to pay more attention, and you can't let your mind drift. You can't look elsewhere. You just have to stay focused on the road ahead, otherwise it can be very dangerous to yourself and others. The same is true in a fast-paced environment. If you're a leader in a fast-paced environment, you just have to pay more attention, and you have to be more present. I'm not sure that that's changed the content of leadership; it just means we have to do it more frequently than we may have been doing it before when things were slower. We didn't have to be as attentive, perhaps, as we do today. Further, when you're on a racetrack by yourself, it's just you, the track, the walls on the sides, and the infield. You don't have to worry about other drivers. But when there are a lot of other race cars going fast on the track with you, it certainly increases the skill you need as a driver. Analogously,

Figure 9.6: Leaders Make the First Leap of Faith

Source: Photo by Sammie Vasquez on Unsplash.

now that we have all these other forces moving fast, it's increasing the need for us to be more skillful and competent than before. That's the intensity part.

We are in that intensity now. You are a race car driver and your focus and situational awareness are essential (Figure 9.7).

Model the Way: The Best Leaders Are Curious Learners

In their book *Human + Machine*, Paul Daugherty, chief technology and innovation officer, and Jim Wilson, managing director of research, both at Accenture, suggest that we start thinking, and leading, like the navigation application Waze. Long ago, we navigated through physical space by using the stars as our guide, and then cartographers developed maps, which were eventually printed. In time, these maps were digitized and linked to powerful global positioning satellites (GPS) to pinpoint

Figure 9.7: Racing Takes Great Situational Awareness

Source: Photo by Max Böttinger on Unsplash.

our place on them. Now, we are hyperconnected and interdependent and we navigate through real-time flows of data. When we drive using the Waze application, we are contributing to the flow of data that is directing our car and others to avoid traffic, accidents, and police speed traps. It is a symbiotic relationship. We need to start thinking this way as we navigate leadership by sensing and responding in order to tap into our adaptation advantage.

In 1979, Fritz Machlup coined the terms "stocks of knowledge" and "flows of knowledge" to delineate the difference between how knowledge is recorded and how it is transmitted.[9] Back in 1979, knowledge was transferred primarily in three ways: person to record, record to person, and person to person. Although those methods have remained, the Internet has added a fourth dimension to all those transmissions; now knowledge can flow from record to record without human involvement, as evidenced by the Internet of Things—sensors that collect, share, and act on input without human intervention.

In this world of increasing data, flows of knowledge, and accelerated change, a leader must be a constant learner. In their *Harvard Business Review* article "The Best Leaders Are Constant Learners,"[10] Kenneth Mikkelsen, coauthor of *The Neo-Generalists*, and consultant Harold Jarche suggest leaders follow a simple Three Ss formula: seek, sense, and share. Seek is about filtering the most important emerging data for what is important through trusted networks that can help check your blind spots and bridge your gaps. Sense is how we make meaning of the uncovered information to ourselves and our organizations. Share is how we transfer that knowledge back through our networks and with our teams and colleagues to elevate everyone's situational awareness. Sharing also builds respect and trust across our networks and with our teams. To build a team that continuously learns and adapts, that learning has to start with you. Your own learning must be evident in your ability to say, "I don't know" and in your willingness to admit errors and explain failures so you learn from and through them.

Enable Others to Act: You Do Not Need to Know Everything

In the past, leadership often meant the person at the top of the organizational chart was the unquestionable expert. No longer. While we encourage you to be a curious learner, we also want you to realize that you do not need to know everything. We are moving from a complicated world to a complex world (Figure 9.8). A complicated world has many intersecting parts, yet it is largely deterministic. A complex world, on the other hand, has plenty of moving parts whose properties and behaviors emerge and change as situations vary. In a complicated world, you can predict outcomes. In a complex one, you need to constantly adapt in order to direct outcomes.

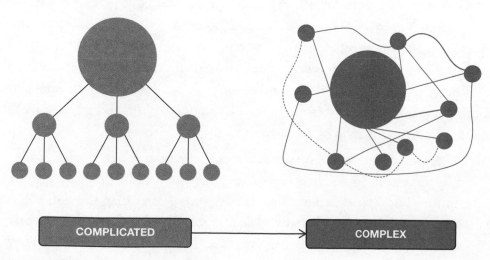

Figure 9.8: Complicated to Complex

In a complicated organization, the leader likely has sat in most of the chairs she came to manage. Even if she skipped a couple of roles, she probably has most, if not all, of the skills and knowledge to do the work of those she manages. In complex environments, new flows of knowledge, skills, and activities continually reshape the organization in ways leaders may not even be able to predict, let alone be trained for.

That lack of knowing leaves many leaders uneasy. We often hear from leaders that they have people reporting to them who have skills and knowledge that they themselves lack. Some leaders even become concerned that their team members, with their specific skills, could take over the leadership role. But even if you can't do the work of someone on your team, you can do yours. Leadership is not about you having more talent than each of your direct reports; rather, it's about your ability to integrate and orchestrate their talent toward your goals. This leadership style is the essence of the adaptation advantage because it enables talent to learn, expand, and reorganize in preparation for as yet unseen opportunity.

Enable Others to Act: Establish Psychological Safety

By now, we hope we've made the case that vulnerability is essential to establish the trust necessary to set the stage for your teams to engage. If you are a leader and you are concealing your shortcomings, you are actually creating a weakness—the bad kind—for your team. Let us say that again: hiding your weaknesses or pretending you know the answers is not positioning you to be a better leader. Instead, you are encouraging your people to hide their knowledge and skills gaps, creating a team that is weak and compromised. Having the courage to show your weakness, embracing not knowing, and admitting mistakes is how you model vulnerability so that your people will be open with their own gaps and raise their hands when they need help. When you model vulnerability and encourage your team to do the same, you establish a safe place for your team to create, collaborate, learn, and adapt. And that is essential to the foundation of effective teams.

In 2012, Google set out to use their data expertise to understand what made some teams successful while others failed. They code-named the project "Aristotle" because of the philosopher's famous line "the whole is greater than the sum of its parts" and to signal their theory that we can do more together than any one of us can do alone. They studied 180 teams from around the globe for over two years to find the answer to the question "What makes an effective team?" They looked at everything from IQ to gender and racial compositions to social connections. What they found was striking. It mattered far less who was on the team than how the team worked together.

The number-one determinant for the most successful teams was psychological safety or "the individual's perception of the consequences of taking interpersonal risk."[11] Or, as Dr. Brown would say, the safety to be vulnerable. Even at Google, an organization filled with intellectual stars, it wasn't IQ that mattered; it was how those stars worked together.

Google determined that in addition to psychological safety, it was essential that teams had dependability and accountability, structure and clarity, meaning, and purpose. Teams must hear from all members, respect all perspectives, and know that all players must feel comfortable to disclose failures and gaps of knowledge as well as skill in order to pursue the team's mission with a clearly defined mandate.

The term psychological safety, made popular by Google, was originally coined in 1999 by Amy Edmondson, PhD, from Harvard Business School, in her groundbreaking paper "Psychological Safety and Learning Behavior in Work Teams." Dr. Edmondson discovered the concept of psychological safety in the 1990s when doing research into team performance in healthcare—specifically looking at how and why medical errors occur. Edmondson sought to understand why some teams performed better than others. Was it because they made fewer mistakes?

She was surprised to find out that they did not, in fact, make fewer mistakes. Rather, they had a team dynamic that made it more comfortable to admit, discuss, and learn from errors. She synthesized her 20 years of research in her book *The Fearless Organization: Creating Psychological Safety in the Workplace for Learning, Innovation, and Growth.* In the book, Edmondson suggests that since so many of our economies are now based upon knowledge work, "for knowledge work to flourish, the workplace must be one in which people feel safe to share their knowledge!"[12]

In our research for this book, we spoke with Duena Blomstrom. While her background is in finance and technology, Blomstrom recently founded a new company called Peoplenottech that has built a machine learning–powered software solution using a proprietary algorithm to redefine employee engagement, team formation, and health, all with a focus on psychological safety. As her company name implies, Blomstrom, despite her deep knowledge of and experience with technology, believes that it is not the technology tool that counts most, but rather the people and how they use those tools.

Blomstrom told us she defines a psychologically safe team as "one that feels like family and moves mountains together. Think back to the last time you made some magic with the team, how you were open and debated and vulnerable and learning, creating, and getting stuff done. That well-oiled machine that felt fun to be a part of. That was psychologically safe."

In order to achieve this optimal team, Blomstrom thinks we need "employees to trust they have permission to be authentic without fear of any repercussion and bring their entire selves to work, they need to see leaders who admit when they fail, don't sugarcoat it in acronyms, say so often, and ask prying, emotionally involved questions that show they truly care about their employees. Needless to say, for them to show this they need to start with managing it within their own leadership groups first and transform those which are now nothing but impression management showcase stages today into psychologically safe management teams."

Impression management, a term coined by Erving Goffman, is "a conscious or subconscious process in which people attempt to influence the perceptions of other people about a person, object, or event by regulating and controlling information in social interaction."

Harvard's Edmondson centers her definition of impression management on the four things leaders typically try to avoid: appearing incompetent, seeming ignorant, looking unprofessional, or acting intrusive.

In order for transformational learning to occur in a learning and adaptive environment, we believe individual workers must be comfortable with not knowing, with ambiguity, and with potentially being wrong—all things not possible without psychological safety. Unless you were a trapeze artist, you would not feel safe on a trapeze letting go of one bar and reaching for the next if the net was removed. Psychological safety is the net necessary for optimal team performance, engagement, and adaptability.

Enable Others to Act: Encourage Respectful Discourse and Dissent

In their most recent State of the American Workplace report, Gallup found that only 3 in 10 employees felt their opinions were valued at work. Gallup predicts that by "moving that ratio to 6 in 10 employees, organizations could realize a 27% reduction in turnover, a 40% reduction in safety incidents, and a 12% increase in productivity."[13]

Moving that needle, though, is a real challenge. You may avoid tough conversations to spare people's feelings. Maybe you are avoiding your own discomfort. Avoiding tough conversations, though, robs your team of the feedback that may help them grow or adapt. Dr. Brené Brown puts it succinctly: "Clear is kind. Unclear is unkind."

Harvard's Edmondson built her book *The Fearless Organization* on the notion that we can care about our team members personally and still give brutally honest feedback to help them change directionally to evolve and adapt to maximize their human potential. This concept of radical candor unfolds in a three-step process: (1) setting the stage, (2) inviting participation, and (3) responding productively. Setting the stage is about framing the reality of your challenge for maximum engagement. Inviting participation is really all about the leader and how you make it safe and okay to admit, explore, and learn from mistakes. Responding productively is holding trust by not penalizing the engagement you worked so hard to elicit and instead expressing appreciation for participation, destigmatizing failure, and creating an environment for continuous learning. This ultimately is a process that is deeply respectful and uplifting.

Remember the 70–20–10 rule: 10% of our learning comes from structured instruction, 20% comes from working with others, and 70% comes in the flow of work. When you consider this in total, what the rule is really reflecting is that 90% of learning at work happens in collaboration. It benefits us as leaders, then, to set the conditions to maximize our teams' learning from both success and failures.

Enable Others to Act: Prioritize Wellness

As our world has become increasingly complex, tenure in jobs has become shorter, and continuous learning has become a nonoptional requirement for staying relevant, it's no surprise that stress levels have skyrocketed. According to the World Health Organization, 300 million people report being depressed.[14] Add anxiety to this mix and that number goes up significantly, though it is difficult to know for sure just how high; fewer than half of those folks suffering from depression seek treatment. The global professional service firm Aon's "Global 2020 Medical Trends Rate" report cites stress as being in the top five global concerns for healthcare costs and risk.[15]

To better understand the impact of stress and mental health on performance, we spoke with recently retired Major General James Johnson, former executive director of human resilience for the US Air Force. Johnson was responsible, he told us, for "optimizing human performance using strategies focused on wellbeing and resilience."

What he learned in that role is valuable to leaders in every type of organization. Johnson shared that insight in an email to us:

> Essentially, we found that the success of our strategies ultimately hinged on leaders consistently using approaches that leveraged research. In this vein, we knew we had to focus first on equipping leaders, because if leaders, from the most senior officer down to the front-line supervisor, don't understand the strategy and underlying science, they won't buy-in, and they won't adequately communicate the strategy to subordinate levels, and, at the end of the day, organizations won't buy-in, and you won't achieve your desired outcomes. In fact, without relying on research-based strategies, not only do we jeopardize positive progress, we run the risk of implementing programs that could actually do more harm. A good example of this is the DARE (Drug and Alcohol Resistance Education) program, which ignored scientific evidence, and continues to inspire more kids to turn to drugs rather than "just say no."

> This focus on leaders and research-based strategies is so important to our work, especially when you consider we share some of society's most distressing human problems that are resistant to simplistic ad-hoc solutions; everything from depressive illness to sexual assault, family violence, and suicide. A study that highlights the challenges (Heyman, Slep, & Nelson, 2011), found that one in three of our people anonymously reported problems with these kinds of issues, including substance abuse, suicidal ideation, and family violence. We also found that two out of three of them indicated these were secretive problems. That's a significant and surprising issue, in our case negatively impacting over 100,000 people.

> Ultimately, we'll see real success with our human wellbeing and resilience strategies, even those dealing with issues as difficult as suicide prevention, when we equip leaders with research-based strategies and implement programs strengthening social support, promoting development of life skills, and changing policies and norms to eliminate mental health stigma, while encouraging effective help-seeking behaviors.

If the military sees mental health as an essential driver of performance, we believe it is high time that corporations make mental health and stress reduction not just a human resource benefit but a core business strategy. Globally, 1 in 7 individuals suffers from either a mental health or substance abuse disorder. In aggregate, that's *over one billion people.* The most common mental health challenge is anxiety, affecting about 4% of the global population.[16]

Simple math: if you have more than seven direct reports, there is a good chance that at least one of them is suffering. How aware are you of the mental health of your team? Adaptation is harder, if not impossible, when in a mental health crisis.

Transformational Leadership

The term *digital transformation* is used ad nauseum in popular and business literature. Most of us think of it as a one-time thing when you shift to a paperless office or when you do everything through a software application. In truth, digital transformation is a multiyear, multiphase process of transforming to a learning-centric environment that leverages data for insights and learning. Web strategist Jeremiah Owyang identifies seven components of digital transformation: strategy, data, customer experience, organizational alignment, analytics and AI, people and culture, and innovation.[17] We'll talk more about this in Chapter 10.

Considering that most companies, except those born digital, are in various places across these dimensions, we turned to Jim Kouzes again to talk about how leadership can make the difference in such profound business and organizational change. "Exemplary leadership makes a significant difference in organizational performance," he told us. "For example, in a survey of 94 large companies, researcher Richard Roi asked executives to rate their company's senior leadership on transformation leadership using The Five Practices of Exemplary Leadership® as the framework. What he discovered in his analysis of the data was that there was a dramatic relationship between transformational leadership practices and company performance. Companies with a strong and consistent application of The Five Practices had net income growth of a positive 841% versus a negative 49% for companies with a low incidence of leadership practices. Similarly, stock price growth was 204 percent for strong transformational leadership practices companies compared with only 76% for companies with a weak implementation of practices. The harder business measures, as well as measures of employee engagement, all indicate that organizations over the long term will produce better results when they exhibit transformational leadership than when they are merely transactional."

We spoke at length with David Walsh, an entrepreneur, investor, and business operator who served as CEO at Genband (which merged with Sonus Networks in 2017 to form the publicly traded Ribbon Communications) and has gone on to found cloud communications platform company Kandy.io. Walsh witnessed firsthand many evolutions and adaptations in telecommunications over his 35-year career in that sector. Speaking specifically about the leadership required for transformational change and continuous adaptation, he says, "Change in organizations is very hard. People cling to the skill they learned and the culture they built around it. This is particularly true in technology companies. People hold onto the original technology that made them successful often long past its usefulness. They ignore the change happening around them until it's too late to pivot, as others have already made the shift and the opportunity is gone."

Timing, it turns out, makes all the difference when navigating change. Walsh makes this particularly insightful observation:

> Often companies at their peak of profitability are at their greatest risk of failure, which makes it even harder to accept that change is needed. I've found that being a benevolent dictator helps drive change in the early stage of the pivot. Bringing in talent from outside the organization with different skills and experiences is key. To reduce resistance, it's also important to repurpose talent from within so people believe they can be part of the future. In order to pivot, the mission has to be clear, the goals have to be well defined, and everyone has to be bought in, from the Board all the way through the entire organization. Then you align your troops along a narrow front and attack with overwhelming force, landing and expanding until you succeed. The people you pick for the mission not only have to be able, they need to believe in the mission. Placing the talent into a separate division or establishing a new brand helps send the message that something new is happening and helps united the team around its mission. I've done this a few times, pivoting from voice trading to electronic trading, from making hardware and software to a business of connecting them together and from using the software of a company to building a SaaS business out of it. All of these pivots required a different culture and business model and the ability not only to fight externally for customers but to fight the "enemies from within" who resisted change at every pass.

Transformational Leadership and Change Management Models

In 1947, German American psychologist Kurt Lewin introduced a simple three-stage model for change management: unfreeze (today we might say unlearning), change, freeze. Lewin's model was a breakthrough in change management because it acknowledged the letting go of old mindsets and behaviors in the unfreeze phase and the crystallization and standardization of processes in the freeze phase. The challenge of this model today is that change is a not a one-time thing; freezing, then, is probably never a good idea.

Fast forward a few decades from Lewin's three-phase model to the time when change management gurus adopted the Satir Change Model. Created by family therapist Virginia Satir in the 1970s, the model assumed change was a one-time thing, a single process from one state to another with five phases: (1) late-stage status quo, (2) resistance, (3) chaos, (4) integration, and (5) new status quo. Satir's model acknowledges both resistance and chaos but still keeps an implied promise that you will only need to be uncomfortable and vulnerable once as you go through a single transformation.

To refer to digital transformation in this transactional way is wrong. Transformation is continuous and moving from phase to phase is a series of learning processes. In order to learn and adapt, you need to unlearn and let go. To deal effectively with this continuous change, you need to get comfortable with being uncomfortable—comfortable being wrong, comfortable not knowing, and comfortable learning from failures. This requires stretching as well as changing your perspective as often as possible (Figure 9.9).

Figure 9.9: Become Comfortable with Being Uncomfortable

Source: Photo by André Noboa on Unsplash.

Years ago, Heather had a colleague who explained the difference between mistakes and failure. He said, "Mistakes should be avoided, and failures embraced. Mistakes are things that go wrong and we do not know why. Failure implies a theory from which we can learn from the results. Embrace failure, avoid mistakes."

Leading with Fear: The Burning Platform

In the scalable efficiency and shareholder-value era, many business leaders used the phrase "create a burning platform" (Figure 9.10) to signal an environment that forces human behavior changes. That phrase originated from a story of an oil rig explosion in the North Atlantic sea off the coast of Scotland in the 1980s. One hundred and sixty-six crew members and two rescuers lost their lives when the rig caught fire. Andy Mochan, a superintendent on the rig, and one of the 63 survivors, was asked how he managed to live when so many perished. Mochan noted that the oil had surfaced and ignited, debris littered the water, and he knew that because of the water's temperature, he would likely survive for only a few minutes if not quickly rescued. Despite the bleak information and training to the contrary, Mochan jumped 15 stories from the platform to the water. When asked why he leaped, he did not hesitate. "It was either jump or fry," he said. His was a choice between probable death or certain death. Mochan jumped because he felt the price of staying on the platform was too high.[18]

Figure 9.10: Beware the Burning Platform

Source: Photo by Stephen Radford on Unsplash.

Figure 9.11: From Burning Platform to Burning Ambition

Source: Peter Sheahan, CEO, Karrikins Group.

Fear is a powerful driving force. We have used the concept of creating life-threatening fear to motivate human behavior change. Fear can work in the short term, but fear as a motivator does not endure. We spoke with Peter Sheahan, founder and CEO of the Karrikins Group, a global behavior change firm. Sheahan suggests we drop the term "burning platform" and instead "create constructive tension by choosing to create a burning ambition over a burning platform" (Figure 9.11).

If you consider the phases of value creation we discussed in Chapter 7, we move from exploration of the problem space to experimentation with ideas to execution of a product or service to expansion of that value through scaling to finally (limiting) your exposure and risk in decline. If you consider these phases, the burning platform metaphor is most applicable to the late stages of potential expansion. More likely, though, the burning platform concept feels most real when you seek to limit your exposure and risk (Figure 9.12).

As David Walsh pointed out from his experiences in telecommunications, these phases are far too late to successfully pivot. The greatest challenge may be leading the behavior change from protection in expansion and (minimizing) exposure to exploration and experimentation. For example, Apple successfully did this by introducing the iPhone when the iPod was still ascending rapidly. If you focus on creating the conditions for burning ambition, leaning into scalable learning rather than relying on scalable efficiency, you will be better positioned for the pivots and

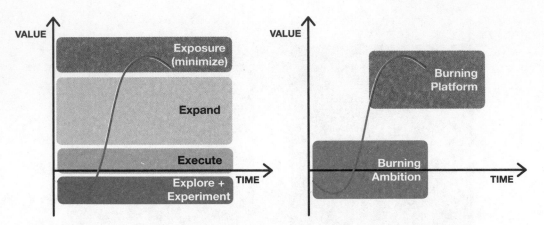

Figure 9.12: Phase of Value Creation and Protection and Burning Platform versus Burning Ambition

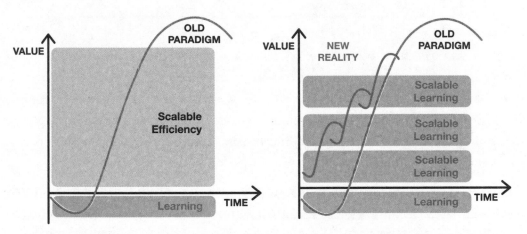

Figure 9.13: Old Paradigm versus New Reality and Scalable Efficiency versus Scalable Learning

continuous adaptation in accelerated change (Figure 9.13). The reskilling and upskilling we've discussed throughout this book are not only for those displaced by change. Rather, they are an essential part of all work. We need both our teams and our leaders to be continuously expanding (reskilling) and deepening (upskilling) their capabilities and knowledge as an integral part of work. Work is learning and work should be organized as a successive series of learning tours designed to expand our individual and collective capacity (Figure 9.14).

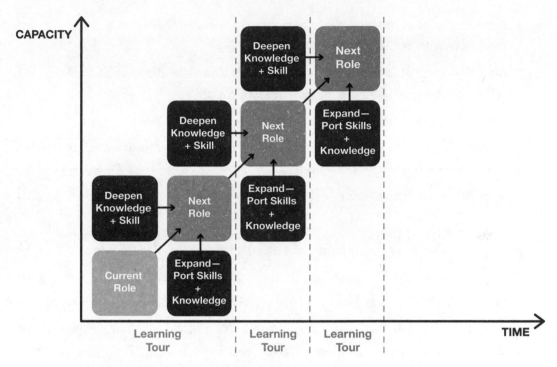

Figure 9.14: Learning Tours to Increase Capacity

Putting It All Together

This is a long chapter so we will keep the summary short. Drop the cookie. Forget the super chickens. Be vulnerable and tell your people what you care about so they can align with your values. Establish safety, trust, and accountability. Check your blind spots and mind your gap by committing to your own learning plan. Own it and apologize when you fail and get up every day with the goal of making your company the one that your team will look back on and say, "That was the best place I ever worked."

Do that, and you'll have a strong foundation for your adaptation advantage.

Notes

1. https://haasinstitute.berkeley.edu/uc-berkeley-professor-dacher-keltner-explains-how-power-makes-people-selfish

2. https://www.weforum.org/agenda/2019/07/the-real-reason-your-boss-lacks-emotional-intelligence

3. https://evolution-institute.org/when-the-strong-outbreed-the-weak-an-interview-with-william-muir/

4. https://www8.gsb.columbia.edu/cbs-directory/sites/cbs-directory/files/publications/Too%20much%20talent%20PS.pdf

5. https://hbr.org/2016/01/collaborative-overload

6. https://blog.ted.com/vulnerability-is-the-birthplace-of-innovation-creativity-and-change-brene-brown-at-ted2012/

7. https://lrn.com/news/moral-leadership-report/

8. Ibid.

9. https://onlinelibrary.wiley.com/doi/abs/10.1111/j.1467-6435.1979.tb02614.x

10. https://hbr.org/2015/10/the-best-leaders-are-constant-learners

11. https://rework.withgoogle.com/print/guides/5721312655835136/

12. Amy Edmondson, *The Fearless Organization: Creating Psychological Safety in the Workplace for Learning, Innovation, and Growth* (Hoboken, NJ: Wiley, 2019).

13. Gallup, 2012–2017 State of the American Workplace Reports, https://news.gallup.com/reports/199961/7.aspx?utm_source=SOAW&utm_campaign=StateofAmericanWorkplace&utm_medium=2013SOAWreport

14. https://www.who.int/news-room/fact-sheets/detail/depression

15. https://healthresources.aon.com/reports-2/2020-global-medical-trend-rates-report?_ga=2.68170193.1752020940.1568645833-1249706872.1568645833

16. https://ourworldindata.org/global-mental-health

17. http://www.web-strategist.com/blog/2019/09/30/digital-transformation-culture-business-model-change/

18. https://www.connerpartners.com/frameworks-and-processes/the-real-story-of-the-burning-platform

10 The Adaptive Organization: Creating the Capacity to Change at the Speed of Technology, Market, and Social Evolution

Key Ideas

1. The most important tool of an adaptable company is culture. Culture is the context in which a company exercises and expands its capacity to learn, grow, and identify and capture new opportunity.

2. To adeptly adapt continuously, organizational leadership must focus on inputs (culture and capacity) rather than outputs (brand, products, and services).

3. Coupling culture and capacity is key to becoming a scalable learning organization and gaining the adaptation advantage.

What Should We Measure?

When William Muir set out to study productivity, he used hens as his test subject because measuring their egg-laying productivity was simple. She who lays the most eggs is the most productive. (If you skipped Chapter 9, you'll want to go back and give it a quick scan to learn more about this intriguing experiment.) For much of the Second and Third Industrial Revolutions, we measured human productivity in the same way. Count the number of acres plowed, the cars produced on the line, the barrels of crude pulled from the earth, the new accounts opened, or the clicks and page views on a website, and you get a measure of productivity.

But what if, in the Fourth Industrial Revolution, we are measuring the wrong things? Does optimizing the production of Product A matter as much when market winds shift to Technology B before you can even complete an inventory of the first? What if production output matters far less in the future of work than does production process? What should we measure then?

That's the conundrum for many organizational leaders as they rethink how they construct and lead their teams for greater learning and adaptation.

Fortunately, Dr. Muir's productivity experiments light the way.

Recall that in Muir's experiment the "super chickens"—the hens that were the most productive layers—were also the most caustic. They outperformed their peers by intimidating, abusing, and in some cases even killing them. In short, the super chickens were bullies. They looked good because they made others look bad.

While attempting to foster a breed of high-performing hens, Dr. Muir inadvertently gave us a lesson in the importance of culture. The toxic "work environment" inside those cages didn't just kill chickens, it killed productivity over the long term. Similarly, as Dr. Muir found, the best environments fostered productivity. When Dr. Muir selected *all* the hens—and not just the top performers—from the best-producing flocks, productivity increased 160%.

As we cross the bridge to a digital economy, we need to shift from measuring output to optimizing throughput. In other words, the conditions in which we create and produce will matter more than the product itself. That may sound like a radical idea, but consider this: the *things* we produce—because they may be transient— are a product of our organization's capacity to identify and rapidly respond to new opportunity and capture new value. Products and services will be short-lived. Rather than optimizing for specific production, our best work will be in establishing the conditions that enable continuous and continually shifting methods of value creation. These conditions result in an agile, learning, and adaptable company able to thrive in the new realities on the other side of the digital economy bridge.

Those conditions we call culture and capacity.

The Power of the Culture and Capacity Focus

It's a radical but remarkably straightforward concept: companies are nothing more than culture and capacity. Period. Of course, neither culture nor capacity is a simple construct. Still, if you can break apart these two elements to understand them, you can rejoin the ideas to create a framework for highly effective organizational leadership. So, let's break it down.

When we put culture and capacity together, we create a powerful force for transformation of the business, one that shifts the focus from output to input. Culture and capacity are the conditions—the inputs—of an effective business. To the outside world, culture shows up as a brand, an expression of the company's purpose and values. Capacity is evident in the products and services a company puts into the market; these products and services are the outputs of an organization's ability to learn and create (Figure 10.1). Drop culture and capacity into a market context—a market need, an industry, a geography—and you have a business. To put culture and capacity to work in our organizations, then, we need to better understand both. Let's dive deeper.

Culture at the Core

Every organization has a culture. Culture is a sense of purpose and a way of doing things that structure daily life at work. Over three decades of observing culture in early-stage technology companies, Chris developed a theory: culture is either intentional or accidental. An intentional culture is a deliberate construction of

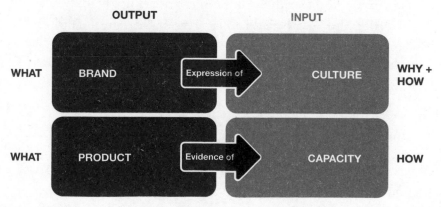

Figure 10.1: Focus on the Inputs: Culture and Capacity

organizational leaders, created in collaboration with all those who are led. An accidental culture is an environment that emerges without intention from a collection of experiences. Accidental cultures, Chris has observed, are almost always toxic.

Too often, the trappings of a workplace—onsite daycare, free gourmet meals, dog-friendly offices, and the like—are mistaken for corporate culture. At best, these benefits are evidence of a culture, but they are not the culture itself. In an intentional culture, a company might declare a lofty purpose: to "unlock human creative potential," for example. Among its operating principles might be a statement like "We believe our employees are at their best when they are at their healthiest." Dozens of decisions can extend easily from that statement of values, allowing the company to say yes to an onsite gym and no to junk food–stocked vending machines. The workplace benefit reflects the values, rather than the other way around.

If that's not clear, let's try another example. You walk into an office space and notice that every desk is outfitted with a Herman Miller Aeron chair, list price $969. These ultra-comfortable, highly ergonomic chairs were once all the rage with well-funded Silicon Valley startups. What do they say about the company's values? On the one hand, it might project a core belief that employees are most productive when they have a comfortable work environment (intentional). On the other—as is too often the case in the profligate boom cycles—it might just mean "we raised a lot of money and we're spending it on ourselves instead of on our business objectives" (accidental). Like we said, the workplace benefits reflect the company values.

Intentional culture begins with organization's leadership. Frankly, it *is* organizational leadership. So, where do you start to build a great culture?

Start with Why, the Foundation of Culture

Author and leadership guru Simon Sinek delivered one of the most watched TED Talks of all time, "How Great Leaders Inspire Action." In this brief talk, well worth the 18 minutes to view, he reminds us that transformational leaders of all kinds set clear targets. From Martin Luther King Jr.'s leading the civil rights movement to the Wright Brothers' chasing the dream of flight, great leaders craft a big vision and give their people a reason to follow them. We join our efforts with great leaders because we share a sense of purpose and live by common values. Or, as Sinek would say, start with why.

*The center of every great culture is a clear sense of purpose.

One young company that has identified its purpose with unmatched certitude is Unreasonable Group. Born from a series of pilot projects and experiments, Unreasonable Group has always had a clear-eyed purpose: "to create a world in which the most valuable and influential companies of our time are those solving humanity's most pressing challenges." Unreasonable Group runs immersive development programs for growth-stage companies building solutions to "seemingly intractable challenges," from alleviating poverty to reversing climate change. The organization partners with global companies as diverse as Nike and Barclays because it is dedicated to driving resources to and breaking down barriers for entrepreneurs who solve the biggest problems.

That sense of purpose runs through everything the company does. Even its name—Unreasonable Group—comes from founder Daniel Epstein's sense of purpose to change the world. "The reasonable man adapts himself to the world," George Bernard Shaw wrote in *Man and Superman*. "The unreasonable one persists in trying to adapt the world to himself. Therefore, all progress depends on the unreasonable man"—"and woman," Unreasonable Group adds to its appropriated mantra.

About three years into building the company, Epstein realized that as the team and community grew, they were rooted in purpose and operating from shared values, but "if we were ever going to have a chance at scaling culture, our values needed to be articulated and expressed in a way that resonates with us," Epstein told us. "Codification of those values is remarkably important. Not just to feel, but to point to. We took what we were living by and put it into words."

Now, the Unreasonable Group's manifesto is front and center of everything the company does (Figure 10.2).

unreasonable

Our values drive everything we do.

We think this is the most important webpage we've ever built. Unreasonable, from its inception, has been a values-driven organization. To be clear, the manifesto below is not a gimmick. All our moves are guided by the constraints set within our values. Without them, Unreasonable Group wouldn't be Unreasonable.

WHY WE EXIST

Our mission is to drive resources into and break down barriers for entrepreneurs solving BFPs. Our vision is to create a world in which the most valuable & influential companies of our time are those solving humanity's most pressing challenges. Below are our values but we want to make clear that we have one law: entrepreneur-centricity. Come hell or high water, we exist to support the entrepreneurs that make up our global community.

OUR VALUES
LONG TERM > SHORT TERM

We put an emphasis on long-term value and impact over short-term gains. In fact, impact is the sole reason we do anything & everything. It is our only bottom line. Although we believe in the power of profit to drive lasting and scalable change, when evaluating an opportunity, we examine its worth via the depth and breadth of the impact we envision possible.

CLIMB THE RIGHT MOUNTAIN

The speed at which you climb the mountain is important, but only relevant if you choose the right mountain to climb. Effectiveness is more important than efficiency and it needs to be intentionally measured over time. We constantly ask ourselves if we are climbing the right mountain and look to leverage data to ensure we are on course and heading towards the chartered summit. Read more about this value on Unreasonable.is.

NO BULLSHIT

We believe humility is paramount and we view vulnerability as strength. We push for open communication even when it's tough, whether that means being transparent about our failures publicly or creating the conditions for authentic communication within our teams. We have chosen to embrace honesty, and sometimes awkwardness, as the path to an incredible team and a brand worth believing in. It's simple: Don't bullshit yourself and don't bullshit others.

LEARN ALWAYS

We believe in the potency of a curious perspective and we are obsessed with prototyping. We strive to learn both from failure and success and we believe that teams often forget to value learning as a measurable outcome to any project. We constantly push ourselves to learn new things (personally, professionally, physically, and spiritually). We continually set and test hypotheses that help us to rapidly evolve towards our mission. WE believe that the best way to learn, is to do.

MAGIC IS IN THE DETAILS

Design matters, the details matter, personality matters, and intentionality is critical. We are tired of hearing that the devil is in the detail. We believe magic is in the details. We have a culture that takes as much pride in a perfectly placed pixel as we do with the design of a page. Overtime, we believe our obsession over detail will speak volumes.

WE > I

We stand on a belief that the world's greatest challenges will never be solved by one person, one team, or one company. We believe in pathological collaboration and strive to turn competitors into partners. Within our own team and community, we always assume good intentions and when circumstances demand it, we are committed to going through hell or high water for each other.

GYSHIDO // VISIT THE SITE

We look for a team-player mindset with an autonomous work practice. Unreasonable is not a micro-management culture. We operate under the assumption that everyone on the team will Gyshido and we all hold ourselves accountable. We only work with people who never let others wait for their part of the job. We hold a conviction that nothing grand comes easily. We love the grind.

YOUR ENERGY > YOUR TIME

If you choose to start your workday at noon or at 5 a.m., so long as you Gyshido, the decision is entirely yours. If you want to go on a hike for three hours in the middle of the day, awesome. We will shape your work around your life. That said, we only work with teammates who feel a deep connectedness to their work. Put another way, we seek out individuals who agree that this is not a 9 a.m. — 5 p.m. job...it's more than that.

WE ARE ENTREPRENEURS

We leverage creativity and the resources at-hand instead of looking elsewhere for the answers. We believe in the importance of maximizing partnerships, realizing the potential of our team, seeing money not as "the answer" but as a tool to be intelligently leveraged, running a skillfully lean operation, and in short, doing as scrappy entrepreneurs do.

GLOBAL IDENTITY

We strive to ensure that the demographics of our team and the community we support are reflective of the globally diverse world we operate within. This is not a gimmick, this is a strategic imperative. It is self-evident that the most productive breakthroughs and creative solutions arise from bringing together people and partners across geographies, religions, ethnicities, political affiliations, genders, abilities, and creeds. From our board of directors to our teammates, to the entrepreneurs and mentors we support, we aim to ensure our community and our brand is representative of the world we are seeking to impact.

NO ASSHOLES

Our greatest asset, the global unreasonable community, thrives implicitly on kindness and generosity at its foundation. We seek out team members, partners, investors, entrepreneurs, collaborators and mentors who choose humility over arrogance, assume good intentions amongst one another, and though we will have many differences of belief and perspective, always treat one another with respect. Though we are a community where creative and social misfits seek refuge, assholes will find no home at Unreasonable. There are no exceptions to this rule.

FAMILY AND HEALTH FIRST

We know it's ironic that this value is last on the list, but there is nothing more important. Your family and health are always prioritized. If you are sick, if someone is getting married, if there is an urgent family need, we will insist you drop everything and take care of your family and your health above all else.

Figure 10.2: Unreasonable Group Manifesto

Epstein is clear, though, that putting a purpose and values into words is just "Step 1 to creating a culture that can actually scale. Step 1 doesn't matter if they don't show up in space and time."

Having documented values "immediately changed policy across the company because they conflicted with our values," he told us. One policy that changed was the company's unlimited paid vacation. "So one of our values is that managing your energy is more important than managing your time," Epstein said by way of example. "I don't know if anyone on our team ever took any time off. It was so intense that people on our team asked if we had to work on Christmas. 'Well, no,' I told them, 'but if we want to get ahead …'" Epstein's voice trailed off as he recounted the story. Even in remembering the conversation, he was struck at the absurdity of an entrepreneurial drive so intense it plowed through major holidays as a sign of commitment to the mission. What he learned from that moment, though, became an important part of Unreasonable Group culture.

"It's not about how efficient you are, it's how effective you are. We needed to have policy to reflect that. Unlimited paid vacation seemed like it supported that value, but almost no one was ever taking vacation. If we actually cared about the value, we had to have policy that reflected that. We now have a minimum of two weeks of vacation. We track the time and if someone works too many days in a row, we force people to take time off. We had to fine tune that one."

Epstein told us that his team embraces the "gravitas of the values" and every employee signs the manifesto when they join the company. Far from a static document, Unreasonable Group's manifesto evolves as the company grows. "Our values are never completely written in stone," Epstein says. "Every two years or so, the team pushes back as our thinking evolves a bit." The organic nature of the company's values also lends to its authenticity.

To Build a Thriving Culture, Celebrate—and Sanction—Behavior

That maintenance of values, the building of a culture true to values, requires great care. Culture needs to be modeled and celebrated daily. And, as importantly, anti-culture behavior must be called out and sanctioned when it occurs. If the corporate culture says that every input builds a better outcome, then it's important for business leaders to solicit new ideas across work roles. If you have a "don't be a jerk" value statement, as many companies claim, you can't allow bad behavior to go unchecked, even if the perpetrator is your best-performing sales representative.

That seems like a tall order for even the bravest of leaders, but Unreasonable Group's Epstein told us that "it's actually not tough, because it is just so clear to me that if you strive to do the right thing for the right reasons, then in the long term everything is going to be better." And sometimes, doing the right thing is parting ways with people who demonstrably fail to share organizational values. "We have turned down business and let go of people who were exceptionally qualified, but they have this hue of arrogance around them. We have taken mentors and investors out of the community who are revered publicly because of things like harassment. In the end, it strengthened us," he said, adding that "It's easy to live by your values when everything is great; it's more powerful to live by your values when in the short term you'll be worse off."

What has living these values meant for Unreasonable Group's business success? Ten years in, this relatively small yet ambitious company has built enduring partnerships with some of the world's platinum global brands. They have a four-year runway for current programs. They have worked with 181 emerging companies in 180 countries, helping them raise $3.7 billion to solve the world's toughest problems. They estimate that through their community of entrepreneurs, mentors, investors, and partners, they have positively impacted the lives of more than 350 million people worldwide. That's the power of intentional culture.

Not All Cultures Work so Well

Consider Airbnb and Uber. Both emerged around the start of the Global Financial Crisis as so-called "sharing economy" companies that offered affordable access over often cost-prohibitive ownership. Both companies offered on-demand and flexible work—gig work, as it has become known. Both raised billions of dollars at sky-high valuations, making their young founders very, very wealthy.

They are different, however, in one very important way. Airbnb was culture driven from the start, whereas Uber was not. Airbnb's culture was intentional. Uber's, arguably, was accidental.

When Airbnb closed their Series C in 2012, cofounder and CEO Brian Chesky asked investor and board member Peter Thiel for his most important advice. Thiel reportedly told Chesky (in words more colorful than ours) that he had to get the culture right. Chesky wasn't expecting this response from someone who just invested $150 million in the company, but he took that advice to heart. The company not only defined their values, they made them the central driving force of their brand. Airbnb now fully embraces their tagline: "to belong anywhere."

Uber, in contrast, established a culture around what it does, rather than why it does it. Their early slogans were "Your own private driver" and "To make transportation as ubiquitous as running water." Both are great aspirations, but neither tells you what Uber believes or why it exists. Arguably, Uber would become the winner-take-all startup driven by the now-legendary early CEO Travis Kalanick. His combative, no-holds-barred and arrogant personality fueled a toxic culture where breaking rules was the norm, women were subjected to frat-boy antics, and public criticism was met with caustic response.

Airbnb and Uber were two rapid-growth companies that had similar sharing-economy platforms, and both were dramatically shaped by their leadership.

"People don't buy what you do, they buy why you do it," Simon Sinek reminds us. Airbnb's aspirations helped it remain focused, even in the midst of inevitable and very challenging events with hosts and guests. This has given Airbnb the tools to respond to failures swiftly, make appropriate corrections, and preserve its brand.

In contrast, Uber's failures with drivers, customers, and employees were dragged into public forums. Polled in the midst of the public airing, nearly one third of Uber's customers said they were less likely to use the service as a result of reported bad behavior.[1] Ultimately, the Uber board needed to remove the company's founder and CEO, Kalanick, and launch a public campaign to polish the company's image.

In the best of circumstances, a company operating in the new frontier of the platform economy will face public scrutiny and unforeseen challenges as it disrupts ways of working, takes on regulatory policies, and reshapes entire industries. The grow-at-all-costs strategy to succeed in such endeavors requires a clear purpose and a strong culture to achieve escape velocity with an enduring brand and clear promise intact. As Airbnb and Uber drove hard into the market, one had the culture to respond and adapt to challenges. The other did not.

"Aspirational values almost always come from, and must be rectified at, the top," writes Dr. Cameron Sepah, a psychologist and professor at UCSF Medical School.[2] "No behavior will persist long term unless it is being perpetuated by either a positive reinforcer (providing a reward, such as a promotion or praise) or a negative reinforcer (removing a punishment, such as a probationary period or undesirable tasks). Thus, when companies start, leaders set the company's values not by what they write on the walls, but by how they actually act."

The very best organizations—those with the strongest culture and greatest capacity to pursue new opportunity—operate with values and performance aligned, recognized, and rewarded.

Capacity: Culture's Partner

By this point, we hope you are embracing culture as the structure in which to manage change. By nurturing culture with care and intension, you create the conditions that strengthen your adaptation advantage. Throughout the book, we've preached that the future of work is lifelong learning and adaptation. For you, individually, that means taking responsibility and initiative for learning. You'll be able to power through the continuous cycles of change and adaptation by connecting to your own motivational driver, the power source that is your sense of purpose. As a leader, you can tap into that purpose and inspire your team to a collective mission when you make culture the foundation of your operating principles.

But culture alone is not enough for *effective* adaptation. To get there, you must also nurture culture's partner, capacity. This is where you need to connect the two concepts for effective leadership.

If culture is the heart of a company, capacity is its brain. Simply put, capacity is an organization's ability to respond to opportunity. But it is much more than the available space, time, and talent needed to address a new opportunity. Capacity is *how* we think about new information and ideas in order to assess and respond to opportunity. In other words, it's not enough to ask whether you have the people—or even the *right* people. You also need to ask whether your people have the mindset to think about this opportunity in the right way.

Autodesk's Randy Swearer and Mickey McManus talk about this type of capacity in terms of bias. To be clear, we're not talking about the bias—unconscious or implicit—that pigeonholes people into stereotypes. Rather, bias can be a useful tool in thinking. "Humans have to be biased, because the world is a complex place," Swearer told us recently. "Frankly, our brains are not all that powerful. Biases are a way that we simplify the world and make sense of it but being aware of them is tremendously important."

McManus makes the point even more clearly with a familiar analogy. "If you have a piece of fabric, like corduroy, it's biased in one direction. You can slide your hand right down the corduroy in one way, but if you slide it 90 degrees, it's really rough and harder to slide. Bias is just a word used for basically creating a shortcut. It requires less energy," he told us.

For us to channel and leverage biases, however, we need to become mindful of them. "We're very interested in thinking about ways to make people aware of those biases and understand the biases that they use to kind of see the world in the sense of making things, but also beyond making things, because it's so crucial today just to exist and to thrive in an environment," Swearer says. "We feel like the tool itself needs to be, or I should say, the platform itself needs to be a learning platform that is giving people feedback constantly on the biases, even nudging them aware from their implicit biases." When we apply this concept to technology, we see that technology, which we once needed to learn to use in order to simply work, now becomes something that we learn with and that we learn from and that, in fact, even learns from us. That's the power of digital transformation when tools and humans learn together.

Capability and Context: The Scissors Metaphor

Nudging people to be aware of their biases, as Swearer puts it, is all about context. Too often, we treat our companies as if they exist without context until something changes in the business environment that upends all our assumptions—our biases. It might be a change in the technology that breaks the business model, a change in the market conditions that shifts customer expectations, or a change in public policy that adds friction to the supply chain, for example. When these changes of context occur, it is helpful to step back and look at the relationships between the company and its environment, the worker and their team, the human and the technology tool.

McManus introduced us to the world of Herbert Simon, an American economist and cognitive psychologist who won the Nobel Prize for his concept of *bounded rationality*, essentially the idea that humans don't act as perfectly optimizing economic decision makers. Instead, the effectiveness of our decision making must be understood in context. Simon depicted his idea using scissors as a metaphor. One blade is our environment and the other is our capability to respond, what Simon referred to as our "cognitive limitations."

"It's not like you can look at one blade and understand a pair of scissors," McManus explains. "The interesting action of a pair of scissors is where the blades push against each other. One blade is the brain running these rules. It's got a limited amount of cognition … but it's pushing against this other blade that is the environment."

To lighten our cognitive load, we rely on assumptions—biases—about the environment in which we're doing our thinking. "These biases are kind of shaped by the environment we're in, so we can actually help you see the thinking about your thinking," McManus concludes.

If we keep this interplay in mind, particularly as we experience a whirlwind of change, the necessity of nurturing culture and expanding capacity becomes self-evident. Doing so in harmony becomes essential. Our role as organizational leaders, then, is to expand both human and machine capabilities and collaboration, while celebrating and protecting the organizational culture to optimize environmental conditions—at least internally.

In Accelerated Change, Focus on the Inputs Rather Than the Outputs

In an age when change came slowly and products and brands had long market lifecycles, an executive might be forgiven for conflating culture with brand and capacity with production. It's a mistake that brings a near-sighted focus to the business that often misses shifting context. Consider a classic example. Kodak was really good at silver-halide chemistry, which worked well for decades before digital transformation disrupted the photography industry. Unfortunately, the company had neither the capacity to reimagine how they defined themselves as a business nor the culture to pivot, which is ironic considering that Kodak invented the digital camera. Kodak invented and owned the intellectual property for the very invention that sank a $28 billion business. If Kodak had embraced the purpose in its "Kodak moments" motto and imagined a business beyond (and significantly bigger than) film and print imaging, the company might have endured. Instead the company that invented the digital camera in 1976 reached its pinnacle in 1996 with a $28 billion valuation and 140,000 employees, only to file for bankruptcy 16 years later in 2012.

Kodak, of course, is not alone; dozens of companies, for lack of a culture-capacity dynamic, withered in the face of digital transformation. Barnes & Noble struggles to compete with Amazon. Apple's iTunes sank the record business. Perhaps most famously Blockbuster fell to Netflix, the former plummeting from $6 billion annual revenue to bankruptcy in six short years. Countless retail outlets are failing in Amazon's wake, yet a few—like Target, Walmart, and Kohl's—are running innovative experiments to blend online and in-store shopping and, in the case of Kohl's, a partnership with Amazon for a competitive—dare we say it: adaptation—advantage. It's anyone's guess where those businesses will come out, but it's refreshing to see large organizations leveraging their capacity to evolve.

It is important to understand the distinction between capacity and capability. A focus on capability, rather than capacity, ties a company's success to a workforce hired to execute the specific tasks to produce a specific product. As change accelerates and product life cycles shorten, capabilities-focused businesses will find themselves stuck in the Sisyphean task of firing and hiring for new capabilities to meet the changing market context.

This "spill and fill" model of corporate capability sets companies on an unending chase for talent when they could otherwise be catching opportunity. Worse, it's incredibly disruptive to the workforce and business continuity across three measures: loss of morale and employee engagement among those who remain in the organization, loss of business momentum as new talent is onboarded and existing employees shift roles, and loss of the tacit knowledge often essential to business continuity as employees leave the company.

Tacit knowledge is exemplified by—and embedded in—the rituals of how companies work. It is where the "why" of work informs the "how." It's the stuff you don't know if you don't work in an organization and it's the stuff that is so embedded in daily work habits that you would be forgiven if you forget to mention it to a new employee. Because tacit knowledge is the unwritten history and habits of a company, it is often impossible to regain once lost.

Whether tacit or explicit, knowledge is nearly impossible to codify and transfer fast enough to stay ahead of the waves of change. Instead, we can build capacity to learn and adapt by making on-demand learning an integral part of organizational culture. How, then, do strong leaders leverage culture and capacity to drive agile and adaptive learning companies?

Curiously, in a scalable learning world, the assets of an organization are measured not in what is produced, but by what an organization can learn. Randy Swearer at Autodesk sums up that idea nicely:

> You've got these brains that are created at these companies. Those intelligences change over time, but fundamentally, that's all you have. Autodesk doesn't own any buildings. Autodesk owns very little. We lease everything. We're a 10,000-person company, but we lease everything. What Autodesk has is some computers and furniture. It probably rents a lot of the furniture, but basically what it has is talent."

Shift Culture to Expand Capacity

We recently spoke with a senior executive who was hired to turn around a traditional, analog company that was struggling with digital transformation. The company's revenue had declined 35% over the prior three fiscal years. Products were missing, and ship dates and technology was failing. As she assessed her team, she discovered a culture of certainty where answers, even if inaccurate, were accepted if they were offered with surety.

"Yes, the product will ship on time."

"No, there is not a problem."

"I know how to get this done. I do not need help."

These familiar statements, perhaps initially reassuring to management, masked big problems. Yet the culture did not afford employees the luxury of reporting problems or asking for help. If a worker's capabilities were not up for the task, she risked losing her job.

In order to transform the company and create capacity, the executive needed first to change the culture, and that started with her. If she tried to manage her team's impression of her—masking her own gaps to avoid appearing incompetent—she would be giving her team permission to do the same. Instead, she needed to create an environment of psychological safety to make the space for her team to raise their hands when they need help.

This executive now seeks difficult and sometimes painful answers earlier in the process of transformational projects and pairs resources and support with struggling workers in order to expand the collective capacity of her organization. This culture shift requires trust in leadership. If seeking truthful answers becomes a process to identify poor performers, the cultural transformation will fail, and the company will be trapped seeking talent for short-term fixes rather than freed to build long-term capacity. In other words, real leaders show vulnerability and model the culture to empower and strengthen their teams.

While we may find it impossible to predict the talent and new skills we'll require in the future, one thing is sure: our old models of expecting skills to be taught in educational programs so that companies can hire for capabilities no longer works. Instead, we need to focus on developing the capacity to learn and adapt while we work, rather than on the capabilities our workforce brings to the job. Capacity-focused leaders build capabilities-retooling into their workforce, hiring people for their learning agility and workplace adaptability in constant cycles of reskilling and upskilling.

We're not naming names here, but we're willing to bet this company's story sounds a lot like a company you know. Indeed, the reality is that most companies face this challenging problem.

Products Are a Souvenir of Culture and Evidence of Your Capacity

The products or services you sell today are likely built with the evidenced capabilities you hired yesterday. What is your plan to create products and services levering the capabilities you don't yet even know you need?

You can begin to answer that question by asking several others:

Where will you find newly identified capabilities if they are not yet part of an academic or workforce-training curriculum? How do you articulate and socialize your culture? How do you reinforce culture by celebrating cultural wins and calling out cultural missteps? Do you screen new talent for cultural fit? Do you have a hiring plan that focuses on learning agility and capacity for change rather than specific capabilities and past experience? Do you have a learning plan that enables your organization to retool for new opportunities and continually build your capacity?

The answers to these questions are the beginning of your own turnaround story. We encourage you to create a plan based on the answers to these questions; it will be the basis of your adaptation advantage strategy.

Becoming a Learning Company

Transforming any organization is a daunting, and often risky, endeavor. But it's possible. Many companies are putting the building blocks of scalable learning in place as they make their digital transformations, often without even realizing it. Whether it's the product or service you create or the methods and means used to market it, every digital interaction is a learning opportunity.

Few are doing this hard work as clearly as industry analyst Jeremiah Owyang, founding partner at Kaleido Insights. Owyang's consultancy works with *Fortune* 100 companies to navigate the challenging waters of digital transformation, creating and implementing strategy to make the crossing from the Third to the Fourth Industrial Revolution. Owyang identified seven components of the Digital Directive—modules, he calls them—that measure the maturity of a company's digital transformation. Each of the seven modules—strategy, data, customer experience, organizational alignment, analytics and AI, people and culture, and innovation—measures a series of specific attributes across all departments to arrive at a deep understanding of the company's ability to cross the digital divide.[3]

"Many companies talk about 'digital transformation,'" Owyang writes on Kaleido Insights' blog, "but use it in a limited fashion, such as just turning paper into PDFs or using web tools to communicate to customers, but in the end, the core culture, and even the business model, has changed." The Digital Directive is a deep dive that provides a thorough diagnosis of the organization's progress toward—and roadblocks to—true digital transformation.

Not surprisingly, Owyang writes, "The most commonly overlooked item is the mindset of workers, managers, and leaders to be a 'digital-first' culture." What's a digital-first culture? Owyang's answer echoes our own. It's a culture that is "making decisions based on data analysis, understanding how to harness information and data as a product, not just physical assets, rapid iteration, acceptance of failure as a means for progress, and developing a culture that is pliable and nimble."

Most importantly, it is a culture that depends on shared values. "Teams have to be empowered to make decisions based on common vision and common values because in a digital-first company you are making real decisions in real time based on real time data," Owyang told us. "A hierarchal culture won't work. You need to have the culture that works in real time."

In some cases, the learning through data is obvious. In others, not so much. When you take a ride with Uber, for example, you are contributing to their mapping of human movement and their learning about traffic patterns and demands. When you use a Roomba robotic vacuum cleaner, you are helping the company create floor maps of homes to better inform smart home design and create better products. When you click on a sponsored story on Facebook, you are refining the algorithm that targets ads to you. When you engage in news stories on curated sites like Apple News and Flipboard, you are refining the type of content pushed to you in the future. When you ask Amazon's Alexa a question, you are building your customer profile for the sale of future products and services. When you drive a Tesla car, you are contributing to their fleet's learning network that seeks to improve future autonomous driving. And on and on.

In each of these cases, the "product" is a means to better understanding of the customer, the market, and future opportunities. The data becomes the basis of learning, which leads to new insights, which leads to new value creation through new products, and the cycle begins again (Figure 10.3).

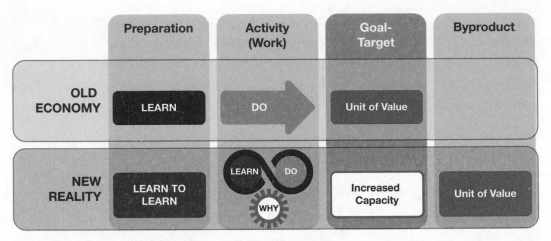

Figure 10.3: Value Created Becomes the By-Product of Increasing Capacity

Data provides transparency in creating information about things we previously could not see or measure—new patterns and insights emerge. As our friend and *New York Times* columnist Tom Friedman puts it, data allows us to digitize, sensorize, automatize, customize, prophesize, localize, optimize, and, we would add, visualize things we could not comprehend before. More succinctly, data allows us to learn.

The key to staying on top of corporate lists, then, is learning and adapting. And keep in mind that there is a clear distinction between flexibility and adaptability. Arizona State University organizational behavior professor Jeff LePine puts it best:

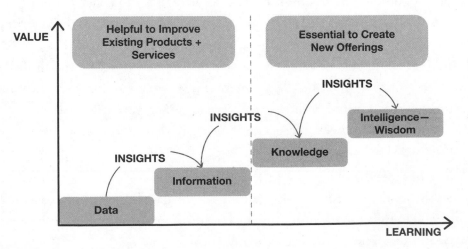

Figure 10.4: Hierarchy of Business Intelligence

"Flexibility is the ability to pivot from one tool in your toolbox to another or from one approach to another. Adaptability may require you to drop that tool and forge a new one or drop that method, unlearn it, and develop an entirely new one."

Every company has the unique opportunity to learn from the market experience and the data afforded by their digital offerings. Every user interaction becomes a data point from which to learn. Indeed, the products themselves may be only Trojan horses to collect data from which they can learn.

Consider the Hierarchy Ladder of Business Intelligence, where the more you move up and to the right, the greater the value (Figure 10.4). Insights extracted from data are sufficient and necessary to improve products and services. To create new value by offering new products and services, those data-derived insights must couple with intelligence and wisdom—in other words, culture and capacity.

Notes

1. https://morningconsult.com/2017/06/22/uber-poll-kalanick/
2. https://medium.com/s/company-culture/your-companys-culture-is-who-you-hire-fire-and-promote-c69f84902983
3. http://www.web-strategist.com/blog/2019/09/30/digital-transformation-culture-business-model-change/10

11 Capability Is King: Looking Beyond the Resume to Design Your Adaptive Team

Key Ideas

1. To build an adaptive team, leaders must break the narrow definitions of jobs and organizational structure.

2. Adaptive teams start in the hiring process, one that de-emphasizes past skills, credentials, and experience, and instead seeks values alignment and both inquiry-based problem finding and framing coupled with fluid problem solving capabilities.

3. Culture fit doesn't mean homogeny, in fact quite the opposite; the best teams bring diverse life experiences, world views, and skill sets, especially cognitive diversity in an environment of psychological safety.

No More Little Boxes

Imagine: it's Christmas Eve and you still have presents to wrap. A small piece of jewelry. A child's bicycle. A sweater. A drum set. Theater tickets. Some power tools. You want to surprise your family with these gifts in the morning and all you have is a roll of wrapping paper, some tape, and a pile of 8 × 10 boxes. How are you going to wrap these different-sized gifts with these uniform supplies?

Every day across the globe, business leaders attempt this same packaging trick when they look at their workers as boxes on an organizational chart wrapped neatly in a job description.

This inside-the-box thinking worked well enough when processes and responsibilities were constant, skills and credentials were fixed, and boundaries between roles were well defined. Executives could manage people in roles, conducting business like a concert master running a well-rehearsed score. The business changed slowly enough that the boxes and people in them could quietly evolve until, at last, a company-wide re-org came along to shake things up.

But today there is a consequential problem with these static organizational structures. They tend toward homogeneity of thought that misses even the most obvious signals that business is changing. Strict roles can lead to a "stay in your lane" mindset that discourages workers from speaking up when they see challenges and opportunities that fall outside their clear job definition. If you've ever heard someone in your organization say, "It's not my job," you have experienced this kind of trapped thinking that assumes that someone else, in some other role, has a better view and clearer responsibility. That is never a safe assumption, particularly in the fast-moving future of work.

Almost paradoxically, these staid structures can also lead to groupthink. Workers hired for the same style, skill, experience, and credentials—what some might mistakenly call a "culture fit"—create uniform teams that think uniformly. It's not that workers are afraid to rock the boat; rather, with everyone rowing in exactly the prescribed direction and tempo, the boat doesn't rock at all. That may feel good and steady in the moment, but it doesn't set organizations up for success.

Still, this dangerous approach to hiring and organizing workers has been the anchor of employee management for decades, if not centuries. And to be clear: the job description and the organizational chart have never been a good proxy for real human talent. We need to rethink the organizational chart. New knowledge is entering your organization at all levels. That information needs to flow throughout the organizational chart, rather than up and down hierarchical maps. That alone demands that you think differently about your decision-making process and, more importantly, how you form your teams.

We are moving from a time when we hired and organized teams based on past experience at solving known problems to a new era that will harvest value

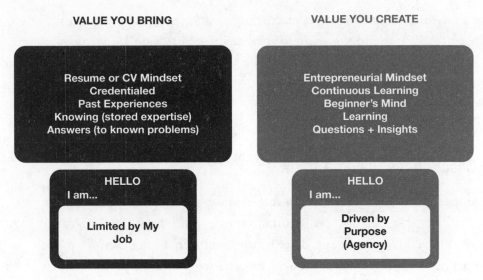

Figure 11.1: From the Value You Bring to the Value You Create

from a beginner's mindset and entrepreneurial outlook well suited for identifying new opportunities and innovative approaches to addressing them. In short, the ability to find new insights will be more valuable than answering known problems (Figure 11.1).

The Job Description Is History

Job descriptions have been around for centuries, evolving from hand-painted "Help Wanted" signs in shop windows in the 1600s to employment ads in newspaper classified sections that emerged in the 1800s and on to detailed and searchable listings of Internet-based job boards in the 1990s. Today, digital technology and algorithmic tools claim to be able to remove bias of race, gender, and culture in job descriptions on sites such as textio.com.

As we continue into the future, modern technology will absorb many explicit tasks that achieve known results. In other words, anything mentally routine or predictable may be done by an algorithm, leaving the less predictable, creative, and insightful work to humans. The funny thing about "less predictable work" is that it's difficult to codify in a straightforward, easily posted job description. So, let's be very blunt: in the fast-changing future of work—where workforce management is a process of continually aligning talent to current and changing needs—the structured organizational chart and the written-in-stone job description are virtually useless. In fact, they may be dangerous because they discourage workers from learning and adapting and instead encourage them to rely on their potentially outdated skills and knowledge.

Job Descriptions Become Traps

As the speed of change continues to accelerate, so will future work requirements. We can hire for next-generation skills as they emerge, but by the time we identify a need, approve a new hire, specify and describe those skills in a job description, seek out and hire qualified candidates, and onboard and acclimate new employees, the need for those skills is replaced by the next wave of skills coming up after them (Figure 11.2).

More challenging, a focus on specific skills risks missing out on tacit knowledge that often makes those explicit capabilities come to life in an organization. Explicit skills are the "what" and "how" of productivity; tacit knowledge is where the "why"

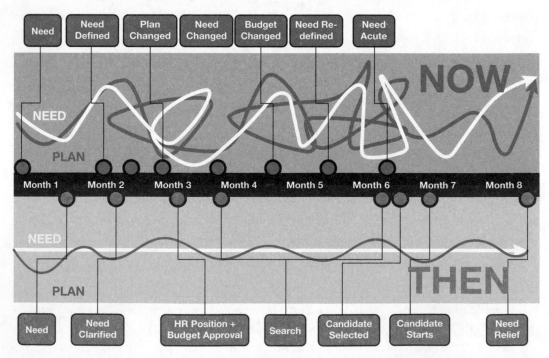

Figure 11.2: Accelerated Change Can Eclipse Long Hiring Timelines

meets the "how" that help workers know when to put those explicit skills to work. Assuming an organization wants to attract and retain the best talent, the question becomes how to identify workers who bridge these essential capabilities.

Job descriptions, almost by definition, describe capabilities and attributes without the context of a dynamic organization, and almost always these descriptions are of roles in isolation from each other. Most importantly, "jobs" as we have known them—tasks to do—will become less and less relevant as workers "do" less and create, collaborate, adapt, and learn more. As the *Harvard Business Review* study discussed in Chapter 8 found, collaborative activities at work have increased by more than 50% over the past two decades. Beyond "work well with others," we need to find a better way to address this shift and move beyond old-fashioned job descriptions.

For insight into how to start doing this, consider what Joanna Daly, vice president of human resources at IBM, told us: "The half-life of skills is getting shorter. Hiring someone because they know something that's in demand today is going to be of limited value. In the past, it might have been a good recruitment strategy, because maybe that skill or that domain knowledge that's needed today, it's going to be in demand for 10 or 20 years. But if now it's going to be five years or fewer, then that's no longer the sole basis on which you should make a hiring decision."

Instead, she says, "We need to consider learning agility, growth mindset, adaptability. These are aspects that we need to consider because I don't want to hire someone to do one job for the next two years; I want to hire them for the ability to do the next five jobs over the next 10 years, and I have no idea what those jobs are going to be. They may be in skill areas that we don't even have the names for today."

As we talked with executives and hiring managers, we've come to see that traditional understanding of roles—full time, part time or temp, manager or rank and file, and the like—don't position organizations for maximum flexibility. After a lot of exploration, we identified five types of talent that each work in and contribute to organizations is specific ways (Figure 11.3), The talent types—executive producer, transformational, contingent, rotational, and foundational—each play a different role in the organization. Executive producers, for example, tend to be more project based, bringing specific expertise to coordinate a team to deliver a specific outcome. Contingent workers participate with an executive producer to bring specific skills to the project on a short-term basis, leaving the project when their contribution is

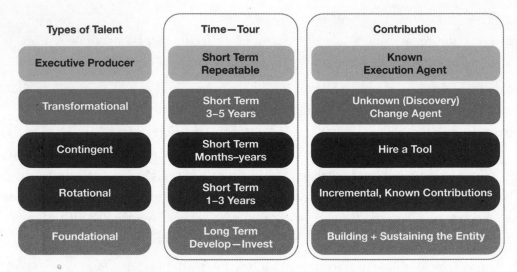

Figure 11.3: Types of Talent

Sources: Reid Hoffman (foundational, rotational, and transformational talent) and Heather E. McGowan (contingent and executive producer talent).

delivered. These workers may be full-time employees of a company, moving from project to project, or they may be more loosely tied to the organization, on call as consultants or freelancers in an arrangement that gives maximum flexibility to both the organization and the individual worker. The television and movie industries have long engaged talent on a per-project basis, assembling the array of talent—from script writers to set designers, actors to accountants, directors to dolly grips—in order to bring together a Hollywood-style production. Increasingly, this engagement model works across all forms of business. Expertise, and the flexibility to apply it as needed, is the key principle at work here. LinkedIn cofounder and now Silicon Valley investor Reid Hoffman dubbed these short assignments "tours of duty" in a 2013 *Harvard Business Review* article cowritten with Ben Casnocha and Chris Yeh. It's a model that requires all of us to think differently about affiliation and retention on both sides of the employer–employee relationship.

Fire Your Job Description

If you've been in the workforce for any time at all, you know that all your instincts ask what you will *do* in a job. What tasks will you be responsible for *doing*? How will you be expected to get the work *done*? How will you prove that you have the skills necessary to *do* the job? Hiring managers answer those questions when they write a job description. Leadership reinforces those answers when they organize their teams. If we are going to hire workers who show the adaptive resiliency to continuously learn and embrace change, we have to ask different questions.

Pymetrics emerged as a company to help employers look for, and look at, candidates beyond job descriptions and resumes. Looking at movie recommendation systems like those used by Amazon or Netflix for inspiration, the company developed a deep analysis of both jobs and individual experience to harness "the power of the long-tail [of data] to match people to the jobs where they were most likely to succeed," the company's website explains. Today, companies as diverse as fast-food chain McDonald's and mineral and mining conglomerate Rio Tinto use Pymetrics to better hire the most appropriate candidates.

We reached out to Pymetrics founder and CEO Frida Polli to talk about the challenges of recruiting for adaptability and learning. When asked specifically about the challenge of finding talent, Polli responded, "I don't think it's because we don't have the people that can fill that role," she told us. "It's because you're not evaluating them properly. If you're evaluating people based on the resume, that's a mistake. The resume is basically a backward-facing, static document that tells you what someone has done in the past. It tells you nothing about what they can potentially do in the present or in the future."

Instead of asking what a candidate has previously done or even what they can do, we have to talk about how potential employees think, how they see themselves, the vagaries of the job, and how they might see themselves in our organization. We need to toss aside the template that lists title, responsibilities, qualifications, and preferences in favor of one that enables applicants to see themselves in service to the mission of the company. We have to describe jobs not as a set of tasks, but as a series of tours in which people apply their experience and expertise, build upon that foundation, and then move on to new applications and learning in continuous cycles. Because our job role, if it exists at all, will inevitably change, we need to focus on our alignment with the company's values and our fit between leaders and teams. Chapters 9 and 10 discuss further how to do these things.

Let's examine a little more closely what's wrong with most job descriptions and what might be done to better connect applicants with organizations. Most job descriptions begin by outlining what would be required of the applicant. And let's be honest, even organizations with the most foresight can only predict what might be required in any position across 12 or maybe 18 months. Instead, start with describing not the job, but your organization. Make your mission and values clear. This statement serves as both a magnet to attract the applicants who feel kinship with your mission and a filter to screen out those who have no affinity for the work you do.

Consider this posting from a digital media startup where Chris serves as chief operating officer and used this language to recruit a top-notch marketing executive:

> About Us: We are a digital media company that leverages the power of storytelling to engage citizens more deeply with their communities, believing that everyone has the power to start something good … We are seeking a Head of Marketing to drive brand awareness and build a deeply engaged user community around our mission …

The posting goes on to describe the ideal *candidate,* instead of the functions of the job. Sure, you want to hire someone with a proven track record, but, more importantly, you're looking to hire someone with something to prove.

> About You: You are a marketing genius and you're ready to prove it in a challenging, high-growth market. Your work has touched on many aspects of marketing— branding, social media, audience attraction and engagement, and market metrics— and you're looking for a place to bring that experience together to make a huge impact on a growing startup. You work hard, know your stuff, and deserve to be recognized and rewarded for it. You don't need to be micromanaged because you have a big vision and are motivated to turn ideas into action. You are eager to contribute your unique talents in a collaborative effort to bring a world-class media property to reality. Most importantly, you stand ready to lead in a dynamic environment where every day brings new opportunities and challenges. As important as it is to develop the strategy, your best work will come when you inspire, empower, and enable your team to deliver it.

Rather than speaking to credentials, past experience, or demonstrated skills, this description addresses the aspirations of the applicant. It gives them the opportunity to see themselves in the job. As importantly, it makes very clear that the company will hire someone who can lead, rather than manage, a team. That's a critical distinction. Managers direct a process, they tell workers what to do, and, often, how to do it. Leaders, on the other hand, are catalysts for good work. They inspire people to do their best work and they provide the direction, resources, and coaching to deliver it. In times of change—and face it, it's all change now—you want to hire leaders, not managers.

Finally, the posting talks about the job; not just the requirements of the job, but how the company expects a winning applicant to embrace the job.

> About the Job: A super-successful digital media company lives or dies on sustained attention—user attraction, retention, and engagement with its content. Our company wants to hire a thoughtful, talented, unique-thinking head of marketing who will be responsible for establishing and implementing the company's product growth and national roll-out strategy. You will own marketing across the company, working collaboratively as part of the company's leadership team, and ultimately building a first-class team of digital and brand marketing pros.
>
> Our head of marketing will have experience with product marketing, brand engagement, social media, budget management, and digital media, and is eager to take that experience to the next level and beyond. Our head of marketing embraces experimentation (growth hacking) and does so with a discipline that respects metrics and deadlines. We will hire someone who is as comfortable working independently as collaboratively, who communicates easily with team members, accepts feedback and critique as tools to improve, and most of all is ready to grow into an exceptional and critical member of our leadership team.
>
> We have no bias for degree or specific experience, and we absolutely respect and expect to hire someone with intelligence, self-awareness, motivation, and ambition. We are moving quickly, so you will need to show that you can think creatively, deliberate clearly, and move decisively. We expect your prior work and current interests to represent what you can do for us. Most of all, we hire people who prove themselves through their work, and who share our ambition to create the world's largest digital-first news platform.

It's not a typical job description, to be sure, but it does hold up a mirror for potential applicants to see themselves working in that organization.

Please, consider the text as a template for your organization if you like. We offer it with empathy because breaking old hiring habits is *really, really* hard. We're accustomed to defining the repeatable and measurable aspects of most jobs—"The successful candidate will have demonstrated product marketing skills," our job descriptions might say—but we forget to talk about how those skills might be applied differently or how they might even become outdated in a world where marketing trends shift overnight. We're comfortable asking for Ivy League credentials or a platinum brand experience, but much less at ease trying to understand how those experiences mesh with the workplace we aspire to have.

To help that process, Frida Polli's Pymetrics developed a matching platform that pairs jobs and candidates based on less tangible attributes of both the role and the worker. Using company data to identify the attributes of high performance in a specific role, the Pymetrics platform puts candidates through a series of tasks to assess a candidate for those attributes. Being careful to remove bias from the system, Polli told us her clients are better able to place high-quality candidates in jobs where they have a higher probability of success. One surprising outcome of the Pymetrics platform was that hiring diversity improved significantly. One aspect of that diversity was a drop in new hires with Ivy League credentials—often the presumptive proxy for a highly qualified candidate—as the platform identified highly competent candidates without prejudice for degree or affiliation.

If we are to build adaptive teams, we have to start with adaptive hiring requirements. What might it mean to hire a really, really smart and intuitive person who's not graduated from college? How might someone with a deep passion for your market and customer overcome a deficit of experience you profess to look for? In our experience, we've found that it is often that person without a fancy degree—or any degree at all—who delivers amazing performance. They have to overcome a bias for credentials, work hard, and prove that they can get work done. More importantly, they bring a perspective that breaks from the homogenizing training of many elite academic programs.

Stop and think about it for a moment. What do those prestigious degrees and flagship companies really signal? Prestigious degrees are often held by people who had a pathway to get them into the school the first place. So, does that degree signal someone who is especially high achieving or someone who is entitled? Or maybe both? Is experience at flagship brands really the most reliable signal when looking at a much larger pool of potential employees? Might longevity at an organization actually be a false signal of success when many times those with long tenures are best adept at organizational politics or, worse, fly under the radar by not challenging the status quo? The career signals that we've often used to identify candidates are as unreliable as they are reliable. By looking beyond conventional signals and tapping into unusual sources of talent, you're more likely to attract a phenomenal and diverse team.

We cannot stress enough the power of diverse teams in the future of work. Too often, problem solving can be reductive as like-minded teams using existing knowledge to narrow, perhaps without even realizing it, possible solutions. We need people who are divergent thinkers to help us find and frame problems, then find novel solutions. Without sufficient "outside mind"—outside of what we've always done, outside what we were trained to think and do, outside the norms of the past—organizations will slip into a default mindset trying to frame and solve new problems by force-fitting old solutions on them.

Hire for Cultural Alignment

To be clear, we're not suggesting a criteria-less hiring processes. Rather, we're recommending that hiring managers embrace the idea that the need candidates fill today will be entirely different a year from now. The optimum thing to do, then, is to build flexibility and adaptability into the job description. The successful candidate will do X today and be able to pivot to Y tomorrow. This expectation builds adaptation into the job requirement. That's key when the future unfolds faster than we can predict.

Make no mistake: it's far easier to write that far-ranging job description than it is to live and hire by it. Over the past few years, we've struggled to put a "future of work" lens on the team building of companies with which we've consulted. We might start with a forward-looking job description, but in the end, we get a mountain of resumes, thrown over the transom by people who just want a job with a stable organization. The easiest way to sort them out is to look at credentials and experience.

So how is a modern business leader expected to build an adaptive future-resilient work force?

Yes, screen for capabilities, and, as importantly, screen for fit. In fact, credentials and experience should be just the price of entry. Too often, "cultural fit" describes an employee who's happy to grab a drink after work, dress in a particular fashion, or bring her dog to work. We want to encourage you to rethink cultural fit to embrace candidates who think broadly and openly in the face of changing workplace dynamics. Cherish the interviewee who asks the probing question for which you did not have an easy answer. The best leaders don't hire for skills alone; they hire for mission and mindset while being open to candidates who make them a little uncomfortable because they think differently. They hire for cultural fit, knowing that many skills can be learned, but culture has to be felt and mission needs to be shared. What matters is whether the candidate can be "one of us," where "one of us" means someone who can think, adapt, challenge, change, and grow. These abilities are paramount in the workforce that needs to find and frame problems not yet known. For that we need diverse and divergent thinking, creativity, curiosity, and talent that asks probing questions even when it makes us a little uncomfortable (Figure 11.4).

Hiring for fit requires a very different process, one that is inclusive of workers from across organizational functions. A hiring manager might have a pretty good bead on the capabilities of the ideal candidate, while potential coworkers can exercise their instincts as to a candidate's ability to cooperate and collaborate in line with the company culture.

At Unreasonable Group, Epstein told us, hiring for culture is critical to the company's remarkable growth and scale. During the interview process, candidates are asked to consider various scenarios, each designed to elicit a response that reflects the candidate's alignment with Unreasonable's manifesto. "We try to bake in a way for our core values to show up," Epstein says. In one such scenario, for example, a candidate was taken through a project where just about everything that could go wrong did. The goal of the exercise wasn't to see how the candidate would fix the problem, but whether she would own it. The goal was to see if the candidate's values aligned with the company's core tenet that states in part, "We push for open communication even when it's tough, whether that means being transparent about

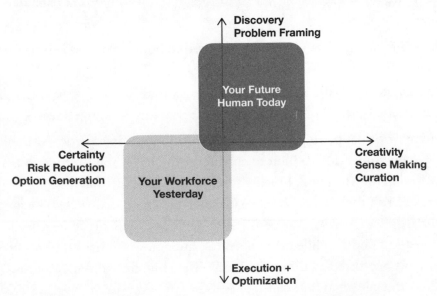

Figure 11.4: Workforce of Yesterday versus Workforce of Tomorrow

our failures publicly or creating the conditions for authentic communication within our teams."

By the time someone is hired at Unreasonable Group, they have talked to at least five teammates. "We have a final huddle to decide who we are going to hire," Epstein says, adding that as much as they discuss qualifications they also "walk through how it feels" to engage with the candidates.

The risk of hiring for cultural fit, however, is that over time your team becomes very homogenous, particularly when an organization perceives "culture" as style over the substance of its values. Epstein admits to making this mistake in the early days of Unreasonable Group. "I hired people close to me, people I knew and had fun working with," he told us. Today, Unreasonable Group hires for "cultural add," Epstein says. Cultural add, he explains, starts with alignment with the company's core values and then looks to see if a candidate is "bringing something new to the team."

If the hiring process at Unreasonable Group is a trial run of sorts, the hiring process for leadership positions at Amazon is a labyrinth. The first stage of the online retailer's process is straightforward: job seekers meet basic qualifications and move to an interview stage, or not. But there's more to applying than sending a resume to a recruiter; applicants are asked to frame their qualifications and experience in the context of the company's 14 leadership principles. Like many of the best companies, Amazon puts their values—their leadership principles—on their website to make clear exactly what they are looking for in coworkers.[1] (This kind of bold statement can both attract talent that aligns with the principles and enable other applicants to recognize they don't fit with the organization.)

If you are passed to the initial interview, you'll meet with a hiring manager who screens for qualification and capabilities. In other words, the interviewer is assessing whether you can do the job. Clear that hurdle and you'll be asked back to meet with a number of Amazon employees, some of whom would work with you directly, and others of whom are really just there to assess if you fit in the Amazon culture. After a day of interviews, your candidacy could end in one of three outcomes: a recommendation to hire because you are both qualified and a fit, a recommendation to pass because you are either not qualified or not a fit, or a recommendation to put your candidacy on hold because you are a fit, but not right for this particular job. This is a considerable investment in the hiring process. While a longer, more involved hiring process may seem counterintuitive in the age of rapid change, this method allows Amazon to screen applicants for other adjacent jobs, knowing full well that what they had in mind when they started looking has probably changed.

It is important to stress here, though, that culture fit doesn't have to mean building a team of like-minded people cut from the same cloth, hewn by the same experiences, and practiced in thinking the same thoughts.

The concept of culture add, in fact, is essential if the company is to adhere to its core value of "global identity." "We care that our team is reflective of what is happening globally," Epstein says. "Culture add lets us give that value an actual identity." The idea of culture add is "a lot like religion," he went on to say. "Whether you're Jewish or Christian or Buddhist, or any other religion, you hold a core set of values prescribed by that religion. It doesn't matter what your race or gender or age or country is. Those things all bring diverse experience, while you still hold your core beliefs."

Hire Adults and Let Them Do Their Jobs

With practice, you'll begin to loosen your grip on branded credentials and instead seek hires who demonstrate the open-mindedness and adaptability needed to navigate a constantly changing work environment. You will find people who fit well with your culture without blending into a bland soup of compliant employees. Argodesign, a strategy and design consultancy with offices in Austin, Brooklyn, and Amsterdam, does just that. The company, one employee recently told us, values individual contribution to fuel their creative processes and deep engagements with a diverse roster of clients. We "hire adults and let them do their jobs," one executive told us.

The bravest of leaders go a step further. They hire not just open thinkers, but ones who are actively almost antagonistic. Call them "devil's advocates" or something else, but those who are able to shine a light on alternative points of view and can disagree without being disagreeable are cherished gifts in a fast-moving organization. These are the people who dare to question the status quo. They are the ones who see disruption and opportunity on the horizon. They are the ones whose voice, if allowed to be heard, can be the scouts of necessary adaptation. These workers bring cognitive diversity to your organization. They are the contrarians who check your blind spots and prevent strategic wrong turns … if you give them the psychological safety to do so. (If this idea doesn't resonate, go back and reread Chapter 9.)

Turn the Right People into Great Teams

Often, we hear leaders talk about their "teams," by which they too often mean the portfolio of people who work for them. In the context of work, we forget that "teams" are a collaboration of individuals, each bringing essential skills and perspectives to a project with the intent of delivering something bigger and better than anything they could do on their own.

Where the teams of the past might have looked like a vertical reporting structure, modern teams swarm around projects and objectives, rather than traditional roles within reporting hierarchies. When workers come together to take on a business opportunity—bringing a new product to market, shepherding a substantial partnership, brokering a market relationship between product and marketing executives—they are leveraging the strength of teamwork to advance the interests of the business. These partnerships might well include skills and capabilities that at one time had been housed in organizational silos.

To shift from the traditional organizational charts that previously channeled people into siloed functions to adaptive organizations, we must organize in purpose-built teams. But how?

For decades, companies have organized by functions: engineering, marketing, accounting, and so one. Hierarchical structures pushed cooperation up and down the vertical structure in order to get anything done. Although that structure and its communications might have been tiresome for many, that top-down organizational structure worked in slow-moving markets. Now that the pace of change has accelerated faster than most companies can organize a meeting, hierarchical structures are far less effective. Consider your work environment, remove anything mentally routine or predictable (that is, much of the processing work), and you will be left with learning. That being the case, how would you hire, organize, and develop your talent to optimize learning and adapting?

The answer, we think, is to organize workers into purpose-built groups to tackle specific challenges. They may work on a project over a period of months or even years in what LinkedIn founder Reid Hoffman refers to as a tour of duty, a period of focused work framed by objectives and measured by outcomes. A worker might be involved in a particular mission for only a short period during which her skills are required, or for a longer engagement where a long-view perspective and deep and relevant past experience will be valuable throughout the life of the project.

In this model, workers might be assigned to a product team with responsibilities for specific inputs and deliverables, even while they have a primary assignment to a functional department. One might be both a part of the company's accounting department *and* be deployed to identify revenue-sucking contract compliance breeches.

To accommodate such fluidity between roles, agile and adaptive companies are organizing physical space and project management to engage diverse perspectives and necessary skills.

At one product design consultancy for which Heather consulted, for example, each employee is organized into three groups. The first group is the person's professional discipline (e.g., engineer, marketing, design, etc.). The second group is their project work team (e.g., solving a client problem) and their assignment to this team will frequently rotate, meaning that they will be moved to a potentially entirely new project as the company determines best deployment of their capabilities as existing projects complete and new projects emerge. The third group is a research group, charged with scanning the horizon for new opportunities such as understanding the potential of the Internet of Things or autonomous vehicles, for example. By experiencing each group, workers bring a more holistic understanding to whatever task is at hand. Moreover, this structure is a catalyst for the socialization that breaks down clans and groupthink and aids the development of a bridging (action) network (Figure 11.5).

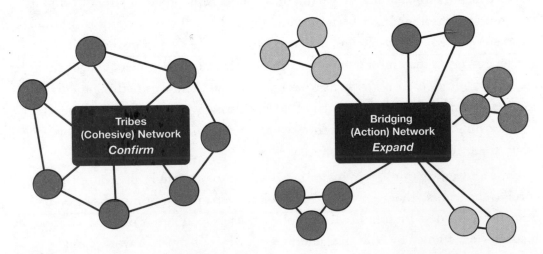

Figure 11.5: The Shape of Your Network Matters

Concept Credit: Anne-Marie Slaughter (author of *The Chessboard and the Web*) and Julie Battilana and Tiziana Casciaro (authors of "The Network Secrets of Great Change Agents" in the *Harvard Business Review*).

This structure becomes especially important during times of change when closed or clan-like networks can become pockets of resistance. In their article, "The Network Secrets of Great Change Agents" for *The Harvard Business Review*, writers Julie Battilana and Tiziana Casciaro shared the story of the United Kingdom's National Health Service to illustrate the point.[2] The giant, bureaucratic agency underwent a massive transformation process, putting a clinical manager—a doctor, nurse, or some other person with a healthcare background—in charge of each local implementation. The authors tracked 68 of these projects and found that the "personal networks—their relationships with colleagues—were critical" in the success of these projects. "Change agents who were central in the organization's informal network," they wrote, "had a clear advantage, regardless of their position in the formal hierarchy."

In the early days of the Internet, TellMe Networks developed an early platform for telephone-based automated voice services. In their Mountain View, California, offices, founder and CEO Mike McCue decided as both a practical and philosophical matter that his growing employee base would work better together if they better understood jobs other than their own. In a retrofitted printing factory, TellMe organized its workspace around pods that accommodated three or five desks. As new employees started their work for the company, they could pull up a chair at any available desk. It was not unusual, then, for an engineer to sit next to an accountant who was next to a marketing guru. Through osmosis, if not direct intent, employees got a broader view of their company and the interdependency of different flows of work.

TellMe, which was acquired by Microsoft in 2007, is not alone in this approach to an integrative and more transparent view of company operations. O'Reilly Auto Parts has its human resources staff tour every functional area of the business so that they can best understand the organization as they recruit new talent. PayPal has implemented a two-year leadership training program that functions a bit like a medical residency, rotating management candidates through the organization, expecting them not only to learn about these areas, but to cross-pollinate ideas from one group to the next.

These models, while different, have the same effect. They give workers a holistic—and empathic—understanding of parts of the business that fall outside their immediate jurisdiction and help form the human relationships that enable workers to openly share ideas, concerns, challenges, and opportunities. Perhaps even more importantly, these open networks transfer tacit knowledge that is so essential to any organization. The often unspoken know-how that makes the organization work, tacit knowledge that lives in humans, is not easily codified, and, therefore, can never be automated. By intentionally organizing individuals to interact beyond the tasks, you may be helping spread tacit knowledge.

Embrace Cognitive Diversity

Even the best team structures will fail if they are not rooted in fundamental business strategy. It is more than popular these days to talk about "diversity" as a human resources (HR) strategy. An HR-centric strategy might advocate for a racially, culturally, and generationally diverse workforce in order to reflect both the customer and market. That's progress, but it is not enough. Diversity, especially cognitive and cultural diversity, needs to become not just HR strategy, but broader business and corporate strategy.

Study after study demonstrates that diversity of thought and cultural experience yields better business results than homogenous teams. A 2018 Boston Consulting Group (BCG) study found that "increasing the diversity of leadership teams leads to more and better innovation and improved financial performance." In both developed and developing countries, BCG found, greater diversity in leadership resulted in higher earnings before interest and taxes (EBIT). Leadership teams with greater diversity had 19% higher revenue from new innovations and 9% higher EBIT than those with lower leadership diversity.[3]

Interestingly, though, in their paper "Teams Solve Problems Faster When They're More Cognitively Diverse," published in the *Harvard Business Review*, Alison Reynolds and David Lewis uncovered what seems at first to be a contrarian discovery. After running hundreds of strategic execution exercises with executive groups, they found no correlation that proves that the more demographically diverse a team is, the more creative and productive it will be. To make sense of this finding, they decided to look beyond gender, ethnicity, and age to consider the impact of *cognitive diversity*, the differences in perspective and information processing styles.

Reynolds and Lewis adopted a model developed by psychiatrist Peter Robertson that looks at knowledge processing and perspective. In knowledge processing, we depend on our existing knowledge or seek new knowledge to address a new situation. Perspective either relies on our expertise or seeks out the expertise of others. By plotting the results of their strategic exercises onto Robertson's matrix, called the AEM cube, Reynolds and Lewis discovered "a significant correlation between high cognitive diversity and high performance."[4]

"Tackling new challenges requires a balance between applying what we know and discovering what we don't know that might be useful. It also requires individual application of specialized expertise and the ability to step back and look at the bigger picture," the researchers concluded. "A high degree of cognitive diversity could generate accelerated learning and performance in the face of new, uncertain, and complex situations, as in the case of the execution problem we set for our executives."[5]

Cognitive diversity is tricky; it's not visible in the way race, gender, and age are. Cognitive diversity is also a cultural challenge for organizations that "screen for cultural fit" when "fit" often means "being one of us" and "thinking about the world the way we do." It's tremendously difficult—and, frankly, highly evolved—to bring contrarians into your work sphere. About this, though, Reynolds and Lewis advise leaders to "find someone who disagrees with you and cherish them."

In a follow-on article "The Two Traits of the Best Problem-Solving Teams," published in the *Harvard Business Review,* Reynolds and Lewis combined their research on cognitive diversity with work on psychological safety. In this study, they found that to tackle volatile, uncertain, complex, and ambiguous (VUCA) challenges, the teams with both cognitive diversity and psychological safety were the most adaptable and "generative" teams. These groups, they found, "treated mistakes with curiosity and shared responsibility for the outcomes."[6]

In this model (Figure 11.6), Reynolds and Lewis identified four team types: defensive, uniform, oppositional, and generative. Defensive is when cognitive diversity and safety are low; folks think the same and distrust each other. Uniform is when folks feel safe because they share groupthink. Oppositional is when folks have diverging perspectives and thinking styles but in a dynamic that can lead to combativeness. And generative is when team members think differently but in a safe space that allows for divergent perspectives. By now, you

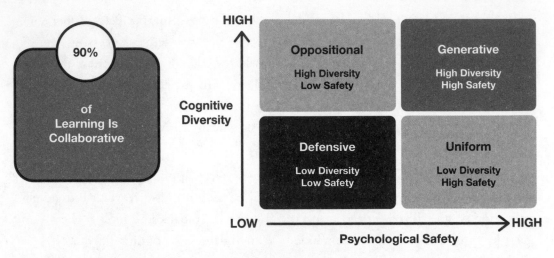

Figure 11.6: For Accelerated Learning, Seek Cognitive Diversity and Psychological Safety

Source: Alison Reynolds and David Lewis, Using the QI Index, from "The Two Traits of the Best Problem-Solving Teams" in the *Harvard Business Review*.

shouldn't be surprised to learn that the optimal teams for accelerated learning, and in particular tackling VUCA challenges, are generative. They are most able to create a new framework in which to understand problems, generate new ideas, and devise new solutions. This sort of framework is essential in accelerated change.

Now consider the 70–20–10 model of learning, we introduced in Chapter 9. In this model, 10% of learning is coursework or direct instruction, what we typically think of as "formal education." The next 20% of learning occurs in shared experiences with others and 70% is learning that happens in the flow of work. By these definitions, 90% of learning is social and collaborative. Couple this with the rise in collaborative work, and the importance of psychological safety and cognitive diversity are even more clear.

Get Comfortable with Failure

Demographically and cognitively diverse teams *will* make better and more productive decisions. They will also make mistakes. Leading these teams demands that you create a safe space for failure.

When we spoke with theoretical neuroscientist and cofounder of Socos Labs, Dr. Vivienne Ming, she stressed the importance of the psychological safety we discussed in Chapter 9. "When it comes to workforce preparation and learning more broadly," she told us, "we need to get much more comfortable with failure. Learning how to fail and pushing through it is a huge predictor of success in a job." And, we would add, for teams.

Dr. Ming contends that in pursuing productivity, efficiency, and scale, organizations have "designed failure right out of the system."

"If you want something that grows, changes, explores, and pushes boundaries, there's just nothing in the fields of AI that does anything like that right now … That's the unique value proposition of humans, and we have to rethink how we help more humans work through failure in the creative economy."

The best leaders are incorporating learning post-mortems into the feedback loops of every step of every project. At Unreasonable Group, for example, Epstein takes regular occasions to ask his team to provide feedback. He invites project participants to answer three seemingly simple questions: What worked? What could be better? What should we celebrate? Participants in turn share in a format of "I liked," "I wish," and—our favorite—"reasons to dance." In a quick round robin, Unreasonable Group identifies and affirms what is working and commits to do more to reinforce that good work, identifies what could be better and immediately follows through to affect change and improvement, and finally gives team members a moment to feel joy and share appreciation for one another and their work together.

Live in a State of Continuous Learning

Companies that are successfully navigating between the Third and Fourth Industrial Revolutions have invested deeply in workforce learning and enrichment because they understand that the future of work is lived in a state of continuous learning. Research by Willis Towers Watson found that "Ninety percent of digitally maturing companies anticipate industry disruption caused by digital trends, however, only 44% are adequately preparing for it."[7] In those that are preparing, consider the often-cited example of AT&T. The company was built with a workforce of people whose job descriptions detailed the skills needed to climb telephone poles and dig trenches to lay cables, operate a switchboard to connect calls, and manage the thousands of workers who made telecommunications work.

Today, the company supports a workforce of more than 250,000 people who manage a cloud-based business requiring cyber security, data analytics, and other technology-dependent tasks, along with the labor-intensive work required to maintain a modern data network. That transition has been anything but easy, yet AT&T took the unprecedented step of investing $1 billion in learning and training programs to lead its workforce into the Fourth Industrial Revolution.[8] Rather than only reskilling workers for new jobs, however, the company encouraged workers to pursue the learning that most interested them, leaving them with the potential to form new jobs around each worker's capabilities and experiences.

Today, AT&T is much more than a telecommunications giant. Its acquisition of Time Warner in 2018, for example, puts AT&T at the center of media assets, including HBO and CNN. AT&T launched Xandar, a data-based advertising business, to tap into new revenue streams. As the company continues to expand from its traditional position, the investment in training and discovery reveals a business that recognizes that its staying power will be realized through learning.

"We're working constantly to engage and reskill our employees, and to inspire a culture of continuous learning," AT&T's William Blasé told us. "For us, the reskilling effort is about transparency and empowerment—creating learning content, tools, and processes that help empower employees to take control of their own development and their own careers."

In other words, AT&T didn't only train workers to fit into new job descriptions. Instead, they built a robust educational infrastructure with a predictive skills and knowledge dashboard that could allow for jobs that fit the abilities and interests of the worker. Just like at AT&T, future jobs will form around workers, rather than workers being plugged into job constructs built on a list of known tasks, knowledge requirements, and set capabilities.

Manage a Multigenerational Workforce

We have arrived at a unique moment in human history where more generations are participating in the workforce than ever before. Prior to the turn of the century, older workers, those the Bureau of Labor Statistics (BLS) defines as 55 years of age or older, were the smallest segment of the labor force. Throughout this century, that age group's share of the workforce has increased as younger age groups have declined.[9] Today, most organizations have four generations working within them, and the BLS projects that more than 10% of people over the age of 75 will be in the workforce in 2026.[10]

Managing a cross-generational team of individuals who variously grew up listening to Billie Holliday, Billy Idol, or Billie Eilish is a challenge, to say the least. That their cultural touchstones are so wildly different might make for challenging conversations … if they can find a common method to communicate at all. Communication is the foundation of collaboration in VUCA work. Those at the older end of the spectrum grew up with synchronous communications, either face to face or by telephone. Gen Z and Millennials grew up with mobile smartphones and quickly shifted from synchronous calling to asynchronous texting and a range of apps. And when they do engage in synchronous calls, they are comfortable with telepresence, using video apps of varying quality in preference to "in person" meetings.

It may be challenging to lead a multigenerational force to collective collaboration, but the effort can pay off in spades. Older workers are the repository for much of the tacit knowledge of an organization, not to mention the wisdom that comes from the experience of developing tacit knowledge across a series of organizations. At the same time, the digital skills of younger workers are vital in a transforming economy. Together, these skills span the depth and breadth of knowledge to create the most formidable teams. (Figure 11.7)

How Do We Get from Here to There?

Perhaps the biggest challenge in the future of work is imagining what that future might look like. Leaders might just have to take a leap of faith and invent a future organization that optimizes for adaptability over everyday reliability. Frankly, that old-fashioned "reliability" will become increasingly unreliable in the face of change. Just ask the former executives at Blockbuster and Kodak.

We need to build teams with clear eyes focused on an unclear horizon, resisting the urge to stare into the rearview mirror and assume that what worked yesterday will be adequate for tomorrow. We need to optimize for sense making and risk taking rather than for efficiency of production.

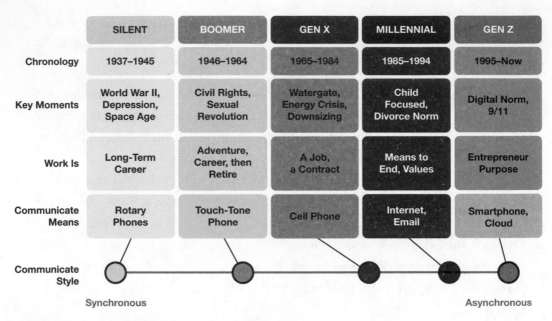

	SILENT	BOOMER	GEN X	MILLENNIAL	GEN Z
Chronology	1937–1945	1946–1964	1965–1984	1985–1994	1995–Now
Key Moments	World War II, Depression, Space Age	Civil Rights, Sexual Revolution	Watergate, Energy Crisis, Downsizing	Child Focused, Divorce Norm	Digital Norm, 9/11
Work Is	Long-Term Career	Adventure, Career, then Retire	A Job, a Contract	Means to End, Values	Entrepreneur Purpose
Communicate Means	Rotary Phones	Touch-Tone Phone	Cell Phone	Internet, Email	Smartphone, Cloud
Communicate Style					

Synchronous   Asynchronous

Figure 11.7: Five Generations in the Workforce

We need to build fluid work groups, rather than work structures. Groups will assemble for a task or project, then disassemble when that project is complete. Group members may be free agents for a time once the group is disbanded, and they will use their free agency to retool their skills and learning for the next opportunity. Or they may find themselves quickly recruited to a new work group project in need of the experience gained from the prior project. Workers really will work in teams, just not permanent ones.

The New Leadership Imperative

As important as inspired hiring and agile organization structures are in the new reality of work, inspired leadership is even more critical.

In his book *Excellence Wins: A No Nonsense Guide to Becoming the Best in a World of Compromise,* cofounder and former president of the Ritz-Carlton Hotel company Horst Schulze makes this point clear. "There is no business," he writes, "There are only people … Reading the economic forecasts and the indicators and the ratios and the rates of this or that, someone from another planet might actually believe that there are really invisible hands at work in the marketplace."

Leaders, he continues "are in the people game" and then makes a clear distinction: "Managers push; leaders inspire."

Make no mistake: hiring for capacity to learn, for alignment of purpose and values, and for an agile mindset is no simple task. Organizing and enabling teams for a future that is uncertain except in its potential for disruption requires dramatically new ways of thinking about work and workers. To put it bluntly, the future of work sets a new and very high bar for leadership.

As marketing guru Seth Godin says, "Managers manage process and leaders lead change." It is all change now, and that requires a shift from management to drive productivity to leadership to inspire human potential, as we discussed in Chapter 9.

In the course of researching and writing this book, we spoke with dozens of researchers, organizational experts, and business leaders, asking each what they believed the future of work held. Those answers are woven throughout this book, yet it seems most fitting—most honest—to close this chapter with this insight from a conversation with Pymetrics' Frida Polli. How, we asked her, can business leaders support and inspire their teams to their best and most fearless work?

"Humans," she said, "sometimes are very limited. They see a pattern. They just want to put a pattern onto the next 20 to 30 years. But, we have no idea. We literally have no idea what's going to happen."

In that context, our best advice is to buckle up. As leadership guru Jim Kouzes reminded us, "When you're moving fast, like a race car on a track, you have to have to pay more attention." That attention will be your greatest tool in leading the Future of Work. That attention allows you to Let go. Learn Fast. Be Adaptable. And make it the future you want it to be.

Notes

1. https://www.amazon.jobs/en/principles
2. https://hbr.org/2013/07/the-network-secrets-of-great-change-agents
3. https://www.bcg.com/en-us/publications/2018/how-diverse-leadership-teams-boost-innovation.aspx

4. https://hbr.org/2017/03/teams-solve-problems-faster-when-theyre-more-cognitively-diverse

5. https://hbr.org/2017/03/teams-solve-problems-faster-when-theyre-more-cognitively-diverse

6. https://hbr.org/2018/04/the-two-traits-of-the-best-problem-solving-teams

7. https://www.willistowerswatson.com/en-US/Insights/all-insights#sort=%40fdate13762%20descending

8. https://www.cnbc.com/2018/03/13/atts-1-billion-gambit-retraining-nearly-half-its-workforce.html

9. https://www.bls.gov/careeroutlook/2017/article/older-workers.htm

10. https://www.bls.gov/opub/ted/2019/labor-force-participation-rate-for-workers-age-75-and-older-projected-to-be-over-10-percent-by-2026.htm

12 Getting Ready to Seize Your Adaptation Advantage

"The Robots Are Coming! The Robots Are Coming!"

Some version of that hyperbolic headline appears near daily as journalists, pundits, scholars, and politicians, among others, struggle to make sense of a world in the midst of digital transformation. The stories often paint a dystopian scene where automation displaces workers and humans become the subjects of their smarter AI overlords. One pundit once told an audience of academics and executives that with the digital transformation complete, the only jobs left would be "oiling the robots." We chuckled at the thought, realizing that oiling the robots is a task so utterly routine and predictable that surely another robot could do it. We aren't alone in our skepticism. American scholar and organizational consultant Warren Bennis is reported to have said in the 1990s, "The factory of the future will have only two employees, a man and a dog. The man will be there to feed the dog. The dog will be there to keep the man from touching the equipment."

This view of work after robots, though, entirely lacks imagination.

In fact, that lazy summation is exactly how we started the conversation that led to this book. We met at an innovation conference that seemed to us steeped in fear of technology and its power to disrupt our lives. Coming at the topic from different directions, we agreed then and still believe that the idea that technology will take down humans is, in a word, absurd. Autodesk's Mickey McManus puts it better than we could: "Humans are what we call passionate, but passionate is such a weak word. Humans can't help themselves. Humans riff on stuff. Humans putter and create. They can't be stopped."

As long as there has been work, which is to say always, humans have fashioned tools to make that work easier, safer, and more productive. We have ceded the heavy lifting to machines, off-loaded memory to recordings, and delegated calculations to computers. Yet there are still plenty of jobs. There may be little demand for stagecoach drivers, blacksmiths, buggy whip makers, or boilermakers, but there is so much else that needs doing. And there always will be.

So, we end this book much where we started it.

"Human beings are works in progress that mistakenly think they're finished," we quoted psychologist Dan Gilbert as saying in the introduction to this book. Observing the "ease of remembering versus the difficulty of imagining," he continues, "most of us can remember who we were 10 years ago, but we find it hard to imagine who we're going to be, and then we mistakenly think that because it's hard to imagine, it's not likely to happen. When people say, 'I can't imagine that,' they're usually talking about their own lack of imagination, and not about the unlikelihood of the event that they're describing."[1]

The world *is* changing, and fast. It is hard to imagine. We will change, too. The work we do and the way we do it will differ almost from day to day. It will always be easier to look back and remember than it will be to look forward and imagine. That practice of looking back and forward, and it is a practice, is incredibly intimidating when you are tightly bolted to a professional identity that measures how you walk in the world. On the other hand, it's incredibly exciting to imagine a future of work that lets us explore *why* we walk in the world.

When we talked with neuroscientist Vivienne Ming, she reminded us that nurturing the emotional, social, and creative skills at the center of a new digital economy takes courage. She sees a schism opening between what she and others call the creative economy and the service economy. As we transition from the Third to the Fourth Industrial Revolution, many people have moved into the service economy, unprepared to participate in the creative economy. No doubt, some of those service jobs are rewarding pathways to career success by many measures, and we need to value those roles in service to one another. Too many service-sector jobs, though, are way stations for automation with paychecks that will never match union jobs in manufacturing. Or, as Ming puts it, the service economy is that work that is "not worth building a robot to do because, frankly, humans are cheaper. It's low autonomy, it's low meaningfulness."

The creative economy, on the other hand, requires more and different education and learning. The creative economy, Ming says, is all about exploring the unknown, learning and creating pathways to new value. Then, she adds, "I think our mission in the world should be: How can we pull as many people as is imaginable into the creative economy?"

We agree. Still, we can only pull those willing to let go. That's the first step. Then, free from the anchor of a fixed identity, we can seize our adaptation advantage and learn fast and thrive in the future of work. It may be helpful, then, to think of education an as investment in your future value. In that context, learning becomes the new pension, accruing value all along the arc of your career.

We crafted this book for you from thousands of conversations, as brief as a Twitter chat or as deep as an after-dinner debate. We hope the conversation continues with you. Please share your story with us on Twitter: @AdaptationAdva1. We can't promise to answer every message, but we do guarantee that when you do get a response, it won't be from a robot.

—Chris and Heather

Note

1. https://www.ted.com/talks/dan_gilbert_the_psychology_of_your_future_self

ADDITIONAL RESOURCES

If you'd like to delve further into the future of work, we recommend the resources provided here. For continually updated resources, visit AdaptationAdvantage.com or follow Adaptation Advantage on LinkedIn and Twitter. We also invite you to connect with us directly @heathermcgowan and @cshipley.

Books

Thank You for Being Late: An Optimist's Guide to Thriving in the Age of Accelerations by Thomas L. Friedman. Building on the concepts he first drafted in *The World Is Flat*, Tom explains how we are in the middle of three climate changes—technology, the market, and Mother Nature—and how those changes are reshaping politics, geopolitics, community, ethics, work, and learning.

Business Model Generation, Value Proposition Design, and *Business Model You,* by Alexander Osterwalder, Yves Pigneur, and Tim Clark. Osterwalder, Pigneur, Clark, and their colleagues create business tools that help you think through your company's business model, your personal business model, and the elements of a value proposition.

The Leadership Challenge by James M. Kouzes and Barry Posner. For more than 40 years, Kouzes and Posner have delivered thoughtful work on the art and science of leadership.

Daring Greatly and *Dare to Lead* by Dr. Brené Brown. Dr. Brown is an authentic, relatable, researcher-storyteller who has her finger on the pulse of the concepts of psychological safety, trust, vulnerability, and shame.

The Fearless Organization by Dr. Amy Edmondson. Dr. Edmondson coined the term "psychological safety" in the 1990s as she sought to identify the qualities of high-functioning teams.

Range: Why Generalists Triumph in a Specialized World by David Epstein. Epstein makes the case that a range of experiences and abilities best positions one for continuous adaptation.

Videos

How Great Leaders Inspire Action, Simon Sinek, https://www.ted.com/talks/simon_sinek_how_great_leaders_inspire_action

The Power of Vulnerability, Dr. Brené Brown, https://www.ted.com/talks/brene_brown_on_vulnerability?language=en

Why Good Leaders Make You Feel Safe, Simon Sinek, https://www.ted.com/talks/simon_sinek_why_good_leaders_make_you_feel_safe

Listening to Shame, Dr. Brené Brown, https://www.ted.com/talks/brene_brown_listening_to_shame

How to Turn a Group of Strangers into a Team, Dr. Amy Edmondson, https://www.ted.com/talks/amy_edmondson_how_to_turn_a_group_of_strangers_into_a_team

Forget the Pecking Order at Work, Margaret Heffernan, https://www.ted.com/talks/margaret_heffernan_why_it_s_time_to_forget_the_pecking_order_at_work?language=en

The Power of Believing You Can, Dr. Carol Dweck, https://www.ted.com/talks/carol_dweck_the_power_of_believing_that_you_can_improve?language=en

ACKNOWLEDGMENTS

It should be clear from the cover onward that this book is a collaboration, and not just that of the authors. Every page of *The Adaptation Advantage* is made better by the contributions, direct and otherwise, of many people. Many of those people we know well and so many others picked up our cold calls and shared with us their most precious resource—their time. All provided insights and perspectives that helped us light a path to a more inclusive and inspirational future. We are deeply indebted to them all.

Had Annalie Killian, now vice president of strategic partnerships at sparks & honey in New York and previously founder of Amplify Festival, not invited each of us to speak at a corporate innovation conference halfway around our world, we might not have met, even though we lived just a few miles apart. What started as casual conversation in a speakers' lounge has grown into a deep, intellectually honest, and deeply fun friendship.

Once we decided to write this book, we were both cheered, encouraged, and sometimes simply prodded into productivity by our wives. Patricia Coryell reviewed multiple drafts of our proposals through her often-critical and always supportive publisher lens and encouraged us to keep at it until we landed the book with our excellent publisher. Nancy Latta proved she has endless stores of patience, putting up with late-night editing sessions and even enduring cross-country driving duty as Chris turned out chapters from the passenger seat.

Beyond family, no one has been more insistent that we write this book than Tom Friedman. We are grateful for his encouragement early in the process, humbled by his full-throated endorsement of Heather's work, and deeply honored by the insightful Foreword he wrote for this edition.

Early readers provided invaluable feedback. We are grateful to Clare O'Brien, Susie Shipley, Robin Wright, Lisa Rioles-Collins, Maria Calkins, David Walsh, Donna Patricia Eiby, and Jim Kouzes, who read early chapters and helped us find our voice.

Melissa Kang, thank you from the bottom of my heart (says Chris) for keeping Heather organized and on task. Nicole Ochoa, thank you for all your assistance with Heather's operational needs.

For nearly four decades, Chris has been guided, edited, and encouraged in her writing by Jeanne Braham, and she is forever grateful that a once professorial relationship evolved into an abiding friendship and for all the wise counsel that has come with it.

Among the industries enduring massive disruption is publishing. We are grateful to Richard Narramore at Wiley for having the foresight and courage to shepherd this book to market. We may fancy ourselves thinkers and writers, but we know we have blind spots. Kelly Talbot shined a light on them and guided the manuscript to a much better place. Even if he wouldn't allow us to use a few choice words, we are thrilled to have worked with him.

The infographics in this book were transformed by Olga of Josephine and Paul Design, an outstanding visual designer we were fortunate to find using one of the online gig platforms that will become even more mainstream in the future of work. The incomparable portrait photographer Asa Mathat captured Steve Jobs in a public moment of whimsy; we are honored that he allowed us to share this rare photo with our readers.

Special thanks to Steven Duarte for enduring a very cold day to take very cool authors' photos. We hope his track record of providing author photos for best-selling books continues.

Throughout the book, you will learn, as we did, from amazing business leaders, educators, scientists, thinkers, and provocateurs. Many people shared their insight, experience, and wisdom with us as we formulated and supported the thesis at the heart of this work: that when we let go of restrictive professional identities and embrace our uniquely human skills, the future of work is a place where we can all thrive.

Finally, over the years of our collaboration, we have been blessed to test and groom our ideas on hundreds of audiences around the world. Each person who listened, questioned, challenged, or simply nodded from the front rows provided the inspiration and encouragement to bring this book to light. Thank you all; you inspired this book.

ABOUT THE AUTHORS

Heather E. McGowan and Chris Shipley have become the leading voices in the Future of Work movement. They have been collaborating on the nature of work, culture, and innovation since 2015. Their essays on these topics have been widely read and shared by more than 1.5 million people. They have spoken to executive audiences around the world and their work has been used by the World Bank, the Brookings Institution, the Ohio Governor's Office of Workforce Development, Credit Suisse, Citi, Nexxworks, Cisco, Deloitte, *Inc.* magazine, *Forbes*, and *New York Times* bestselling author Thomas L. Friedman, among others.

Future-of-work strategist **Heather E. McGowan** helps leaders prepare their people and organizations for the Fourth Industrial Revolution. The Third Industrial Revolution was marked by computerization and automation of physical labor, laying the foundation for the Fourth Industrial Revolution, which will be notable for the rapid advancement of technology tools into the domain of human knowledge work. In this world, humans must continuously learn and adapt, and with this transition comes information overload. Heather gives lucidity to the complex topic of the future of work through her illuminating graphic frameworks and powerful metaphors, all backed by deep research. In 2017, LinkedIn ranked her as its number-one global voice for education. In 2019, Swinburne University in Melbourne, Australia, appointed her to the faculty of their Centre for the New Workforce. Pulitzer Prize–winning *New York Times* columnist Thomas Friedman frequently quotes Heather in his books and columns and describes her as "the oasis" when it comes to insights into the future of work. Heather gives nearly 50 keynote talks a year, through which she assists employees and leaders alike to prepare for and adapt to jobs that do not yet exist. Heather is a regular *Forbes* contributor.

 **Chris Shipley** has documented, influenced, and predicted the impact of technology on business and society for more than 30 years. As a journalist, analyst, executive producer, and startup mentor, she has witnessed firsthand the transformation brought about by digital innovation. She covered the tech industry for leading publishing companies throughout the 1980s and 1990s, and was among the first to identify emerging technology trends, including the rise of web applications, early smartphone technologies, and social media. As the executive producer of the DEMO Conference for more than a decade, she ushered groundbreaking products such as salesforce.com, TiVO, and VMWare to market. Were those companies an investment portfolio, they would have a market value exceeding $300 billion today. Chris now spends her time curating and advising communities of entrepreneurs, journalists, and technology thought leaders as they navigate toward an empowering digital future.

INDEX

Page numbers followed by *f* refer to figures.